Networks and Institutions in Europe's Emerging Markets

Do ties between political parties and businesses harm or benefit the development of market institutions? The post-communist transition offers an unparalleled opportunity to explore when and how networks linking the polity and the economy support the development of functional institutions. A quantitative and qualitative analysis covering eleven post-socialist countries combined with detailed case studies of Bulgaria, Poland, and Romania documents how the most successful post-communist countries are those in which dense networks link politicians and businesspeople, as long as politicians are constrained by intense political competition. The comparison of original network data sets shows how this combination allowed Poland to emerge with stable institutions. Bulgaria, marred by weak institutions, corruption, and violence, cautions us that in developing economies intense political competition alone is harmful in the absence of dense personal and ownership networks. Indeed, as Romania illustrates, networks are so critical that their weakness is not mitigated even by low political competition.

Roger Schoenman is Associate Professor at the University of California, Santa Cruz.

Cambridge Studies in Comparative Politics

General Editor
Margaret Levi *University of Washington, Seattle*

Assistant General Editors
Kathleen Thelen *Massachusetts Institute of Technology*
Erik Wibbels *Duke University*

Associate Editors
Robert H. Bates *Harvard University*
Stephen Hanson *University of Washington, Seattle*
Torben Iversen *Harvard University*
Stathis Kalyvas *Yale University*
Peter Lange *Duke University*
Helen Milner *Princeton University*
Frances Rosenbluth *Yale University*
Susan Stokes *Yale University*
Sidney Tarrow *Cornell University*

Other Books in the Series
Christopher Adolph, *Bankers, Bureaucrats, and Central Bank Politics: The Myth of Neutrality*
Ben W. Ansell, *From the Ballot to the Blackboard: The Redistributive Political Economy of Education*
Leonardo R. Arriola, *Multi-Ethnic Coalitions in Africa: Business Financing of Opposition Election Campaigns*
David Austen-Smith, Jeffry A. Frieden, Miriam A. Golden, Karl Ove Moene, and Adam Przeworski, eds., *Selected Works of Michael Wallerstein: The Political Economy of Inequality, Unions, and Social Democracy*
Andy Baker, *The Market and the Masses in Latin America: Policy Reform and Consumption in Liberalizing Economies*
Lisa Baldez, *Why Women Protest? Women's Movements in Chile*
Stefano Bartolini, *The Political Mobilization of the European Left, 1860–1980: The Class Cleavage*

(continued after Index)

Networks and Institutions in Europe's Emerging Markets

ROGER SCHOENMAN

CAMBRIDGE
UNIVERSITY PRESS

CAMBRIDGE
UNIVERSITY PRESS

University Printing House, Cambridge CB2 8BS, United Kingdom

Cambridge University Press is part of the University of Cambridge.

It furthers the University's mission by disseminating knowledge in the pursuit of
education, learning and research at the highest international levels of excellence.

www.cambridge.org
Information on this title: www.cambridge.org/9781107031340

© Roger Schoenman 2014

This work is in copyright. It is subject to statutory exceptions and to the provisions of relevant
licensing agreements; with the exception of the Creative Commons version the link for which is
provided below, no reproduction of any part of this work may take place without the written
permission of Cambridge University Press.

An online version of this work is published at https://doi.org/10.1017/CBO9781139381628 under
a Creative Commons Open Access license **CC-BY-NC 4.0** which permits re-use, distribution and
reproduction in any medium for non-commercial purposes providing appropriate credit to the
original work is given and any changes made are indicated. To view a copy of this license, visit
https://creativecommons.org/licenses/by-nc/4.0.

All versions of this work may contain content reproduced under license from third parties.
Permission to reproduce this third-party content must be obtained from these third-parties directly.

When citing this work, please include a reference to the DOI 10.1017/CBO9781139381628

First published 2014

A catalogue record for this publication is available from the British Library

Library of Congress Cataloging-in-Publication Data
Schoenman, Roger.
Networks and institutions in Europe's emerging markets / Roger Schoenman.
    pages cm – (Cambridge studies in comparative politics)   1. Business and politics–Europe,
Eastern.   2. Business networks–Political aspects–Europe, Eastern.   3. Post-communism–
Economic aspects–Europe, Eastern.   4. Institution building–Europe, Eastern.   5. Europe,
Eastern–Economic policy.   I. Title.
HD3616.E8523S36 2014
322'.30947–dc23   2013045299

ISBN 978-1-107-03134-0 Hardback

Cambridge University Press has no responsibility for the persistence or accuracy of
URLs for external or third-party internet websites referred to in this publication,
and does not guarantee that any content on such websites is, or will remain,
accurate or appropriate.

To my family

Contents

List of figures		*page* x
List of tables		xi
Acknowledgements		xii
Introduction		1
PART I FOUNDATIONS		
1	Approaches to institution building	29
PART II THE ROLE OF NETWORKS		
2	When broad networks increase cooperation	55
3	Tracing ownership networks	84
PART III THE ROLE OF UNCERTAINTY		
4	When uncertainty increases cooperation	131
5	Tracing elite career networks	145
PART IV BRINGING IT TOGETHER		
6	Institutional development in new democracies	167
7	Conclusion: political varieties of capitalism in emerging markets	185
List of interviews		196
References		200
Index		216

Figures

2.1	Ownership structures	*page* 61
2.2	Bank and industrial ownership across east central Europe, 2005	71
2.3	Membership of business organizations	73
2.4	Perceived value of business associations in resolving disputes with other firms, workers, and officials	74
2.5	Value of business associations in lobbying government	75
3.1	Firm networks in Poland, 1995	111
3.2	Firm networks in Poland, 2000	112
3.3	Firm networks in Poland, 2005	117
3.4	Ownership network of Bank Handlowy, 2000	119
3.5	Romanian ownership network, 1995	120
3.6	Romanian ownership network, 2000	121
3.7	Romanian ownership network, 2005	122
3.8	Bulgarian ownership network, 1995	124
3.9	Bulgarian ownership network, 2000	125
3.10	Bulgarian ownership network, 2005	126
5.1	Yearly average of elites changing jobs	156
5.2	Sequence entropy by country	158
5.3	Bulgarian network of ties between social sectors, 1993–2003	160
5.4	Polish network of ties between social sectors, 1993–2003	161
5.5	Romanian network of ties between social sectors, 1993–2003	162
6.1	Progress on six major policy areas, 1990–2005	176
6.2	Competition policy, 2000–2005	178
6.3	Securities market and non-bank financial institution reform, 2000–2005	180
6.4	Banking regulation reform, 2000–2005	181
6.5	Rule of law by cluster	182

Tables

I.1	Percentages of private sector's share in GDP	*page* 16
I.2	Imperial legacy and progress on reform	19
1.1	The effect of networks and uncertainty on the state	50
2.1	Ownership concentration, 2000	59
2.2	Owners, ownership structures, and resulting functions	60
2.3	Agency problems, diversity of assets and the likelihood of collective action	67
2.4	Ownership concentration and diversity of assets	72
3.1	Top owners by type and their ties, 1995, 2000, 2005	89
3.2	Mean degree and normalized mean degree, 1995, 2000, 2005	113
3.3	Top twenty most connected firms, 2005	115
5.1	Comparison of cases	153
5.2	Coding of data	154
5.3	Most common career transitions	163
6.1	Networks and uncertainty in the Baltics, east central Europe, and the Balkans: final cluster center scores	173
6.2	Networks, uncertainty, and state types	174
7.1	Summary of findings	188

xi

Acknowledgements

This book has been long in the making, and the journey to its completion has had many twists and turns. Consequently, the list of individuals and organizations to whom I owe a great debt of gratitude is long. Along the way, many incredible people I met in a professional context have become dear friends, which I count as one of the great payoffs of this process.

At its core, I have hoped in this book to understand how social worlds are transformed by historical shocks and their remnants reassembled by those left in the wake of sweeping change. For this curiosity, I have to first thank my parents, Henry and Helen, and my grandmother, Rosa. They shared with me the insights and experiences gained from life in turbulent pre-war Poland, the Holocaust, deportation to the Soviet Far East, post-war Polish reconstruction, and new beginnings in the United States in the 1970s. They and many others emerged from each of these trials to start new lives. Despite the many hardships they faced, my parents maintained an enthusiasm for life and a curiosity that I hope I have inherited in some small part. I am deeply grateful to them for inspiring me and setting me on this journey and many others.

My wife, Eleonora, has been an intellectual counterpart and loving and devoted companion through every stage and deserves the most credit for supporting me through the whole process. She has followed me across the post-socialist region since the mid-1990s, and championed my work even when I was discouraged by some defeat along the way. I am deeply grateful for her encouragement, assistance, meticulous editing, and patience.

Three mentors deserve special recognition. My dissertation advisor in the political science department at Columbia, Ira Katznelson, has believed in the project since its inception and supported me throughout. I am deeply grateful for his kindness and direction. David Stark has been an extremely generous, warm, and supportive advisor since graduate school. He introduced me to new ideas in sociology, pushed me to sharpen my thinking, and was enthusiastic about the argument in this book as it took shape. At his invitation and with his

Acknowledgements

support, I also had the opportunity of spending a postdoctoral year at the Harriman Institute at Columbia University as part of a project on "Networks and institutions in post-communism." Bruce Kogut has been an influence since I participated in the "Small worlds of corporate governance" project he led. Bruce pointed me to literatures outside political science that I had not explored and shaped my thinking in ways that are very different from my graduate training. In every interaction, his energy and enthusiasm have been an inspiration. I can only hope that a little bit of Ira, David, and Bruce's scholarly creativity and style have rubbed off on me in the time I have been fortunate to spend in their company and with their research.

I would also like to thank my colleagues at Columbia University's Harriman Institute: Balazs Vedres, Alexandra Sznajder, and Eugene Raikhel. Interacting with them over the course of a year added not only great richness to this project but also regular doses of fun and an ability to share our fondness for and fascination with the post-socialist region.

I also was extremely fortunate to spend a year in the Max Weber program at the European University Institute. My mentor, Laszlo Bruszt, helped sharpen key parts of the argument. I am grateful to Ramon Marimon, Karen Tilmans, and my colleagues Ben Ansell, David Art, Simon Bornschier, Isabelle Engeli, Jane Gingrich, Silja Hausermann, and Miriam Ronzoni for their insight, encouragement, and comments on my work, as well as their company during an incredible year in Florence.

Throughout the period in which this book was written my colleagues at the University of California, Santa Cruz (UCSC) – Eva Bertram, Michael Brown, Kent Eaton, Paul Frymer, Ronnie Gruhn, Ronnie Lipschutz, Mark Massoud, Dean Mathiowetz, Benjamin Read, Vanita Seth, Megan Thomas, Daniel Wirls, and Michael Urban – have given me their support, feedback, encouragement, and friendship. I am truly blessed to work in a department with such wonderful people.

Along the way, numerous individuals have shown me unexpected kindness. Gerry McDermott, whom I met by chance at the American Political Science Association while still in graduate school, stands out. I have benefited from the insight and encouragement of Josh Aderholt, Andrew Arato, Leo Arriola, Thom Henry Chivens, Ruth Collier, Alex Cooley, Rachel Epstein, Gil Eyal, Timothy Frye, Venelin Ganev, Doug Guthrie, Agata Hanczewski, John Huber, Wade Jacoby, Ira Katznelson, Xiaobo Lu, Isabela Mares, Frances Matthew, Iain McMenamin, Katharina Pistor, Grigore Pop-Eleches, Martin Rhodes, Jack Snyder, and Steve Solnick. I would also like to thank the members of the Berkeley "Comparative politics" workshop. Finally, the manuscript benefited greatly from John Haslam's support at Cambridge, the invaluable comments of three anonymous reviewers, and Mike Richardson's meticulous copy-editing.

The fieldwork on which this book was based has benefited from the support of too many individuals to name. All those who were generous enough to meet for interviews – and there are too many to name here – contributed to the findings in this book. Several individuals went inexplicably out of their way to assist me. Adriana Halpert was extremely generous when I wandered into her office at Capital. I walked in, a perfect stranger, and walked out with a gold-mine and an advocate. Adrian Baboi-Stroe was a constant friend and guide to the world of Romanian politics. Hermina Emirian was my fearless and resourceful assistant in Bulgaria. The Institute for the Study of Politics of the Polish Academy of Sciences provided tremendous support during my research in Poland.

This work would not have been possible without the financial support of UCSC, Columbia University, the Harriman Institute, the American Council of Learned Societies, the German Marshall Fund, and the National Science Foundation.

Lastly, I would like to thank the joys of my life – Oscar and Stella. Their arrival may have slowed me down a bit but their love and invitations to play also gave me the inspiration and courage to bring this project to a close.

Introduction

In 1990 Aleksander Gudzowaty chartered a plane, filled it with cheap consumer goods and Polish fashion models, and flew to Siberia for a meeting with an old acquaintance, the chairman of the Russian natural gas supplier Gazprom. When Gudzowaty returned ten days later, he approached the heavily indebted Polish government as the sole mediator with which Gazprom would negotiate gas supplies to Poland. Poland depended on the Russian natural gas supplied by Gazprom and earned a substantial income from transit fees on gas headed west through the Yamal pipeline, but it found itself in constant negotiations over its gas debts. With winter approaching and Poland's gas supply threatened, the Polish president had to accept the businessman's terms: a percentage fee on all natural gas arriving in and transiting through Poland to western Europe. By taking a remarkable gamble and banking on his connections, Gudzowaty became Poland's first overnight dollar billionaire.

Gudzowaty began to invite a coterie of powerful new friends to visit his walled and heavily guarded home—complete with a private zoo and glass meditation pyramid—in a forest outside Warsaw. Although his first move toward wealth had depended on the protection of foreign patrons, he quickly understood that political allies at home were a key element of any future success in the highly uncertain market environment. As Poland began to practice democracy in fits and starts, Gudzowaty started to finance acquaintances from before 1989 who had entered the new left political party, the Democratic Left Alliance (SLD); to hire former bureaucrats as executives of his holding company;[1] and to purchase shares of other firms. He did not hide his support of the left and openly admitted to good relations with the SLD. He routinely used these contacts to influence regulatory policy and the legislative agenda.

---

[1] His company, Bartimpex, reportedly employed seventeen former ministers.

The party system was sharply divided between the post-communist SLD and the anti-communist Solidarity coalition. Thus, at each change of government, Gudzowaty had to re-evaluate his position and work to maintain the material and legislative goods he had obtained. He became known as a close ally and supporter of the SLD and was received as an almost holy figure at the annual party congress – a strange relationship between a gas magnate and a supposedly social democratic party. Party finances were opaque but it was alleged that he contributed millions of dollars to each campaign.[2] When the SLD was in opposition, his business fared less well, and his ability to participate in privatizations and government contracts suffered because right-wing politicians spoke against his plans and favored other businesspeople. When asked in an interview in 2000 about his ties to political parties, he said: "With the last [left] government we had good contacts. This current [right] government, of Mr. Buzek, is simply aggressive toward us and we have constant conflicts with it. We try to use state institutions – courts, the prosecutor's office – and nothing works out."

The ties of businesspeople to parties remained stable over the first decade and a half of reform. In 2006, when changes in the party system seriously weakened the left, Gudzowaty tried to shift alliances, but with only limited success. In an attempt to distance himself from his old allies, he leaked tapes of a private conversation with the former SLD prime minister, Josef Oleksy, about dealings between politicians and businesspeople. In that discussion, Oleksy told Gudzowaty that the Polish president, Aleksander Kwasniewski, had established "political capitalism" in Poland and cultivated a group of insider businesspeople who supported the left.

By "political capitalism," Oleksy meant that there existed a cohort of businesspeople who were closely allied with political parties and depended on their support for business success. In fact, Gudzowaty operated among a group of such businesspeople. They did not form a strong, united front to speak with one voice, but they were recognized as businesspeople who had benefited from ties to left politicians and were, consequently, eager financial supporters. Similarly, they had all created relationships of reciprocal benefit and commitment with politicians. Their wealth depended on these ties, which allowed them to participate in privatizations, win government contracts and licenses, and influence laws and regulations when the left was in power. And they all actively sought to employ former bureaucrats, ministers, and elected officials to strengthen their ties to government. In other words, "political capitalism"

---

[2] Until recently there was only anecdotal evidence of Gudzowaty's contributions to the left, because party budgets provided no detail of such contributions in Poland. In March 2009 documents surfaced detailing the transfer of 3 million złoty from Gudzowaty's companies to the SLD (*Rzeczpospolita* 2013). Gudzowaty himself confirmed these donations (*Newsweek Polska* 2009). And Marek Belka, long-time SLD member and future prime minister, sat on the supervisory board of one of the donating companies (*Newsweek Polska* 2009).

Introduction 3

was a headline-grabbing label for the embeddedness of the polity in the economy. What Oleksy failed to observe was that Poland exhibited only one of the varieties of embeddedness emerging across the region.

In this book, I examine the emergence of different varieties of links between the polity and the economy: the network relationships between businesspeople and political actors that have emerged across the post-socialist world. In Poland, networks between economic and political elites have been a key component of robust economic development and the emergence of broadly distributive, as opposed to selective advantage, institutions.

I define institutions as "the rules of the game in a society or, more formally, ...the humanly devised constraints that shape human interaction" (North 1990: 3). More specifically, "[i]nstitutions are relatively stable sets of widely shared and generally realized expectations about how people will behave in particular social, economic and political circumstances. Expectations structure behavior by informing individuals about the likely consequences of alternative courses of actions" (Weimer 1997: 2). I focus on formal institutions, which set out these expectations in rules enforced by the state. "Broadly distributive" institutions are those that distribute benefits to broad segments of the affected population, such as whole classes or types of actors. Such institutions are the result of policy making that does not deliver selective advantages and rewards supporters only indirectly (Kitschelt 2000: 849–50). These institutions may provide club or collective goods but they do not bestow private benefits. Further, the redistributive consequences of these institutions are applied regardless of whether an actor supported the party initiating a particular institutional reform. By contrast, "selective advantage" institutions distribute benefits to targeted recipients, and only those who engage in the quid pro quo with political actors receive the benefit. The purpose of this book is to explain the effect of network ties between the political and economic sphere, as well as the effect of uncertainty, on the emergence of broadly distributive institutions.

The negotiated nature of the Polish transition – accompanied by the widespread belief that no single party would dominate post-socialist Polish politics – set Poland on a particular trajectory of political capitalism. As in the case of the SLD, the parties that emerged on the right from the Solidarity movement also sought economic allies. Beginning with Lech Wałęsa's first presidential campaign, parties sought a-legal donations to increase their chances of winning. They found allies in the likes of Jan Kulczyk,[3] partial owner of the privatized telecommunications company TPSA, who had strong ties to the parties on the right.

---

[3] Kulczyk was selected as the buyer of the important Lech and Tyskie Breweries by the privatization minister, Janusz Lewandowski, in the center-right government of Hanna Suchocka. He was also selected in partnership with France Telecom for exclusive negotiations in the privatization of the Polish telephone company TPSA under the Solidarity government of Jerzy Buzek.

Politicians also frequently sought out ties with businesspeople, particularly when their parties depended on business as a source of political finance. The linkage of politics and business was initially very direct. Quite quickly, however, the opportunities for the direct political creation of firms disappeared; they constituted too great a liability for Polish politicians. Instead of politically creating firms, politicians from all parties sought to acquire political control of privatized firms by staffing corporate boards with the party faithful. This became another source of revenue for political parties in addition to the financial support of individual business owners. One by-product of this broad enmeshing of politics and business was that political responsiveness to business interests and effective business regulation came to be in the interest of political elites.

Across post-communist Europe businesspeople and politicians eyed each other as possible allies or resources to different extents. The central place of ties between politicians and businesspeople in the Polish economic transformation is surprising, however, given the emphasis placed on rapid reform in explaining Poland's early emergence as one of the best-performing post-communist countries. The prominence of networks thus challenges the traditional explanation for Poland's success: relatively rapid progress on privatization and economic reform that established functioning markets (Lipton and Sachs 1990b; Sachs 1994; Åslund 1995) and allowed firms to operate with little regulation (Shleifer and Vishny 1998; Frye 2010) while disrupting pre-1989 social networks.

In this book, I re-examine both paradigmatic success stories and frequently cited laggards of political and economic reform in post-communist Europe between 1989 and 2005, by focusing on the neglected role of networks between firms and political parties. My goal is to explain the role of networks and uncertainty in the emergence of broadly distributive institutions in the region. The combination of business and politics was by no means peculiar to Poland or members of the former Communist Party. In the Polish case, however, the purpose of bringing together the two spheres – economy and polity – was quite different from what it was in many other countries, due to the intensity of Polish political competition in the early 1990s. Polish businesspeople sought to secure their place in the economy and approached politicians to offset some of the uncertainty that the early period of transformation to capitalism entailed. Their political counterparts, faced with sharp electoral competition, sought to increase their chances of victory at the polls. Both groups recognized that the changes that began in 1989 would completely change their understanding of politics and the economy, but no one knew exactly how. Because so many different actors were involved, no one could hope to control the process or its outcome.[4]

---

[4] Ostrom refers to such contexts as "unstructured problems" in which individuals are at best engaged in a "trial and error effort to learn more about the results of their actions so that they can evaluate costs and benefits more effectively over time" (Ostrom 1990).

Introduction 5

In an attempt to offset the uncertainty inherent in periods of massive social change, politicians and businesspeople forged networks of social ties, political financing, and favors. In addition, party members moved between political organizations, jobs in the state bureaucracy, and positions in the private sector. The networks linking the polity and the economy grew deeper over time, and with each passing year the links between a particular political party and their business allies grew more intense. As on K Street in Washington, and in many other capitals of established democracies, these businesspeople provided jobs to former party officials and politicians in exchange for access.

There is no question that the first two decades of transformation in Poland were marred by corruption between businesspeople and politicians, as they were in all post-communist countries.[5] Blame was placed on everyone from the socialist *nomenklatura* after 1989 to the new "nomenklatura," composed of elite members of the former opposition, the secret services, lobbying and pressure groups, and "networks" (Żakowski 2009).

Instead, however, in the context of strong networks between the state and business, broadly distributive institutions emerged in Poland. This outcome was not a given, as the trajectories taken by the two other case studies in this book, Bulgaria and Romania, clearly demonstrate. Hence, I seek to understand how the configuration of networks determined the institutional trajectories of post-socialist states. The three basic questions of this study are as follows. Why do networks among firms and between politicians and firms emerge? Why did variation emerge in the types of networks and in relationships between the state and the economy? And what is the relationship between networks and institutional development?

I develop the argument in greater detail in the next chapter. Briefly, I argue that the structure of networks and the level of uncertainty within which these networks operate shape the incentives of elites to act collectively. Networks emerge to fill the space left by incomplete institutions. Broad networks link cross-sectoral coalitions and thus facilitate collective action. The effect of uncertainty on collective action depends on the type of network present. Under high levels of uncertainty, cooperation emerges if networks are broad, because information flows and the threat of damage to reputation undermine defection from agreements between politicians and businesspeople. Under high levels of uncertainty and narrow networks, parties are weakened by high levels of competition and are unable to credibly commit to agreements with business because the narrow network makes their defections hard to detect, and uncertainty lowers the value of their promises. The result is that cooperation between firms and parties is unlikely, and, consequently, business can prey directly on the state. Under low levels of uncertainty and narrow networks, dominant political elites, safe from the threat of political competition, exploit atomized

---

[5] Corruption here means illegal or a-legal exchanges between these groups.

firms. Under low levels of uncertainty and broad networks, dominant political elites enter into collusive relations with firms.

These findings challenge the traditional view by suggesting that broad networks are not anathema to the emergence of broadly distributive institutions. To the contrary, in conditions of widespread uncertainty, networks are necessary for the development of broadly distributive institutions. Chapter 2 develops a theory of how networks function dynamically in times of widespread institution building, how network variation shapes institutional development, and why network variation emerges.

The starting point for this analysis is identifying the distinctive features of Poland in comparison to other post-communist countries. As will be explored in more detail in the pages below, Poland stands out because the networks widely blamed for post-communist corruption were broad at all levels of society. These networks made possible the gradual institution building that took place.

Two types of network are examined in this book. First, Polish ownership networks were much broader than those in other countries, meaning that firms in many different sectors were joined in a horizontal web linking state firms and private firms. Ownership cross-holdings are a common way for firms to enable credible commitments when institutions are still incomplete or when the complexities of market activity are such that contracting cannot cover all contingencies in a practical fashion (Williamson 1985; Gerlach 1992).

Second, Polish personnel networks – those created among the individuals who hold high-level positions within the same organization – included many more individuals than those in other post-communist countries. This came about because appointments were highly politicized in Poland, with the result that high-level employment experienced significant turnover after every election that brought about a shift in the ruling party. These personnel networks spanned the state and the private sector. They had a sharp partisan logic, as bureaucrats and private individuals often depended on party support to obtain elite positions. Although changing jobs frequently imposed regular start-up costs on individuals, it also limited the length of time any one person spent in a particular position of power, increased the level of connection among the elite, and thereby produced another key form of state–economy embeddedness.

As a result of Poland's broad networks, political and economic elites looked to the long run: they all knew their fortunes did not lie in maximizing short-run benefits but, rather, in working within lasting political structures. Alternation in power of the two largest coalitions – center-left and center-right – held for the first four fully democratic elections, in 1991, 1993, 1997, and 2001. Business elites realized that short-run benefits might be fleeting and defecting from a party could lead to future punishment. In contrast, lasting alliances were likely to deliver long-run benefits, even if those benefits were unavailable when the allied party was out of government. They also had invested into developing relationships with political allies that were not so easily shifted to the opposing

Introduction   7

political side. The alternation of parties in power alone was not sufficient to realize coordination, however. Only because networks connected a large group of firms and politicians, providing many points of contact and creating a web of mutual obligation and commitment, were political and economic actors able to focus on the long term. No one group of businesspeople could coordinate to steer the process of institution building in its own direction, because networks included too many different firms with too many disparate interests.

Thus, instead of pushing for narrow, selective benefits, firms and parties eventually sought to turn over power to broadly devised institutions and to empower the state with decision-making authority through a series of compromises. This state functioned both by command and by adjudication, mediating between various competing interest groups that would otherwise face a stalemate. In the process, stakeholders developed a functioning competition policy, built financial institutions and regulation, reformed banking policies, and developed a comprehensive corporate governance system before neighboring countries managed these feats. Polish financial law was more effective in 2000 than financial law in almost all the other countries in the region (Sanders and Bernstein 2002). Corporate governance law more closely approached international standards for the protection of shareholder rights than that of any country in the region. Poland was even comparatively successful in developing a framework to regulate lobbying relations between business and politicians.

Evidence that networks drove this process appears in the surprising persistence of network-based economic activity in an otherwise rapidly developing liberal institutional context. According to a 2005 survey, of all the Balkan, Baltic, and east European countries, Polish firms were most likely to turn to collective associations to resolve disputes with other firms (EBRD 2005b). According to Williamson (1985: 166), recourse to dispute resolution mechanisms other than courts is a key signal that credible commitments are a cornerstone of inter-firm relations and play a larger role in market relations than is customarily recognized. Polish firms also used network-based sources of capital as a primary form of credit (EBRD 2005b). In the first two decades after 1989 Poland underwent a great deal of institutional change in the context of broad networks that played a central role in the day-to-day ability of firms to navigate an uncertain environment. Broad network ties enabled firms to make credible commitments and forge broad coalitions with political actors. The cooperative relationship that developed between business and politics determined the trajectory of Poland's institutional development.

Not all countries fared so well; most much more closely resembled the stereotypical "wild East" that we have come to associate with the post-communism era. For the sake of illustration, the next pages briefly contrast the case studies discussed at greater length later in this book.

In sharp contrast to his Polish colleagues, the Bulgarian businessman Ilya Pavlov, who ranked among the ten richest men in eastern Europe until 2003, had a different impact on institutional development. Pavlov was a well-known wrestler (Bulgaria was an international leader in the sport) who married the daughter of the last communist secret police chief. He was well acquainted with high-ranking party officials and members of the military and security services. As the communist regime was unraveling, Pavlov and others like him – many of them emerging from professional sports circles, the military, and the secret police – began to take part in foreign trade. Pavlov founded a company called Multigroup that, formally, dealt in the import and export of art, although it quickly expanded to trade in other products. Multigroup established a bewildering array of shell companies in offshore tax havens, making it impossible to trace the company's structure. It used these shells and the vast resources the company quickly acquired to avoid the control of the state – even flying products directly out of Bulgaria without submitting to customs procedures (Ganev 2001: 15).

The methods employed by Pavlov and a group of other businesspeople blurred the lines between (semi-)legitimate business activities and mafia methods. They formed companies with names such as Alpha and Beta and business groups such as VIS-2[6] that traded small arms to developing countries, captured the privatizations of large resorts, offered insurance and private security services, and fought among themselves over the division of Bulgaria's valuable tourist infrastructure and industry. As they came to control banks, hotels, and heavy industry, Bulgaria was rocked by car bombings and contract killings of businesspeople in broad daylight. In 2000 the capital, Sofia, averaged three per week. The interior minister even publicly stated that the police were powerless to do anything, but that normal people should not be concerned because the killers were conscientious and rarely involved innocent bystanders. As violence became part of the standard toolkit of business, it ultimately consumed even Pavlov – several times named "Bulgarian businessman of the year" and ranked the eighth wealthiest man in central and eastern Europe – with a single bullet to the heart outside Multigroup's headquarters in 2003.

The business groups behind this violence were in a position of asymmetrical force and influence. Rumors that they had infiltrated the police, the military, and the state bureaucracy were plausible, given the lack of energy with which contract killings, bombings, and illegitimate business deals were investigated.

Pavlov and his cohort show how, despite internal conflicts among business leaders, a small group was able to use its strength to influence the political scene. Bulgarian parties, in effect, became clients of a narrow field of businesspeople. In this context, businesspeople had no interest in creating pacts with politicians and found it difficult to sustain alliances among themselves. Networks among firms and members of the state bureaucracy, as well as those between businesspeople

---

[6] VIS-2 was a successor company to VIS-1, which was blacklisted by the government for selling insurance to owners of expensive Western cars in what was alleged to be a protection racket.

Introduction

and politicians, were much less broad than in Poland and offered fewer points of contact. As a result, businesspeople did not have the same network assets to negotiate broad institutions with a view to the long term. Competition policy remains poorly developed in Bulgaria, and low enforcement capacity means that even the weak existing institutions of market regulation function poorly. Moreover, secured transaction law that regulates the risk of giving credit does little to protect creditors, because influential interests have managed to block institutional development. Despite intense pressure in the process of EU accession, business elites and politicians operate in a highly uncertain environment based on domination, without the network ties that create webs of joint obligation or mutual reassurance, and large areas of the state remain under the influence of narrow, mafialike groups (Andreev 2009).

Romania's transition set in motion yet a third dynamic. One dominant party emerged out of the jarring revolution of 1989 as a national unity government: the National Salvation Front (NSF). The central actors of the NSF subsequently dominated Romanian politics through a new umbrella party, the Party of Social Democracy of Romania (PDSR),[7] which lost its first election, in 1996, to an ineffectual opposition party that spent most of its mandate on internal squabbles. The PDSR, renamed as the PSD in 2001, returned in 2000 to further dominate Romanian politics until 2004. Romanian business elites grew out of this milieu dependent on political support. In turn, they provided financial support to the NSF and PSD. To limit financial extraction, however, some business elites attempted to develop a margin of autonomy by forming their own satellite political parties with strange names and obscure platforms, such as the vaguely liberal Humanist Party and the nationalist New Generation. These personal parties brought their business sponsors some attention and limited autonomy from PSD politicians. In turn, personal parties served the PSD by taking voters from opposition parties by offering similar platforms. For example, the Humanist Party, founded by one of Romania's wealthiest men, Dan Voiculescu, brought votes and the support of Voiculescu's television station to the PSD from 2000 to 2006.

Although this strategy was available only to a few, it contributed to fragmenting the business community and prevented the development of organizations. Networks of cross-ownership were weak and firms rarely shared directors. As a result, institutions were poorly developed until the intense pressure of the EU accession process generated a significant degree of business regulation. At that time, progress was made in the reform of banking law, and the state of secured transaction law improved. Overall, the level of institutional change lay somewhere between Poland and Bulgaria, but networks between firms tended to be weak.

---

[7] I refer to this party throughout the text as the PSD – its current name – to indicate also the period when it governed as the PDSR.

Thus, three sharply different forms of the business–politics relationship emerged in Poland, Bulgaria, and Romania. In Poland, collaborative exchanges between two politically allied sets of business elites and their political sponsors defined the first two decades of struggles over reform, with the effect of a gradual consolidation of state power. In Bulgaria, the dominance of a narrow group of business actors over politicians undermined the development of broadly distributive institutions. In Romania, the dominance of political actors similarly failed to support the development of institutions.

The divergence between these cases points to the role that networks play in reducing uncertainty and complementing the development of institutions. The absence of such networks limits the extent of collective action by promoting the interests of narrow coalitions. By contrast, broad networks allow cross-sectoral coalitions to emerge. Thus, broad networks are crucial for the development of collective action and a necessary but not sufficient condition for the emergence of broadly distributive institutions (which additionally require the condition of widespread uncertainty).

The next chapter reviews relevant contributions in the literature and then moves to develop a theory of how networks affect the emergence of broadly distributive institutions. Before moving to that task, the next section reviews alternative explanations of post-socialist state development.

Traditional explanations of variation in institutional development are largely the product of a long-standing debate between two camps: those who feared widespread popular opposition to painful reforms and those who believed that powerful insiders would impede restructuring or even seek to stall reform. Concern about the political sustainability of reform was one of the motivations behind a lively literature about the appropriate speed of economic reform (Fischer and Gelb 1991: 104). Those who worried about a popular backlash and the sustainability of reform and saw benefits to a piecemeal approach viewed a gradual set of policy reforms as the best way to transform the state socialist economies into dynamic market economies (Portes 1990; Roland 1991; McMillan and Naughton 1992: 141; Dewatripont and Roland 1992a: 292; Aghion and Blanchard 1994; Dewatripont and Roland 1995). Those who feared bureaucrats and insider interests would try to block reform viewed rapid reform or "shock therapy" as a way to kick-start market economies (Lipton and Sachs 1990a; Frydman and Rapaczynski 1994; Sachs 1994; Åslund 1995; Hellman 1998).[8]

Even the brief comparison of Bulgaria, Romania, and Poland brings into question the standard explanations for differences in developmental trajectory

---

[8] As Dewatripoint and Roland point out, some authors took a mixed position, seeing the need for a shock approach on some dimensions and a gradual approach in others. For example, most economists agreed that measures to bring about macroeconomic stabilization should be adopted rapidly but diverged on liberalization, privatization, and the pace of firm restructuring (Dewatripont and Roland 1995).

Introduction

in the post-socialist region. To better understand the institutional development of these countries, this book focuses on the role of elite agency as shaped by network structure and uncertainty. I argue that the differences between these countries are better explained by a combination of social network structures and political factors, specifically levels of political uncertainty. Therefore, this book takes a different approach from the broader literature, and instead builds on the work of some scholars who have explored how networks in post-socialism served as resources during the transformation, and those who have also explored how political competition has promoted institutional development.[9] This book brings these elements together, however, to identify the conditions under which networks running between political and economic actors can, in the context of high levels of competition, support the development of broadly distributive institutions.

The approach presented in this book developed as a response to scholarship that has focused on the speed of reform. The following section explores this existing scholarship on post-socialist reform to situate and substantiate the alternative proposed here.

I also discuss two other alternative explanations. First, scholars have argued that some countries had a better chance in the reform process on the basis of various legacy effects and a history of contact with cultural or physical proximity to the West (Jowitt 1992; Hanson 1995; Jowitt 1996; Ekiert 1999; Kopstein and Reilly 2000). Second, as countries in post-socialist Europe began to negotiate the possibility of joining the European Union, scholars began to study the impact of such external actors and the conditions they imposed on the speed of reform in candidate countries (Moravcsik and Vachudova 2003; Vachudova 2005; Ekiert, Kubik, and Vachudova 2007). This "conditionality," as it became known, is a potentially important alternative factor that may have pushed countries along, and it thus merits discussion as an alternative explanation.

SHOCK THERAPY VERSUS GRADUALISM

Even before the political transition to democracy began in 1989 scholars had begun to consider how experiments with reformed socialism that introduced elements of markets would impact the institutions of state socialism and shift the sources of power and privilege (Kornai 1986; Stark 1986; Szelenyi 1988; Nee 1989). After 1989, as policy makers and academics began to consider how to create market economies in the region, a heated debate about the reform process developed in the literature. A central question of this debate focused on

---

[9] For examples of the network approach, see McDermott (2002) and Stark and Bruszt (1998). Grzymała-Busse (2007), O'Dwyer (2006), van Biezen and Kopecky (2007), and Woodruff (2009) are examples of scholarship on the role of political competition.

the appropriate speed of economic reform. Opposing sides embraced so-called "shock therapy" and "gradualism." The speed of the transformation was central, because each side attached negative consequences to the other's recommended pacing of reform.

Advocates of shock therapy contrasted it with a "muddling along" approach to reform and argued that the only way to create prospering and successful market economies was to carry out reforms quickly (Sachs and Lipton 1989; Lipton and Sachs 1990a). The advantages of the "shock program," as it was initially called, were both economic and political. Supporters argued that, from an economic standpoint, shock therapy would bring a return to growth sooner, generating a sustained rise in standards of living (Sachs and Lipton 1989: 1). It developed out of Sachs' experience in Latin America, and he and Lipton advocated this approach as advisors to Solidarity in 1989. The program began with price liberalization, which had the advantage of bringing macroeconomic stability by controlling inflation, reducing dangerous shortages in retail goods, and creating stable exchange rates. Price liberalization would also eliminate the distortions in investment that plagued command economies. In addition, it was supposed to reduce the costs of foreign debt and inspire confidence, which would make foreign loans and investment available. Price liberalization was to be accompanied by rapid reforms to remove obstacles to private sector activity, and privatization. Altogether, these moves would rapidly increase the allocative efficiency and raise productivity, albeit at the cost of massive layoffs and labor reallocation (Dewatripont and Roland 1992b).

Although there were several parts to the program, privatization was at its core. Describing the consensus approach to reform of post-communist societies in the early 1990s, Zinnes, Eilat, and Sachs (2001: 148) state,

[T]he linchpin of transition was to transfer ownership of the firms in the economic sectors to private hands – and to do so as fast as possible. Once in private hands, a series of self-reinforcing, virtuous, though self-interested, forces would emerge to demand the creation of all the institutions required for private ownership, thereby locking in the market economy.

This "stakeholder lobby" theory was the political argument for shock therapy. It claimed that the privatization of public assets was a policy that would move the reforms in the desired direction because these new owners of private property would then become the lobby that pushed for the development of market-supporting institutions (Fischer and Gelb 1991: 95; Shleifer and Vishny 1998: 10–11). Underpinning shock therapy was the idea that the ownership of private property would promote the articulation of demands for market-governing institutions.

Sachs and Lipton anticipated that privatization would begin with small enterprises, which could be privatized quickly, and move on to the more

Introduction 13

complicated large privatizations as soon as practicable. They also advanced a strategy for rapid large-scale privatization, however (Lipton and Sachs 1990a). As the privatization of large enterprises could take some years, Fischer advocated removing enterprises from the control of ministries and establishing them as independent entities with their own management in the interim (Fischer and Gelb 1991: 98). Fischer's addition highlights the importance attached to creating independent stakeholders in these new market economies. Separating the state from the economy, it was hoped, would also reduce government budgets by removing state-owned enterprises from them, and perhaps create new avenues to power and prestige (Nee 1989: 679). The shock therapists answered the criticism that these measures were too dangerous and would lead to a backlash against reform by saying that there was no other option (Sachs and Lipton 1989: 3).

The stakeholder lobby argument was based on the perceived harmful role that insiders and state actors can play in the reform process. Managers of firms had been recruited on the basis of loyalty to the Communist Party and lacked the technical skills to manage firms properly while operating in an environment lacking an adequate system of corporate governance (Lipton and Sachs 1990b: 314). These insiders might organize to extract concessions from the state, derail the reform process, and engage in a lengthy battle over the terms of privatization. Given their economic power, they might also attempt to influence state actors directly. When shock therapy was pursued a rapidly created large private sector would marginalize insiders and bureaucrats, creating larger sets of stakeholders using the "honeymoon period" after 1989 to quickly push through irreversible reforms (Svejnar 1989; Lipton and Sachs 1990a: 87–9; Sachs 1994; Åslund 1995; Boycko, Shleifer, and Vishny 1995; Johnson and Loveman 1995).

Privatization, preferably using a method that quickly distributed as many shares as possible to outsiders, was seen as a necessary step because it would limit state interference, impose hard budget constraints and private market signals on firms, and thus root out insider interests (Lipton and Sachs 1990b; Sachs 1994; Aghion and Blanchard 1998). Partial reform, by contrast, would produce "early winners" who could stall further privatization and reform to reap the economic benefits of the initial stages of transformation (Hellman 1998). This position was strengthened as the planning structure collapsed, leaving behind a large and directionless state-owned economy and firms that were often no longer under state control but in the hands of insiders with inadequate resources and abilities to carry out restructuring (Lipton and Sachs 1990b: 314; Aghion and Blanchard 1994: 287; Aghion and Blanchard 1998: 89). One of the reasons that rapid privatization would lead to both economic growth and political development, according to the shock therapists, was that it would free the state of actors linked to it by distorted incentive structures and create a large set of "outsider" stakeholders committed to going forward and developing institutions that supported the market (Shleifer and Vishny 1998: 10–11).

Gradualists, on the other hand, argued that shock therapy ignored the political realities and potential economic effects of the reform process. Prominent advocates of this view did not disagree on the destination of reform but envisioned a different "road" (Kornai 1986: 1715–24, 1728–30; Kornai 1990). Again, there were both political and economic arguments. Politically, gradualists argued that the extreme individual and aggregate uncertainty about what the future held could lead to popular opposition to rapid reform precisely because of the high reversal costs that shock therapists viewed as an advantage (Dewatripont and Roland 1995: 1208). A slower pace would instead allow policy makers to rack up some initial reform successes, building support for further reform among those who would need to approve the process. As reforms took place, the status quo ante would increasingly look less attractive than the outcome of a reformist policy (Roland 2002). Partial reforms would thus build support along the way for further reform. Partial reforms are also more acceptable since they are perceived as reversible and may be less costly in terms of compensation payments to losers in the process (Dewatripont and Roland 1995; Roland 2002: 33). And gradual reforms permit a "divide and rule" approach to reform in which governments can build coalitions with different groups affected by reforms instead of facing widespread opposition to rapid reforms that are opposed by a majority (Dewatripont and Roland 1992b: 721).

Gradualists also argued that shock therapists underestimated the budgetary costs of the compensation that would make restructuring acceptable to workers (Dewatripont and Roland 1992a: 292). As such, it had the potential to undermine the return to growth (Portes 1990; Roland 1991; Dewatripont and Roland 1992a: 292; McMillan and Naughton 1992: 141; Aghion and Blanchard 1994; Roland 1994; Dewatripont and Roland 1995; Roland 2002). Kornai argued that reform programs should focus on transferring firms to better owners and developing good corporate governance instead of emphasizing a quick transfer out of state hands (Kornai 1990).

The post-communist state was viewed quite differently by each approach. Shleifer and Vishny drew attention to the potential for states to disrupt the reform process by engaging in pathological behavior (Shleifer and Vishny 1998). Their "grabbing hand" approach attempted to identify ways to prevent government officials from turning to predatory behavior, which they identified as the cause of poor growth. Consequently, they argued that depoliticizing the economy was one of the priorities of the reform process and privatization one of the key tools to achieve it. This view was based on the perception that post-communist states had the ability to meddle with the economy. Political scientists, however, pointed out that post-socialist states were often weak and in need of rebuilding. In other words, the problem was not an excess of predatory or other kinds of state intervention but a lack of state capacity (Grzymała-Busse and Jones-Luong 2002). In the worst cases, this lack of capacity allowed private actors to overrun the state (Ganev 2001; Hellman,

Introduction 15

Jones, and Kaufmann 2003; Ganev 2007). By contrast, some scholars found that, when bureaucracies were more developed, states could play a crucial role in helping firms adjust to the post-reform economic conditions. For example, in a comparison of Russian regions, Brown, Earle, and Gehlbach (2009) found that, when bureaucracies were larger, privatization was more successful and firms more productive.

This discussion cannot cover all the intricacies of the debate, and my goal in discussing this literature is not to resolve the shock therapy versus gradualism debate. Others have already suggested that the emphasis on speed was misplaced (Kolodko and Nuti 1997; Kolodko 1999; Kornai 2000; Popov 2000; Zinnes, Eilat, and Sachs 2001; Popov 2007). Consequently, the central issue of relevance to my argument is the contention that fast reform, particularly rapid privatization and the marginalization of insiders, would yield better outcomes by undermining attachments to the status quo, distancing the state from the economy, and scrambling old networks. The main claim of interest here – that of the stakeholder lobby theory – proposes that the emergence of private owners would promote the development of institutions.

Numerous scholars have raised questions about this argument since it was proposed. They point out that private owners may, in fact, oppose the emergence of market institutions. For example, Hoff and Stiglitz (2002: 38) argue that uncertainty about the impact of the future legal regime may lead insiders to postpone its development or avoid making demands for it altogether. This applies both when privatization puts ownership in the hands of insider oligarchs and when property is distributed widely (Hoff and Stiglitz 2002). Black, Kraakman, and Tarassova (2000: 1753) have similarly shown that privatization did not generate demand for institutional reform because company owners and "kleptocrats" instead opposed efforts to strengthen market rules and push forward with reform after an initial, partial, market opening.

Data on the size of the private economy from the 1990s support the view that the "stakeholder lobby" theory does not account for differences between countries. The size of the private sector, shown in Table I.1, captures the emergence of new firms and privatized firms alike. Examining this data set shows that the supposedly detrimental economic effects of slow privatization are hardly borne out by evidence about the growth of the private sector. The quintessential success story of both growth and the development of institutions – Poland – generated the same percentage of GDP in the private sector as Albania, Hungary, and the Slovak Republic in 1995 and similar levels to Bulgaria and Romania,[10] which were extreme laggards in institutional reform, in 1996. Lithuania, Estonia, Hungary, and the Slovak and Czech Republics overtook Poland after 1995,

---

[10] In the Albanian case, this may be due more to the collapse of the state sector than the productivity of the private sector. In the other cases, however, the private sector grew as quickly as it did in the regional leader of growth and institutional reform.

TABLE I.I *Percentages of private sector's share in GDP*

	1989	1990	1991	1992	1993	1994	1995	1996	1997	1998	1999	2000	2001	2002	2003	2004	2005
Albania	5	5	5	10	40	50	60	75	75	75	75	75	75	75	75	75	75
Bulgaria	10	10	20	25	35	40	50	55	60	65	70	70	70	70	75	75	75
Czech Republic	5	10	15	30	45	65	70	75	75	75	80	80	80	80	80	80	80
Estonia	10	10	10	25	40	55	65	70	70	70	75	75	75	80	80	80	80
Hungary	5	25	30	40	50	55	60	70	75	80	80	80	80	80	80	80	80
Latvia	10	10	10	25	30	40	55	60	60	65	65	65	65	70	70	70	70
Lithuania	10	10	10	20	35	60	65	70	70	70	70	70	70	75	75	75	75
Poland	30	30	40	45	50	55	60	60	65	65	65	70	75	75	75	75	75
Romania	15	15	25	25	35	40	45	55	60	60	60	60	65	65	65	70	70
Slovak Republic	5	10	15	30	45	55	60	70	75	75	75	80	80	80	80	80	80
Slovenia	10	15	20	30	40	45	50	55	60	60	60	65	65	65	65	65	65

Source: European Bank for Reconstruction and Development (EBRD) "Structural change indicators."

Introduction 17

and Poland's performance subsequently trailed many countries in the Baltics, central Europe, and the Balkans.

Traditional explanations thus made much more than was warranted of the impact of privatization while ignoring other factors. The trajectories of countries shown above suggest that privatization is likely part of a more complex dynamic governing the emergence of well-functioning institutions.

In arguing against the shock therapy approach, I do not wish to throw the proverbial baby out with the bathwater. By emphasizing the importance of steady progress with reform, the shock therapists identified the key issue of how emergent economic elites would act in an economic system caught between the opposing logics of state socialism and market capitalism. In other words, their emphasis on the articulation of demands for the development of market-governing institutions as a result of privatization was based on a conception of the reform process as a coordination problem. They worried about the effect elites would have on the future course of reform in the absence of privatization. The shock therapists also believed that, once established as private owners, they would be driven to cooperate in their demand for institutions.

While I have raised questions about the linkage between privatization and institutional reform, underlying this literature is an interest in how economic and state elites interact to push forward the development of formal institutions of government. The literature has yet to provide an account, however, that examines the effect of different forms of this interaction – various network structures linking officials and business leaders – on the development of post-socialist institutions. I propose that to provide such an account requires the incorporation of other factors, such as the context in which firms were being privatized, the role that the state and parties played as the ownership of firms was being transformed, and the availability of networks to help firms coordinate.

LEGACIES AND GEOGRAPHY

A second strand of literature focuses on the radically different historical legacies and the role of geography that, scholars argue, continues to influence decision-making processes and the functioning of institutions (Jowitt 1992; Janos 1993; Hanson 1995; Jowitt 1996; Panther 1997; Ekiert 1999; Kopstein and Reilly 2000; Winiecki 2004; Dimitrova Grajzl 2007). The argument is that certain legacies or proximity to the West lead to better outcomes than other legacies or geographic distance. It often hinges on one of the following factors: the perceived negative influence of Ottoman and Russian rule and the beneficial impact of Habsburg and Prussian institutions (Panther 1997; Winiecki 2004; Dimitrova Grajzl 2007); the continued salience of pre-communist differences (Janos 1993); the negative impact of Soviet influence (Jowitt 1992); the spread of norms via geographic proximity to the West (Kopstein and Reilly 2000); the positive influence of economic contacts

(Hanson 1995); or expectations of EU and NATO membership (Kopstein and Reilly 2000).

Essentially, the argument explains why east central European countries have developed the best-functioning states, whereas southern European countries perform progressively worse by appealing to one or more of these factors. Hence, the farther north one travels toward the Russian imperial borders, the better bureaucratically endowed and culturally advanced countries are, and hence the better they fared under communism (Panther 1997; Winiecki 2004; Dimitrova Grajzl 2007). Similarly, according to this argument, associational patterns – the extent to which political and bureaucratic actors are embedded in webs of obligation with societal interests – increase in southern countries, because such ties became part of the general social fabric and culture under the Ottomans and were much less prominent under the Hapsburgs and Prussians.

Two critiques undermine the legacies argument. First, the empirical validity of such arguments is questionable, as I show below. Second, that specific legacies can be identified as explanations for the characteristics of some later time period, in this case the institutional development of countries a century or more later, is far from clear.

The coming chapters show that the legacy argument does not predict where networks are important. In fact, the opposite of what we would expect is true: networks have developed much more broadly in Poland than in the southern European cases examined here. As such, the mechanism implied by the legacy explanations – that lasting cultural maps are transmitted across generations – is unable to account for the level of network development or the extent to which networks are used.

According to Mendelski (2008), such legacies do not explain well institutional development or any other related variable. In fact, the data in Table I.2 show that geographical features fail to account for variation in measurable outcomes such as progress in the development of institutions. The interactions between interest groups that have brought about these changes are counter-intuitive. Table I.2 shows the complex patterns between imperial legacy, geography, and institutional development. The indicator shows the level of the EBRD reform index for six key areas of reform averaged over the first decade of reform and over the first fifteen years. To compare the longer-term trajectories of these countries, the yearly scores were averaged for the periods 1990 to 2000 and 1990 to 2005. Averages flatten sharp differences between countries that occur in any given year.[11]

---

[11] For example, in 1994 the Czech Republic scored significantly better for the development of securities market institutions than Hungary. The two countries changed places in the following year, however. Looking at the average score over time gives a general sense of both the speed and the extent of progress for the first decade and a half of reform.

Introduction

TABLE I.2 *Imperial legacy and progress on reform*

Country	Principal imperial legacy	Average reform index 1990–2000[12]	Average reform index 1990–2005[13]
Albania	Ottoman	2.1	2.31
Bulgaria	Ottoman	2.43	2.67
Czech Republic	Austro-Hungarian	2.95	3.17
Estonia	Russian	2.73	3.03
Hungary	Austro-Hungarian	3.25	3.43
Latvia	Russian	2.56	2.83
Lithuania	Russian	2.49	2.79
Poland	Russian, Prussian, Austro-Hungarian	3.09	3.28
Romania	Austro-Hungarian, Ottoman	2.28	2.51
Slovak Republic	Austro-Hungarian	2.85	3.06
Slovenia	Austro-Hungarian	2.76	2.94

Source: EBRD.

The data confirm that imperial legacy fails to explain fully the different trajectories. There is significant variation among countries with the same imperial legacy. Neighboring countries such as Slovenia and Hungary, both former Austro-Hungarian territories, have taken significantly different paths. Bulgaria, which the Ottomans ruled with a particularly brutal hand, performs better than Romania and Albania. The Baltic states also progress at rates similar to those of the Czech Republic and Slovenia despite Russian imperial domination.

Some countries that today are unified were formerly split among imperial powers. Romania, which was split between Austro-Hungarian and Ottoman influence until independence in 1878, seems to lend support to the negative influence of Ottoman rule, although we might expect partial Austrian rule to lift it onto a better path than those countries that were subjects only of the Turks. As noted already, this is not the case. Poland, which ceased to exist after 1795 as the result of partition among three empires, performs second only to Hungary on the reform index, despite the negative influence of Russian rule,

[12] Average of EBRD country reform scores on enterprise restructuring, price liberalization, trade and foreign exchange, competition policy, banking reform and interest rate liberalization, and securities market and non-bank financial institution regulation.

[13] Average of EBRD country reform scores on enterprise restructuring, price liberalization, trade and foreign exchange, competition policy, banking reform and interest rate liberalization, and securities market and non-bank financial institution regulation.

tripartite partition, and its difficult re-emergence from that experience, to become a unified state that was quite radically recomposed after both the First and Second World Wars.

The failure of legacy arguments to account well for subsequent institutional development holds also if we extend the analysis to include the communist legacy. Despite the hypothesized negative effect of Ottoman legacy, Bulgaria had a similar level of institutional quality to Habsburg successors Hungary and the Czech Republic in the mid-1980s. Poland's low level of institutional quality in the mid-1980s was close to that of Romania. Poland was also considered one of the economic basket cases of socialist Europe in the 1980s (Frye 2010). Poland and Romania both achieved rapid institutional change until 1994, however, when the two countries began to diverge (Mendelski 2008).

The inconsistencies above raise bigger questions about the legacy approach. Not only is it difficult to identify when but also how and which legacies matter. In other words, why focus on imperial legacy, when we could go further back in time, or forward to consider the legacy of Nazi occupation or some other period (Gross 1989)?

Geographic proximity to the West similarly raises many questions. Although the capital of the Slovak Republic is only thirty-five kilometers from Vienna, it was ruled by the increasingly undemocratic regime of Valdimir Meciar from 1994 to 1998. Kopstein and Reilly (2000: 30) argue that this was only an episode, and ultimately the Slovak Republic ended up on a better path than could be expected on the basis of policy alone. Nevertheless, the episode raises questions about the stability of the path. This is even more the case in Hungary. That country, by contrast, had been on a good trajectory since the beginning of the transformation. Since the publication of their paper, however, Hungary has seen a series of eyebrow-raising institutional reforms by the Fidesz government that took power in 2010. These have included the drafting of a new constitution and the passage of laws that concentrate power in the hands of the government. The far right party Jobbik, often described as anti-Semitic, anti-Roma, racist, and homophobic, has emerged as the third largest party in the National Assembly. While it is plausible that geographic factors have some influence, the effects seem to be weak, and these "trajectories" often change quite dramatically.

While legacies do not offer a compelling account of the trajectories of countries after 1989, Crawford and Lijphardt (1995) point to important lessons generated by the approach. First, considering central features of socialist society, they argue that, because these were dominated by elites that had few societal linkages and the political transitions themselves were largely the result of splits within the ruling elite and challenges from small groupings of counter-elites, an analytic focus on elites in the post-communist region is justified. Second, successes and failures in the transition process were often overdetermined by immediate factors, even where legacies would seem to be relevant (Crawford and Lijphart 1995: 175).

Introduction 21

In this book, I prefer to treat legacies as a background condition with some impact, but to bear in mind that there are complex and inconsistent mechanisms by which legacy affects actors and institutions. My belief is that the agency of actors is of greater interest in understanding contemporary outcomes, and I make that argument in this book.

I can thus better account for variation in developmental paths than the arguments above. This is not to say that legacy plays no role in facilitating or complicating progress on institutional development. The variety of paths followed by countries emerging from the same imperial legacy show that agency, particularly elite agency, can overcome the effects of legacy. As Kitschelt has argued, legacies matter, but we must not dismiss the impact of elite decision on country trajectories (Kitschelt 1999; Kitschelt 2003).

EU CONDITIONALITY

Although I focus on domestic factors in this book, it is worth considering the possibility that external factors may have influenced the development of these same institutions. The most significant of these external factors is the European Union, which could have positively affected the reform process by imposing conditionality on countries throughout the region as part of the accession process. A significant literature has attempted to identify how and to what extent EU pressure on candidate countries might have affected the process being discussed here. Some scholars have argued that the accession process tipped the scales in favor of reform and the adoption of democratic and market institutions (Moravcsik and Vachudova 2003; Vachudova 2005; Ekiert, Kubik, and Vachudova 2007). These accounts do not see the European Union simply as an external actor affecting domestic policy choices, however. The EU's influence is filtered through domestic actors. For example, Ekiert, Kubik, and Vachudova (2007: 11) state that "the benefits and constraints offered by the European Union shaped the character of domestic political competition, informed the agendas of many political and economic actors, and expanded opportunities for reformers."

In keeping with this approach, Jacoby argues that conceptualizing external actors as a "freestanding" influence on domestic policy events holds little promise. In other words, we should view external actors as an additional component of an explanation more than an alternative explanation. In this view, external actors influence the choices of domestic actors in a kind of "informal coalition" (Jacoby 2006: 626). In a review of several studies examining the effects of EU influence, however, Jacoby finds evidence that the success of external actors in influencing domestic policy is rare, even when linkages with domestic actors are present (Jacoby 2006: 643–4).

Other scholars echo the limits of this effect in new member states. Frye and Grzymała Busse argue outright that the pressure of the European Union came too late to explain the paths of institutional change taken by different countries (Grzymała-Busse 2007: 89, quoted by Frye 2010: 16). Jacoby notes that bureaucrats were also able to avoid revealing areas of institutional dysfunction. Although such revelations were a prerequisite to receiving assistance, ministerial elites also perceived them as a potential weapon in the hands of opponents of enlargement and preferred to avoid such disclosures (Jacoby 1999: 62).

Others note the ability of interest groups to resist external pressure (Höpner and Schäfer 2010). These scholars use comparative case studies to show that active interest groups and domestic resistance are a key factor impeding the effects of EU expansion and shaping national variation in policy adoption. For example, Höpner and Schäfer (2010) find strong resistance to pressure to adopt economic institutions that undermine domestic models of capitalism. The latter finding is particularly relevant, because this book explores the formation of these domestic models of capitalism. The policy areas examined here are keenly guarded and influenced by domestic groups. Undoubtedly the European Union at times impacted debates and the progress of reform in post-communist Europe. The literature reviewed here, however, suggests that this impact was often insufficient to affect the course of domestic actor's choices and, when relevant, was layered over existing interest group struggles.

Consequently, I argue that the two dominant explanations for post-socialist development – speed of reform, and legacy or geography arguments – fail to explain well the trajectories that countries in post-socialist Europe have followed on the path to developing economic institutions. In this book I also take the position that the impact of the European Union does not undermine an analysis that focuses primarily on the interaction of domestic interests.

In the coming chapter, I argue for an approach that focuses on two key variables in the process by which state power develops in contemporary societies: networks, which sustain coalitions; and uncertainty, which limits how networks are used.

As I will show, neither variable alone is sufficient to explain the different developmental outcomes. A more parsimonious explanation, that political competition creates a watchdog effect driving countries toward better institutional outcomes, is shown to be false in the comparison of Romania and Bulgaria. Frequent alternation of the party in power alone failed to put Bulgaria on a much better path than Romania. I explain below why competition in the absence of networks is insufficient to allow elites to coordinate toward mutually beneficial equilibria.

CASE SELECTION

In studies of the varieties of capitalism, the focus has been on countries in which institutions are already formed and not on places where the development of market institutions is stalled or in the early stages of development. Hence,

Introduction

the post-socialist countries offer a unique opportunity to pursue a much broader question: how do the institutions that regulate markets and the institutions to govern them develop? The post-socialist countries allow us to observe this process in a relatively compressed and well-documented period of elite struggles over the contours of basic societal institutions that determine the breadth and depth of participation in the market, such as the protection of competition, access to credit via both banks and securities markets, the role of networks in economic activity, and the extent to which government reinforces insider ties.

In broader comparative terms, this study is concerned with a mid-category of cases among capitalist countries. There exist countries in which institutions of economic management have long since stabilized – the advanced industrialized states – and countries that have developed highly effective institutions to steer industrialization before developing democratic institutions – the so-called developmental states (Wade 1990; Evans 1995). The former type of state developed a variety of state forms as a result of class conflict (Moore 1967) and the pressure to raise capital or finance the nation state (Tilly 2001), while the latter type developed capacity in an attempt to catch up with the industrial world.

By contrast, the post-communist countries considered in this study offer an opportunity to investigate states that are neither developmental, in that they have lacked both the capacity and the capital to engage in any substantial industrial policy, nor simply predatory (Bates 1981; Shleifer and Vishny 1998). In the period under consideration they all had governments subject to recall by elections, were open to the flow of transnational capital, and faced considerable external pressure to reform. At the same time, the breakdown of state socialism had severely undermined the power of their bureaucratic institutions. Thus, the transition to capitalism and democracy meant developing institutions by leaps and bounds in a process defined by internal political pressure and external advice. Most countries had inherited and resurrected regulation and law from the 1930s, which had large gaps when it came to regulating much more complicated contemporary economies. Areas of law as basic as the handling of bankruptcy and relations between creditors and debtors were fundamentally lacking. Hence, they have recently undergone a process of often lurching institutional development.

This setup allows for a number of insights. First, it puts in a national context some of the global patterns affecting countries more broadly. By selecting countries experiencing similar shifts over time, this book sheds light on the national-level factors through which international effects – such as the European Union, openness, liberalization, and capital flows – act on these countries. Second, it permits an explanation of divergence between countries that were similar, in that they are all transformed socialist societies, but are now very different on account of internal phenomena, such as the restructuring of social ties and informal organizations.

PLAN OF THE BOOK

This book examines why some post-socialist countries have developed broadly distributive institutions while others have not. My explanation focuses on how different social network structures and levels of uncertainty have affected the types of market institutions – broadly distributive or selective advantage – that political and economic elites can develop collectively.

The book is divided into parts and proceeds as follows. Part I provides an introduction, a review of relevant literatures, and argument. Chapter 1 discusses the contributions of two literatures in political economy that shed light on the institutional impact of state–business ties. The literature on the developmental state offers a point of departure for thinking about how the relationship between economic and state-level actors affects institutional development. A second literature on the varieties of capitalism provides a way of thinking about how firms and political actors develop institutions in the advanced industrialized world. I draw on both lines of scholarship to construct a theory that also incorporates the untreated variable of networks and partisan political competition. Bringing networks and political competition over economic resources to the fore, I develop and extend both literatures to contexts that are democratic but not part of the advanced industrialized world. The result is a theory that prospectively conceptualizes the bargaining moves between political and economic elites as a way of understanding elite collective action. The rest of the chapter develops the argument about networks, uncertainty, and the trajectories of institutional development.

Part II discusses the role of networks in shaping firm behavior and interaction with political actors. Networks facilitate monitoring and the spread of information. In order to demonstrate that networks shape institutional outcomes and not the reverse, Chapter 2 sets out in more detail an argument about how corporate governance – that is, who controls firms – and ownership influence collective action. I show that, when networks are broad, firm collective action increases.

Chapter 3 examines the first type of network treated in this study: the development of the actual ownership and director networks in three post-socialist countries and the trajectories that each case represents. It shows that very different actors have emerged as key owners in each of the societies under study between 1990 and 2005. I focus on the dominance of financial versus industrial firms and find that the former maintain far more ties. As a result, when financial firms dominate, much broader networks emerge. Chapter 3 shows that "who owns whom" – whether key owners are banks, families, or industrial firms – affects the shape of the ownership network and thus structures the incentives that firms have when organizing for collective action.

Part III shows how uncertainty interacts with networks. Chapter 4 investigates how uncertainty affects the incentives of firms and politicians to create alliances. It shows that party financing networks vary significantly across the three case studies, representing three distinct forms of party–firm alliance.

Introduction

Chapter 5 explores the second type of network by mapping the system of influence constructed out of the individual career paths of elite state bureaucrats developed between 1990 and 2003 across the three countries. Political parties manage the promotion and advancement of their cadres into non-state positions as part of a broad informal organization that aims to garner power and control financial resources. How frequently personnel moved, whether their state and non-state positions were stable after elections, and where in society they went from their state positions had a key impact on the distribution of influence in each society.

Chapter 6 carries out a quantitative cluster analysis and comparison of eleven countries in the region to identify the role of networks and the extent of uncertainty in each country. These results are used to individuate different forms of state–society relation that have emerged across the region. The argument of this book is that the social structure of economic interests and their embeddedness with political actors, in combination with the level of uncertainty, determines the trajectory of institutional development. I find three clusters. The first, *concertation states*, in which elites and firms form broad networks under high levels of uncertainty, have made the most progress on institutional development. This comes about because uncertainty constrains political actors, and networks facilitate monitoring, information flows, and credible commitments. Thus, economic and business elites have been able to forge broad distributive bargains. The second, *patronage states*, in which elites form narrow networks under low levels of uncertainty, have made moderate progress because political elites are not constrained and are not able to make commitments, and narrow networks also undermine monitoring. *Captured states*, in which elites form narrow networks under high levels of uncertainty, are extreme laggards on institutional development because monitoring is poor and extreme uncertainty discounts the value of the promises of political actors.

Finally, I present the conclusions of the book in order to offer a comprehensive understanding of how different paths – those based on broad versus narrow networks and high versus low levels of uncertainty – influenced the development and consolidation of institutions. The book ends with a discussion of the implications of this argument for our understanding of the development of market institutions in emerging market economies.

PART I

FOUNDATIONS

I

Approaches to institution building

Political scientists have long sought to understand how relations between economic and political elites affect the development of institutions. This question gained particular salience as the financial crisis of 2007–2009 gripped the global economy. The deregulation of banks, their ability to own such large parts of the US economy and securitize credit markets, and their political access were frequently blamed for the inadequate regulatory institutions that were largely responsible for the economic crisis.

The post-socialist countries offer an opportunity to examine the parallel development of a whole region in perhaps the closest approximation of a social science laboratory. All the post-socialist countries were affected by insider attempts to preserve the status quo of the early 1990s in the context of states undermined by the collapse of state socialism. Yet, after more than two decades, sharp differences in institutional development are apparent even in neighboring countries. Some states continue to be vulnerable to the demands of narrow societal groups, while others are able to pursue institutional reforms that broadly promote economic development.

The general expectation is that networks among businesspeople and linkages between the state and the economy will be an obstacle to the development of well-functioning institutions. Paradoxically, the cases examined in this book show that the causal linkage between networks and institutional development is more complex. The cases in this book show that, when networks of business ownership and personnel are broad, larger coalitions were driven to imbue institutions with the power to regulate the market.

The introduction to this study presented an initial comparison of the three core cases explored in this book: Bulgaria, Romania, and Poland. In Poland, strong networks emerged among a group of crony entrepreneurs allied with the Social Democratic Party and a competing faction supported by the anti-communist opposition, Solidarity. The left faction prospered when the SLD was in power and frequently suffered when Solidarity won elections. Those affiliated with Solidarity also took advantage of political protection. Because political competition was sharp, parties depended on political financing from firms, and thus had an interest in their prosperity. Many firms took advantage of preferential access to privatizations to acquire shares in other firms. Thus, ownership networks among firms became increasingly broad over time. Also as a result of sharp political competition, individuals shifted from positions within the state to jobs in private but politically allied firms. These shifts often happened after elections, with the result that personnel networks also became very broad over time. Both types of networks tightly linked political parties to firms and firms among themselves. The economy consequently became heavily politicized. Because of these broad networks, large cross-sectoral coalitions negotiated over the content of new market institutions. Yet, despite these strong network ties between parties and firms, institutions that were broadly distributive emerged.

This outcome was not a given, as shown in the divergent paths taken by other countries in the region, including the two other case studies of this book: Bulgaria and Romania. Bulgarian political parties effectively became the clients of powerful businesspeople. In this context, businesspeople had no interest in creating pacts with politicians. Networks among firms and members of the state bureaucracy, as well as those between businesspeople and politicians, were much less broad and offered fewer points of contact. As a result, businesspeople did not have the same network assets to negotiate broadly distributive institutions with a view to the long term. Instead, small groups of businesspeople hijacked institutional development for their own purposes. Romania followed a third path, because the nature of its transition created a political party that was asymmetrically powerful. Firms developed under the patronage of the dominant Social Democratic Party. In order to limit extraction, some businesspeople entered the political arena with personal parties. This further undermined business cohesion, and firms did not develop collective bodies to articulate demands. Businesspeople also figured heavily on party lists as part of a broad system of clientelistic exchanges that traded financial support for the protection of business interests (Protsyk and Matichescu 2011). Unsurprisingly, the resulting institutions favored selective advantage – that is, they were narrowly distributive.

The comparison of Poland, Romania, and Bulgaria frames a puzzle: given the generally negative and corrupting role ascribed to networks, how can we explain their positive role in the process of institutional development in some contexts? My argument is that the structure of networks and the level of uncertainty within which these networks operate shape the incentives of elites to act collectively and make broad demands for market-supporting institutions. Networks emerge to fill the space left by incomplete institutions. Broad networks link cross-sectoral coalitions and facilitate collective action. The effect of uncertainty on collective action depends on the type of network present. Under high levels of uncertainty, if networks are broad, cooperation emerges because

Approaches to institution building

information flows and reputation undermine defection from agreements between politicians and businesspeople. Networks also support credible commitments. Under high levels of uncertainty and narrow networks, business elites prey on the state because parties are weakened by high levels of competition and cannot credibly commit to agreements with business. Narrow networks make defections hard to detect, and uncertainty lowers the value of politicians' promises. Under low levels of uncertainty and narrow networks, dominant political elites that do not face the threat of alternation exploit atomized firms. Under low levels of uncertainty and broad networks, dominant political elites enter into collusive relations with firms.

Hence, I argue that the broad incorporation of interest groups is critical to the successful design and implementation of economic policy and market-supporting regulations that are broadly distributive. Strong and broad networks are not anathema to institution building. To the contrary, in the conditions of widespread uncertainty present after political and economic transitions they are necessary for the development of functional institutions.

I examine the trajectories of institutional development by exploring the progression of countries in four areas of policy making that have very direct distributional consequences: competition law, the regulation of banking, the regulation of financial transactions, and the rule of law. These institutions have sweeping distributional consequences for firms.

To understand the extensive bleeding together of economic and political elites that is so prominent in the cases at hand as part of an explanation of the emergence of broadly distributive institutions requires a revision of some views in the literature. To begin, I propose that little leverage is gained in conceptualizing the emergence of institutions through the notion of a unitary and bounded state. Accounts based on a unitary view also fail to deal with the genesis of state power – the authority that comes from being separated from societal influences and yet connected to societal actors in a way that envisions political elites building institutions together with economic elites that meet the needs of both groups and generate long-term stable social equilibria. This is the elusive embedded autonomy described by Evans (1995).

As discussed in the previous chapter, early studies of reform in post-socialist countries suffered from an inability to adequately explain the emergence of capacious and autonomous states in contexts in which reform did not make it quickly through the "valley of transition" – the difficult early period when reforms were extremely painful and required determined leaders while democracy heightened the incentives for them to deviate from the necessary policies to increase short-term welfare (Przeworski 1991) – but instead passed through a long process of negotiation and experimentation. As many countries faltered in the valley, Hellman (1998) has argued that the initial "winners" – those who used arbitrage opportunities present when reforms such as price liberalization were only partially complete to amass vast wealth and power – would hijack the policy agenda, preventing further reform in order to protect their interests.

The implicit conclusion of Hellman was that only fast shock therapy resembling reforms would allow countries to build markets and grow instead of becoming mired in a state of partial reform. By extension, as actors are joined by increasingly broad networks of ties, states should become hostage to a greater number of demands. Consequently, we should expect those states with broader economic networks to be less autonomous and make less progress on institutional reform than those narrowly connected to the economy.

Quite surprisingly, the puzzle of eastern European state building is that this does not describe the progress of reform across the region. Across the post-socialist world, different trajectories of institution building emerged that deviated from the predictions of the early reform literature.

The empirical record shows that countries with broad networks of inter-firm ties and ties connecting political and economic elites have been able to collaborate toward broadly distributive institutions. Those that did not have these networks have not been able to do so. Put another way, networks do the opposite of what the institutional argument suggests. Instead of binding reformers, when networks are far-reaching they can align the interests of a broader group of actors and allow them to work in concert. Networks thus structure the demand making of societal actors. When broad, they also shield states and political actors from narrow interests. The use of networks must be channeled in productive directions, however. This is more likely to happen when a second factor is present: uncertainty.

Two literatures are useful in understanding the link between networks and uncertainty, which are at the center of my argument. The body of research that has grown out of the research agenda on the "varieties of capitalism" (VoC) approach offers a way to understand how the variety of economic institutions that has emerged across post-socialist Europe over the last two decades can be internally stable and coherent (Hall and Soskice 2001). The VoC framework argues that the early institutional preferences of firms create spillover effects that lead to the selection of other complementary institutions. Thus, VoC provides a model for how firms put forward demands for institutions. More importantly, VoC helps understand how these demands can lead to the development of sets of complementary institutions that constitute internally coherent and stable models of economic activity. These can deviate sharply from the liberal model of capitalism. Thus, each of the state types described in this chapter and the institutions associated with them reflect the preferences of dominant firms and the extent to which they can collaborate across network ties. I use this notion of *complementarity* as a way of explaining the persistence of varieties of post-socialist capitalism that have developed out of the preferences of firms and are based on various network structures that link the polity and economy.

A second literature, commonly known as the "developmental state" approach, has sought to identify how the east Asian states, in particular, were able to pursue economic development by aligning coalitions of actors such as

Approaches to institution building 33

business leaders, unions, and bureaucrats behind the goal of rapid upgrading and innovation. The principal contribution of this literature to my argument is the concept of *embeddedness*: the extent to which political actors are able to enlist economic actors in the process of building institutions to govern the market. I focus on embeddedness because it has a role in generating institutional reform that serves the interests of both political and economic actors, but I also develop the notion to show that there can be different faces to embeddedness. Early work emphasized the positive role of embeddedness in allowing information flow. Later scholars also focused on the extent to which single or multiple factions of elites were linked through embedded ties.

Together, insights from these literatures help explain how demand making from firms in collaboration with political actors has generated a variety of trajectories of institutional development. I extend both concepts, focusing on information flows for collaboration but also introducing competition.[1] Thus, while building on the conceptual tools offered by VoC and developmental state scholarship, I add a novel focus on political party competition as a factor that shapes the interests of firms and the way in which embedded ties are used. The rest of this chapter examines the most important contributions of the two literatures, which provide useful tools and a foundation for the typology and argument advanced in this study.

EXTENDING THE VARIETIES OF CAPITALISM

The process of economic reform is one of devising new institutions that frame economic activity and drive economic actors toward broadly distributive institutions. Ideally, these institutions allow firms to pursue profits and politicians to be re-elected while promoting economic growth and development. The basic challenge is to develop institutions that will govern markets so as to support the wealth-enhancing and innovative activities of firms. Not all firms are well served by the same institutions, however, and not all market economies follow the same systemic logic. This point has been well established with the development of a broad research agenda on the varieties of capitalism. The central message of the literature that focuses on VoC in the advanced industrial societies is that different countries develop distinctive institutions that generate strong complementary effects to support economic activity.

The VoC literature proposes two main variants: the coordinated market economies (CMEs) of continental western Europe and the liberal market economies (LMEs) of, for example, the United Kingdom, the United States, and

---

[1] The developmental state literature neglects to consider competition because it is concerned largely with non-democratic contexts.

Australia. In the former, firms depend "more heavily on non-market modes of coordination" such as relational contracting, the use of inter-firm networks, and collaborative instead of competitive relationships with other firms (Hall and Soskice 2001: 8–9, 33–6). In liberal market economies, by contrast, firms coordinate on the basis of competition. The CME/LME framework of the varieties of capitalism project has opened up research on the complexity and variation both between and within these clusters.

The extension of this agenda to contexts in which institutions are still in a developmental phase requires some adaptation. In the post-socialist countries, where market institutions developed to replace pre-existing state socialist institutions, similar institutional complementarities have developed. These support forms of market-based activity that are radically different from either the CME or LME types, however. The main distinction is the extent to which economic activity and actors are politicized and rely on networks that differ from those present in CMEs.

Efforts to expand the VoC framework have been undertaken by numerous scholars. While Feldmann (2006) argues that the two VoC types can be applied to post-socialist countries, most authors find that these types cannot be directly transported. Nölke and Vliegenthart (2009) argue that the post-socialist countries represent a fundamentally different type of capitalism with a heavy transnational component and suggest a third variant: the dependent market economy (DME), in which transnational corporations are the core coordination mechanism. Bohle and Greskovits (2007) also highlight the difference between post-socialist capitalism and the two variants present in advanced industrial societies. They argue, however, that not one but several different variants of post-socialist capitalism have emerged out of the common legacy of state socialism, classifying states by how much they have imposed constraints on private economic activity.

These authors underscore the extent to which firms in post-socialist countries are collectively trying to solve a very different set of problems from those present in the advanced industrial economies, such as much higher levels of uncertainty, a lack of indigenous capital, poorly developed institutions, and lower state capacity. It follows that firms in post-socialist countries address these problems using strategies other than those identified in CMEs and LMEs. Bohle and Greskovits in particular draw attention to the role of the state in light of the influence of transnational actors. Yet the fundamental point of the VoC literature is that different variants of capitalism persist because of the strong institutional complementarities they generate. The DME and the variants identified by Bohle and Greskovits label the distinct qualities of post-socialist capitalism but do not identify the nature of the complementarity of arrangements that underpins it. One such arrangement is the configuration of the relationship between the polity and the economy. In my view, this is the foundation of each distinct form of post-socialist capitalism.

Approaches to institution building 35

How these forms develop is explained in the VoC literature. The process by which countries embark on different paths occurs at two levels according to the framework developed by Hall and Soskice. On the ground, firms seek to create institutions that increase their chances of survival. Once firms choose a particular set of institutions, a macro-social evolutionary logic drives the development of complementary institutions. In the CMEs, for example, Hall and Soskice's argument is that, if the prevailing labor practice is to sign long-term contracts with skilled laborers to ensure the availability of skills, then it is also highly likely that firms will rely on extensive education and training schemes and develop systems for sharing technology with other firms as a remedy for the lack of labor mobility. The benefits of institutions increase as other complementary institutions develop around them. By this mechanism, the initial preferences of firms start countries on an institutional path.

Hall and Soskice's evolutionary vision of the development of economic institutions is useful in explaining the different variants of post-socialist capitalism that have emerged. In the post-socialist countries, early moves toward network-based forms of coordination drove countries toward the establishment of matching institutions in other areas that frame economic activity. For example, if business finds new clients primarily via networks, it is likely that it will also borrow by using preferential access to banks. Over time an insider network logic takes hold in the whole economy, because a hybrid mix of institutions would generate costs and confusion rather than the synergies to be found with complementary institutional forms.

Discovering which institutions will generate the best results for a given group of firms and a particular context is not a simple problem, however. Hall and Soskice (2001) focus on the preferences of firms and to some extent the formation of coalitions of firms. They pay relatively little attention to the interaction of firms with political actors. Yet it is precisely this interaction – the ability of firms to create coalitions and negotiate acceptable solutions with state leaders – that is crucial in the developing world and emerging markets, where the state is often predatory or suffers from insufficient capacity to achieve its goals alone. Further, state leaders can have the wrong motivations or bad information, be under the influence of powerful but narrow lobbies, or even simply harbor bad ideas – all with disastrous effects. Leaders can also pursue their own short-term interests by choosing to serve the preferences of economic allies. All these dynamics were at work at times in the economic and political transformation from state socialism, which involved the readaptation of old institutions and the construction of new institutions to regulate the emerging economies.

Differences between countries persist because the majority of firms in one country might oppose, for example, the elimination of selective benefits that come with the development of a competition-enforcing authority or the protection of minority shareholders (Black, Kraakman, and Tarassova 2000: 1753; Hoff and Stiglitz 2002: 38). These firms might fear the unexpected consequences that accompany a move away from the status quo. Influential firms in some countries might prefer weak shareholder protections and be willing to sacrifice the ability to raise funds in capital markets. Similarly, some firms may prefer a more developed system of banking, credit, and the institutions that accompany developed lending markets, while others will prefer to source credit from within networks.

Later chapters show how firms in the post-socialist countries have settled on different levels of what can be called "selective advantages." Countries across the post-socialist region vary widely in the development of key areas of market regulation, such as banking, financial, and competition law, and the regulation of political finance by firms. The variance of interest here is the extent to which institutions are designed to distribute benefits broadly or narrowly. Over time, as a result of foreign pressure and changing internal economic conditions, key institutions of market regulation may creep toward and ultimately converge on Western norms, such as those established in the EBRD's transition indicators of progress on institutional development. There are many long and tortuous roads to that end point, however. Countries take different paths toward that destination, and it is much too soon to argue for a convergence of institutional types.

Thus, when adapted to the market conditions of countries in the developing world, the conceptual tools of the VoC literature allow us to understand how trajectories of institutional development persist over time despite the pressure of international economic integration. Networks provide the social foundation through which an array of complementary alternative market practices form the basis of national economic models that deviate from competitive markets.

CONSIDERING MULTIPLE FORMS OF EMBEDDEDNESS

Throughout the post-socialist reform period businesspeople sought to influence politicians so that new institutions would benefit their existing or nascent ventures, while politicians sought to secure financial support from businesspeople. In other words, economy and polity were both in the process of developing different forms of embeddedness (Evans 1995; Polanyi 2001). The concept of embeddedness was applied by Evans to explain why some states in the developing world were able to promote growth while others failed. "Embeddedness" signifies the extent to which networks connect the state to the economy. According to Evans, when these two spheres are too closely connected, opportunities for collusion are easily within reach. At the other extreme, when they are too distant, opportunities for entrepreneurs and policy makers to coordinate and communicate are not available, and critical signals and information are lost. Policy makers and businesspeople both fail to understand the goals and priorities of their counterparts. At the ideal balance point for embeddedness, political and economic actors are connected but the state is able to remain autonomous – gathering key information but nevertheless able to make difficult and often unpopular decisions without being too influenced by

Approaches to institution building

the demands of narrow business interests. When this balance is struck, business can receive vital support from the state while also facing incentives that make firms innovate, becoming more productive and competitive.

Evans offers an important foundation for thinking about how state–economy ties are both critical for and able to derail developmental policy. Where Evans's approach and the developmental state literature fall short is in failing to make clear why political elites would want to pursue developmentally oriented policy as opposed to short-run self-dealing. In the developmental state literature, we are told that states able to achieve the miraculous outcomes associated with east Asian development had a special blend of embeddedness and autonomy.

Later studies questioned the benign nature of embeddedness and its sufficiency to explain good economic governance. Kang (2002), for example, instead focused on the importance of a situation he labels "mutual hostages." In this circumstance, instead of a state mediating to bring about good outcomes, Kang sees two social networks of elites that counter each other's power. The conflict between them promotes good governance by limiting the power of each to engage in excessive self-dealing. When the economic and political elites are unified, on the other hand, excessive self-dealing undermines governance. Kang's approach avoids ascribing to the state the almost magical qualities of the developmental state to coordinate economic development, and takes a much more cynical view of the east Asian "miracle." This approach is not sufficient to explain good governance in democracies, however, where there are always at least two separate groups of political elites but very different outcomes obtain across countries.

For both Evans and Kang, good developmental outcomes result from network ties, albeit through different mechanisms: information sharing versus mutual monitoring. In both, the problem of development is essentially a type of coordination problem facing elites. I build on these ideas toward a hybrid position, viewing the problem of development under incomplete institutions as a coordination problem in which multiple elites must collaborate to realize the greater gains to be had after institutional reform.[2] To collaborate requires that they overcome pervasive information, monitoring, and commitment problems.

Such coordination under incomplete institutions is facilitated by networks. According to Beckert (2007a), Polanyi's original notion of embeddedness was precisely one of the glue that allows market actors to operate in stable worlds that are calculable. Polanyi identified three key coordination problems that are exacerbated by uncertainty (Beckert 2007a; Beckert 2007b). First, the problem of *value* refers to the difficulty with which individuals are able to form notions

---

[2] This is akin to Doner's (2009) idea that elites in developmental states were able to coordinate around levels of investment or upgrading that individuals would not pursue alone.

of value of items offered on the market. Value is socially and, more importantly in the present context, politically created. The second coordination problem is that of *competition*. Markets are based on competitive pressures, but profit emerges only when markets are imperfect. Hence, market actors try to create conditions that protect them from pure price competition. Incumbents try to retain their position by using existing regulation, while market actors who are disadvantaged attempt to challenge incumbents (Weber 1978 [1922] and Fligstein 2001, both cited by Beckert 2007a). The state plays a central role here by setting out the rules of the game. Third, *cooperation* problems arise from the fact that not all actors have the same access to information about factors such as "price, product quality and the possible opportunism of exchange partners" (Beckert 2007a: 14). Embeddedness provides a solution to all three problems. Even for Beckert, however, embeddedness is a "mysterious substance which provides...stability in market exchange" (Beckert 2007a: 11).

This book adopts a view of embeddedness as just such a solution to the coordination problems of value, competition, and cooperation that business-people and politicians are trying to solve, and unpacks its mysterious mechanisms. As the coming chapters show, it was precisely these problems that plagued economic actors and led them to form different types of bonds with political elites. Each group articulated a series of demands to their counterparts wherein their common aim was to make the future more legible. As I will show later, certain network structures facilitate that task while also leading to the development of broadly distributive institutions, while others result in narrowly distributive institutions. The structure of networks also can allow economic and political elites to act as constraints on one another. For both reasons, the developmental state literature set an agenda for studying ties between political and economic elites. The rest of this book builds on this foundation to understand the relationship between individuals, the social structure within which they act, and the development of institutions.

HOW UNCERTAINTY LEADS TO INSTITUTIONAL DEVELOPMENT

Two groups of elites have been identified as key actors in the process of state building in contemporary new democracies: business leaders and politicians. Together they operate in emerging markets – sites of high economic volatility where opportunities for economic growth are immense but the institutional framework is incomplete. Since the 1960s emerging markets have been a subject of fervent conversation among social scientists, investors, politicians, and development experts, at times because emerging markets were a source of surging growth, at others because they were sites of financial volatility, desperation, and social unrest. But what does it mean to be an emerging market? Economists tend to think of such markets as places where opportunity and uncertainty are high because political and economic institutions are not yet present or well established but economic dynamism and innovation are present.

Approaches to institution building 39

At the same time, we tend to think of emerging markets as places where social networks fill the gap left by missing institutions, generating other types of uncertainty, such as poor information flow.

Both these circumstances are present simultaneously: markets are based on social structures as well as institutions and impersonal signals (Fligstein 2001). It is the interaction of these in a variety of forms, each with a different political foundation, that determines the extent to which uncertainty and networks are relevant. Hence, family capitalism (Morck and Yeung 2004; Fogel 2006) is different from business group or alliance capitalism (Gerlach 1992; Kang 2002) and institutional capitalism (Black 1992; Hawley and Williams 1997). These capitalisms differ because their institutions vary according to the cultural and political context in which they are embedded (Granovetter 1985). Each of these forms of capitalism presents a different relational solution to the challenge that businesspeople in emerging markets face: how to minimize uncertainty in order to generate profits.

Two decades have now passed since the largest political and economic transformation in recent history swept across nearly half the globe and affected every country lying between East Germany, North Korea, and Vietnam. What this massive transformation did, at the most basic level, was to introduce uncertainty into economies that were previously planned and governed by one party. This was accomplished by expanding the base of stakeholders in the economy and the polity and making them compete.

The ability to reduce uncertainty underlies the paradox investigated in this book. After all, the presumed purpose of introducing elections and markets into previously one-party systems and planned economies is precisely to introduce uncertainty into contexts in which everything was rather certain. But uncertainty can be paralyzing, as actors unable to form expectations about the future will refrain from taking any action at all. Unable to calculate the likelihood of outcomes, economic actors prefer to keep assets buried in the proverbial backyard.

What is the optimal point between too much uncertainty and too much certainty? Should elites coordinate closely and exchange information in the process of development, as the east Asian developmental model suggested? Or does close elite coordination generate bad growth rates and political corruption, as African, Latin American, and indeed the post-socialist cases suggest? In other words, is it true that social networks generate institutions that are narrowly focused and redistribute to narrow coalitions? Current scholarship presents a confusing picture. On the one hand, networks are seen as inefficient except under special circumstances when their impact is limited by elite competition (Kang 2002), acute international competition (Doner, Ritchie, and Slater 2005), or special bureaucratic capacity (Evans 1995), which is extremely difficult to reproduce. Under these conditions, it is argued that networks can be harnessed toward productive ends (Evans 1995; Chibber 2003). Other research, however, finds that even overt corruption does not correlate with lower levels of investment when the environment is predictable and business-people have clear expectations about the outcome of their illicit exchanges (Edgardo Campos, Lien, and Pradhan 1999). In other words, we do not yet have a clear understanding of the boundary conditions under which networks and uncertainty can lead elites toward collaborative and broadly productive outcomes.

My position is that broad networks reduce uncertainty and thus render the future more readable for economic and political agents. The former use networks to facilitate business and exchange information about the changing nature of the economy. The latter use networks to obtain information about the preferences of economic actors and to secure political finance. When these networks are broad, the intense uncertainty of a period of simultaneous and rapid institutional and economic development is reduced for a large number of actors with heterogeneous interests. Thus, networks become conduits for implementing broad preferences rather than narrow ones. Moreover, if political competition is high in combination with networks, it acts as an offsetting force by both limiting the amount of time that politicians have at the helm and making them more sensitive to the preferences of societal actors, thereby raising the incentives for cooperation.

Comparison across the post-socialist region shows that various patterns of influence expression and interest aggregation have emerged. These patterns do not correspond to economic factors such as GDP growth, suggesting that there are multiple paths and political models of functioning markets in the region. Close examination of the interactions of business and political actors since 1989 in three case studies reveals that broad networks play a crucial role in the emergence of broadly distributive institutions, however.

HOW NETWORKS AFFECT INSTITUTIONAL DEVELOPMENT

Granovetter's (1973) theory of weak ties provides the basis for my argument about the value of broad networks. Research spearheaded by Granovetter on the spread of new ideas finds that social systems lacking weak ties will be "fragmented and incoherent" (Granovetter 1983: 202). The effect of this fragmentation is that new ideas spread slowly and individuals are exposed to homogeneous views likely to be held by their friends. Because networks of strong ties are likely to link actors with similar outlooks, such social systems will be deprived of diversity of thought by the failure to "bridge" to other groups with dissonant outlooks.

According to Granovetter, "[A]cquaintances, as compared to close friends, are more prone to move in different circles than oneself. Those to whom one is closest are likely to have the greatest overlap in contact with those one already knows, so that the information to which they are privy is likely to be much the same as that which one already has" (Granovetter 1983: 205). A dangerous consequence of such tight and closed networks is the unchallenged persistence

Approaches to institution building 41

of poor information, bad ideas, or inappropriate strategies, because the lack of exposure to outside information reinforces the status quo even if external circumstances have changed. Thus, particularly when network members' weak ties act as bridges to other groups, they are crucial conduits of information. This is especially relevant in situations when actors are engaged in "searches" for information (Stigler 1961).

Search theory, commonly applied to labor and producer markets, can equally well apply to markets for influence and information in politics. In all these contexts, actors are reliant on information in order to obtain better outcomes for themselves. For example, individuals who maintain weak ties tend to have greater success in job searches (Granovetter 1995) and obtain higher wages (Montgomery 1992). Similarly, maintaining "acquaintance relationships confers an informational advantage for individual lobbyists" as a result of the same weak tie mechanism (Carpenter, Esterling, and Lazer 1998: 439). Granovetter points out that weak ties also generate macro-social benefits, for example by increasing the efficiency of job placements. Stigler argues that lowering the costs of information search lowers price variability and increases efficiency in the target market.

Thus, when networks are broader and link diverse groups, actors (whether people or firms) will be exposed to new ideas, more information, and greater diversity. Such broad networks of weak ties therefore benefit from the challenges that come from encounters between dissimilar actors. If one accepts that heterogeneity and conflict strengthen social systems by subjecting plans and ideas to constant trial as well as causing new ideas to spread widely, then diversity is performance-enhancing. In fact, this is a central premise of explanations for the performance of complex adaptive systems – that is, systems of multiple interconnected agents capable of learning from experience (Axelrod and Cohen 1999; Miller and Page 2007). Broad networks of such ties, therefore, are crucial for the successful design of institutions.

I focus on the breadth of network ties as a key feature of networks because it determines the extent to which networks can act as the conduits of diversity. Networks themselves are arrays of relations between a set of actors that form a structure. These structures can vary in how dense they are, because some actors have many more ties than others. They can be more hierarchical if they have a distinct center around which other actors are organized, or they can be disjointed, with many isolated actors. These and many other properties of networks can be observed and measured to obtain an understanding of the possibilities that different actors have. In other words, networks create a structure of possibility for the actors in them. They also relationally structure the identities of actors in them; much as in a high school clique, we are defined by those to whom we are connected. Those who are connected to many can potentially use their network to mobilize others much more effectively than those who are connected to only a few. They can also control and funnel information more effectively. As a result, networks with such actors may be more efficient at passing news, though also more vulnerable to disruption if the single central actor is removed.

The basic idea of network analysis is that systematic patterns of relations among actors reveal the structure of a system. Networks are defined as lasting relations that generate expectations of reciprocity or provision of some sort (Granovetter 1985). A central consideration of network analysis is how relationships among multiple actors jointly affect individual network members' behavior. In other words, networks capture the structure of opportunity and reciprocity, and can both empower and constrain members.

Networks do not simply present a map of existing social structures, moreover. When we move to a temporal conception of networks, network approaches are able to capture both structure and agency. Kilduff and Krackhardt (1994), quoting Cialdini (1989), present a clear illustration of this mechanism with Baron de Rothschild, who signaled his close link to a would-be borrower by walking across the floor of the stock exchange arm in arm with him. Observers of the display of friendship upgraded their evaluation of the creditworthiness of the baron's apparent friend and would-be borrower. Thus, by observing the same network over time, we can observe the effect that structure has on individual choice within a network.

As in the example of Baron Rothschild, networks can both empower and restrict an individual's ability to act, as the individual is defined by his or her ties. Networks by definition have non-linear effects, as information spreads relationally. The difficulty and the value of network approaches both lie in the relational and recursive nature of network ties. Much as in an iterated game, players update their strategies on the basis of observed and expected behavior alike. As such, neither is a fixed point; their actions mutually affect the choices that the other will make. Taking again the cases at hand, ties between individuals and between organizations structure political outcomes. In the process of building capitalism, politicians and firms both anticipate and adapt to the actions that their counterparts take. Thus, to say that firms adapt their strategies to the policy choices that politicians make would be to tell less than half the story, as politicians are already incorporating both the anticipated and the observed actions of firms in their behavior.

Similarly, firms have considered the reactions of politicians in the earlier moves that led to politicians' current choices. The mutually constructed nature of institutional choice results from this process of anticipation and reaction. Of course, information is imperfect and consequences are often unintended, making the process of institutional design a meandering journey of experimentation and selection. As the chapters that follow show, politicians formulated and altered their strategies to develop firms as a source of political resources that they needed in order to win elections. In parallel, firms forged relations with the political sphere in ways that reflected both their strategic opportunities at any given time and the effects of earlier political decisions that had a constitutive impact on them as political actors.

Approaches to institution building

This relational perspective has the advantage of drawing attention to the internal configurations and external connections of interest groups. By including network features as an independent variable, this book takes networks seriously as part of the political process. In particular, it seeks to understand how networks affect institutional function and development.

What, then, is the relationship between networks and institutions? Institutions provide a set of rules that govern political and economic life. Networks provide a social structure to supplement incomplete rules and indeterminate institutional outcomes. Institutions determine who has the authority to make decisions and who can benefit from and dispose of material goods. Networks enable their members to influence decisions, and sometimes the nature of the institutions themselves.

For this reason, the period during which institutions are being chosen has been of particular interest to social scientists; during such times the participants in the process of institutional development cannot know fully the effects of the institutions they are choosing. Nevertheless, they often have strong beliefs about their likely distributional consequences. Hence, they jockey for individual advantage, form coalitions, strike bargains, share information, and engage in open conflict to arrive at their desired outcome.

Ties between businesspeople and politicians are one place where networks and institutional development meet. Newspaper headlines resonate in the popular imagination when they refer to visible or alleged ties between the economy and the polity. The political goals of businesspeople affect elections, shape legislation, and impact the institutional landscape. Businesspeople lobby, make private deals with politicians, create organizations, and sometimes use violence.

Precisely in the middle ground when institutions are not yet fully developed, social groups – networks of individuals – fill in the gaps, influencing the process by which institutions are built through formal and informal means. I therefore focus on the network that we imagine as the most powerful in contemporary democratic polities: the community of businesspeople and their ties to the political sphere. How does the network that we imagine as most powerful affect a nation's ability to make economic policy and guide economic development? The answer lies, I argue, in understanding the various ties between the economy and the polity.

My argument is not to be mistaken for the "grease the wheels" argument, which states that corruption arises as a solution to the problem of inefficient bureaucracy (Leys 1965). Corruption is generally acknowledged to be inefficient (Mèon and Weill 2010) and harmful to development (Aidt 2009). Nevertheless, some authors argue that corruption can be used to address inefficiencies, such as the extra time needed to deal with a slow or inept bureaucracy (Lui 1985). Others have argued that extra payments related to corruption may attract talent to bureaucratic work in contexts where low government pay would otherwise have the opposite effect (Leys 1965). These arguments suggest that corruption constitutes a second best solution by allowing business to operate in contexts that would otherwise present major obstacles to private sector activity and in which the development of functional institutions is not a viable alternative. By contrast, the argument being made here is not about corrupt payments or "wheel greasing" to obtain certain outcomes, such as queue jumping. Instead, it focuses on collaborative agreements, which may involve electoral support to parties from business in exchange for influence in shaping institutions and affecting legislation, regulation, or other policy-related decisions.

The business owners discussed in this volume used existing networks, reconfigured old ties, and built new coalitions in order to achieve their goals. One of these goals was to influence the basic content of rules, laws, and regulations that were being designed as part of long-term reform projects with potentially huge rewards for the first set of incumbents. Because one key focus of this study is the large business owner, this is also an account of the impact of "who owns what" on institutional development. Ownership is one of the core forms of economic power defined by institutions such as contracting and the rules of property rights. Ownership is therefore a form of politics. And yet we have only just begun to understand how the structure of ownership influences the conduct of politics. Thus, ownership structure is one of the key starting points of the argument. Whenever one firm buys a stake in another firm or one individual owns two firms, ownership creates networks of firms. These ownership networks interact with and reinforce personal and personnel networks. "Who owns what" links with "who knows whom" to create a structure through which some individuals and organizations wield much more influence than others. Therefore, in addition to ownership networks, I examine elite career networks. Both these networks influence the creation and function of social institutions; they are a core part of the construction of markets and the consolidation of state power over them.

ARGUMENT

The post-socialist countries provide an opportunity to explore and trace the process of contemporary institution building because, by the time of transition, these states had lost the capacity to extract resources, control their assets, and effectively issue commands and sanctions. As other scholars have argued, late socialism was a time of state weakness and breakdown (Ganev 2001; Grzymała-Busse and Jones-Luong 2002; Volkov 2002; Ganev 2007). In the early 1990s new democratic governments had weak state structures, as evidenced by the tunneling of resources out of state-owned firms and frequent business-related violence. Actors in control of the state had to create a new framework and rebuild capacity if they had any hope of carrying out political and economic reforms.

Approaches to institution building 45

What enabled them to do so? Two elements are central in the answer advanced by this book, as shown in Table 1.1. First, the *breadth of networks* among members – whether they are broad or narrow – is a key resource that determines how firms behave when calculating and pursuing their interests. The ties of any one individual constrain or enable their opportunities for action. By extension, as discussed in Chapters 3 and 4, the identities of actors are also relevant. Some firms, such as financial institutions, maintain more ties, on average, than industrial firms by virtue of their sector. Thus, the prominence of financial institutions in a given country will shape the network structure. And, as Chapter 4 shows, the structure of firm ownership and control networks affects the incentives of elites to engage in collective action.

A second critical feature shaping the macro-trajectories of countries is the *level of uncertainty* actors face when calculating the future. The nature of political competition generates a key form of uncertainty. It has been argued that political alternation and divided government generate suboptimal behavior because sets of actors with opposing goals make policy decisions that often reverse course on decisions made earlier (Persson and Tabellini 2000; Frye 2010). For example, US states with divided governments have larger fiscal deficits (Alt and Lowry 1994; Poterba 1994). Similarly, the alternation of governments is linked to higher deficits (Rumi 2009). Frequent alternation has detrimental effects on the quality of policy because longer time horizons allow office holders to plan and execute better policy decisions (Rumi 2009). This may indeed be the case in well-institutionalized contexts. The same time-horizon-limiting features that lead politicians to make poor spending decisions, however, or react slowly to budget crises can also force them to concentrate on the present and collaborate with other societal actors. Scholars have found, for example, that frequent government alternation in the post-communist area correlates with lower levels of influence peddling (Horowitz, Hoff, and Milanovic 2009), and, when constructive lobbying is possible, alternation is a substitute for rather than a complement to corruption (Campos and Giovannoni 2008). I find that uncertainty, and especially political uncertainty, promotes collective action between party and business elites by disciplining politicians, who must deliver on their promises to business or risk punishment in the next election cycle.

High uncertainty means that societal actors do not know who will be in power next and thus cannot assess the value of their social networks. They also find it difficult to predict policy changes that may come with the next government. These changes could range from policies such as tax and labor policy to the awarding of public contracts. Uncertainty may come from high levels of political competition in an unsettled party system, such as in Bulgaria, which has seen the regular entrance of new parties. It may also come from high levels of competition in a polarized party system. This does not necessarily mean that the same parties will alternate. For example, in Poland failure at the elections

46   *Foundations*

has frequently meant organizational death for Polish political parties. While the party labels changed, however, the parliamentarians themselves largely reappeared under a new organizational guise. Shabad and Slomczynski (2002) document the emergence of career politicians in Poland, showing that an increasing proportion of the candidates for office have competed in prior elections (Shabad and Slomczynski 2002: 342). Career politicians thus preserve the value of ties between business leaders and political actors even if old party organizations are replaced by new ones.

This is contrasted with low uncertainty, in which it is much easier to identify the dominant political force because the levels of political competition are lower. For example, in Romania not only was there a dominant party[3] but the recruitment of political elites was highly centralized (Gherghina, Chiru, and Casal Bértoa 2011). According to Chiru and Gherghina (2012: 511), for more than two decades major Romanian parties (they examine five) have displayed an "uninterrupted oligarchic inertia," in which parties have highly centralized leadership selection and removal procedures with low party membership and little member involvement.

The view that uncertainty drives elites toward better policy making is echoed by other post-communism scholars. For example, Grzymała-Busse (2007) finds that high levels of competition limit corrupt behavior by political parties. When opposition parties offer a viable alternative, parties resist opportunities for private gain and instead move forward with reform agendas such as institution building and privatization. Similarly, O'Dwyer (2006) finds that high levels of competition reduce opportunistic moves by political parties to expand the size of the state bureaucracy. And Horowitz, Hoff, and Milanovic (2009: 118) find that more government turnover is associated with higher levels of the development of the rule of law.

In both the case studies and the quantitative analysis that follow, political uncertainty is the key form of uncertainty that affects political and economic actors. Political uncertainty specifically is generated by the difficulty of predicting alternation across the dominant left–right (post-communist/anti-communist) cleavage. This corresponds to what Horowitz, Hoff, and

---

[3] I classify Romania as a country dominated by one party, the PSD, and this may raise questions with some readers. My research covers the period 1989 to 2005. During this time the PSD was in government from 1990 to 1996 and again from 2000 to 2004. The country was governed by a broad opposition coalition from 1996 to 2000 that was largely ineffectual and plagued by internal conflicts. Although it came to power as the result of a protest vote against the PSD in 1996, voters were so dissatisfied in 2000 that they returned the PSD to power. This dominance allowed the PSD to shape networks and attract the support of business allies as no other party could. I thus think it is reasonable to talk of one-party dominance during this period. The situation changed afterwards, but this does not affect the argument here, which is focused on the first fifteen years during which the distinct trajectories of each country developed. For most of the period from 1990 to 2005 party competition was mostly between two blocs, the left-leaning PSD and the right-leaning opposition (Fesnic and Armeanu 2010).

Approaches to institution building

Milanovic (2009) refer to as "ideological turnover." This is differentiated from leadership turnovers: a shift in the majority coalition of political parties that does not necessarily imply a shift across the ideological divide. I choose the term "ideological turnover" because it better captures what firms are actually concerned with: that another ideological option to which a firm has no access will come to power. Firm–party networks are often a legacy of the pre-1989 period, and the contacts of business owners often run to a broad group of either post-communist or anti-communist political elites (McMenamin and Schoenman 2007). As also becomes clear in the case studies, ideological turnover matters because the ideological divide is a key factor shaping the personal networks linking economic and political elites.

Ideological turnover is, thus, closer to the argument being made here than regular government turnover. The purpose here is to capture the extent to which changes in party personnel in positions of power limit a firm's ability to extract rents and favors. Despite the emergence of a new coalition, when a government turnover is not also an ideological turnover, the same actors have often been reshuffled into a new leadership coalition.

Without an ideological turnover, the networks of firms to power holders might not be disrupted because leadership turnovers can be the equivalent of rearranging "the thrones of heaven, or the deck chairs on the Titanic, as the case may be" (Horowitz, Hoff, and Milanovic 2009: 110). In fact, they find that ideological turnovers have a slightly stronger effect on the development of the rule of law than leadership turnovers, reasoning that the latter may allow for more continuity of corrupt contacts (Horowitz, Hoff, and Milanovic 2009: 121). Thus, for my argument, ideological turnovers are clearly more relevant.

One question to be answered is how ties between parties and business can be maintained in competitive democracies. Why do citizens not mobilize to disrupt the alliance between business and political parties, withdrawing their votes from parties that are seen as self-serving and serving the interests of business allies rather than those of voters? Kopecky (2006) notes that political parties have traditionally been studied and classified by their connection with societal actors and the representative function they performed. Thus, an earlier literature on parties compared them on the basis of patterns of representation (worker's party, peasant party, religious party) and organizational form (cadre party, mass party, catch-all party). This approach to political parties reflected an era when the key function of parties was to represent societal actors.

In the post-communist context, however, political parties have ceased to function primarily as representative actors. In fact, the decline of the party–society linkage across Europe is well documented in the literature (Katz *et al.* 1992; Mair and van Biezen 2001; Kopecky 2006; van Biezen and Kopecky 2007; Dalton 2008; Whiteley 2011; van Biezen, Mair, and Poguntke 2012). Evidence of this in the post-communist world is seen in the comparatively low levels of popular party identification, strikingly high levels of electoral volatility – the net change in the popular vote across consecutive elections (Lewis 2002; Birch 2003; Bielasiak 2005; Sikk 2005), low levels of party membership, declining voter turnout, and weak links between parties and collateral organizations (Dalton and Wattenberg 2000; Bielasiak 2002; van Biezen 2003; van Biezen and Kopecky 2007).

Numerous reasons are cited in the literature to explain this lack of embeddedness in post-communist civil society. Some have argued that the legacy of repression and forced political mobilization under communism has left post-communist citizens reluctant to become involved with political organizations and skeptical of the political realm (Kitschelt 1992; van Biezen and Kopecky 2007). Alternatively, in what is known as the "tabula rasa" approach, citizens are a seen as blank slates shifting from party to party as they try to make sense of a confusing landscape of new political organizations, learn about political participation, and understand their own interests in an unfamiliar and complex economic system (Kitschelt 1992; Sztompka 1992; Sztompka 1993). In addition, economic interest did little to create stable alliances to parties during the transition, as voters were faced with an array of mainstream parties proposing pro-market economic programs imposed by international economic pressure (Brada 1996; Kochanowicz 1997; Ost 2006). Parties in some countries, such as Poland, also leaned toward making broad appeals to voters instead of narrowly targeting socio-economic groupings, thus undermining the sense that a particular party speaks to a specific group (Szczerbiak 1999).

What is clear from this debate is that the attachment of voters to parties in the post-communist world is remarkably unstable. On the supply side, voters are faced with the frequent entrance of new parties and movements wooing voters (Tavits 2008). On the demand side, voters are shifting alliances from party to party, although not necessarily to new entrants (Sikk 2005). Nevertheless, voter volatility has continued to rise well into the second decade of transformation after multiple elections, by which time we would expect voter preferences to have settled (Innes 2002). While Tavits (2005) argues that party systems are slowly moving toward stability, on the basis of a decreasing trend in volatility after an average eleven years of democratic transition, Epperly (2011: 2) finds that "the passage of time is not consistently associated with decreasing levels of volatility," based on a data set covering a longer period. Regardless of who is correct, both support the view that the voter–party linkage is too weak to interrupt exchanges between interest groups and politicians.

This is not to say that some parties have not made progress in developing connections to constituents. In fact, some differences can be observed in the extent to which programmatic parties have emerged and created ties to societal groups across the post-communist world. The difference, however, is between modest progress in countries such as Poland and Hungary and the poor record

Approaches to institution building 49

of parties in most other countries in post-communist Europe. Moreover, as Innes argues, the impression of stabilization in countries such as Poland and Hungary given by "rational choice" approaches to the study of parties in post-communism is misconstrued. Even in these countries, where there has been a noticeable shift toward programmatic competition among parties, party systems remain "peculiarly vulnerable" (Innes 2002: 101). In this context of region-wide weak ties to societal constituencies, it does not make sense to view post-communist parties as an outgrowth of societal interest groups (van Biezen and Kopecky 2007). Because this linkage is absent, we also should not expect party–society ties to perform the usual function of disciplining parties in their behavior. In other words, the role traditionally assigned to civil society in a democracy is undermined (Katz and Mair 1995; Scarrow 1996; Dalton and Wattenberg 2000; Bartolini and Mair 2001; Detterbeck 2005). As a result of the absent society–party linkage, parties are driven to form other bonds in the direction of the state (Kopecky 2006; Meyer-Sahling 2006; van Biezen and Kopecky 2007). As Kopecky (2006) explains, in post-communist eastern Europe "political parties are weakly anchored in society while at the same time they have strongly penetrated the state." Consequently, in analyzing parties, these authors argue for a shift of attention from the party–society linkage to the party–state one. They point out that political parties and the state are linked through a series of channels: the flow of campaign finance funds from the state to parties is the most visible. Patronage resources such as appointments in the state bureaucracy and state-owned or partially privatized firms also flow from the state to political parties, however. Control of these resources through the appointment of party personnel to the boards of firms is another key manner in which the state–party linkage is reinforced. Building on a paper by Kopecky (2006), van Biezen and Kopecky (2007) propose that the nature of the party–state linkage can be assessed on three key dimensions: the public funding of parties, the public regulation of parties, and party rent seeking. These three dimensions reveal some of the substance of the linkage between party and state. The public funding of parties is an indicator of the dependence of parties on the state for financial resources. Public funding is widespread in the region. Szczerbiak finds that it clearly favors "insiders" and has been increasing in amount in Poland since the establishment of state financing in 1993 (Szczerbiak 2006).

The public regulation of parties is seen as a reflection of the increasing perception that parties are a necessity and that their role must be defined and specified in the law and, increasingly, directly in the constitution. Van Biezen (2004) argues that this has transformed parties from voluntary associations emanating from society to a kind of "public utility" to be regulated and managed by the state. The constitutionalization of parties is an extreme form of the institutionalization of parties (van Biezen and Kopecky 2007).

Finally, party rent seeking is an indicator of the extent to which parties dominate and have penetrated the state. Of the three dimensions, this is perhaps the most commonly associated with post-communism and the widespread political corruption that has been a central part of post-communist political development.

Kopecky finds that public financing is widespread, public regulation of parties is extensive throughout the region, and party rent seeking is also common. Meyer-Sahling (2006), in fact, shows that attempts by governing parties in Hungary to penetrate the state and politically staff the bureaucracy, commonly referred to as politicization of the state, have increased over time and are not just a feature of early post-communism.

The above dynamics support a focus on the interaction of economic actors and politicians. I thus propose that uncertainty and network structure together define potential future costs for individuals or firms calculating the payoffs of strategic behavior. In other words, the availability of networks and the level of political competition determine the ability of businesspeople and politicians to calculate the probable shape of the future and make decisions about collaboration. As uncertainty rises, businesspeople have a harder time predicting who will lead the next government. Thus, uncertainty shortens time horizons. It does not mean, however, that parties know they won't be in power again (it is only post hoc that we know this). In an attempt to increase their chances at the polls, parties turn to business for support. Under broad networks, politicians and businesspeople are able to forge deals because monitoring, information flows, and credible commitments are facilitated and parties have the credibility needed to raise broad support. Defecting on deals under broad networks will undermine the future ability of parties to turn to business. Networks offer informational, binding, or commitment opportunities. They determine the balance of relations between polity and economy, and influence the ability of individuals to calculate likely future scenarios. The breadth of networks among economic actors (firms and their proxies) and between business and political elites thus affects the predictability of the future. Broad networks allow information to flow and provide a structure of mutual credible commitments, but they also include more and heterogeneous actors. The resulting deals are likely to represent broader demands. Narrow networks have the opposite effect.

The combinations of network structure and uncertainty and the resulting state type are summarized in Table 1.1. I present below the characteristics of the resulting trajectories of institutional development.

TABLE 1.1 *The effect of networks and uncertainty on the state*

		Uncertainty	
		Low	High
Network structure	**Narrow**	*Patronage*	*Captured*
	Broad	*Embedded corporatist*	*Concertation*

Approaches to institution building

(1) When <u>networks are broad</u> and <u>uncertainty is high</u>. In this context, political and economic elites are engaged in a process of concertation, and the state broadly functions as a coordinating body by channeling information, mediating among interests, and potentiating network ties. In these contexts, *concertation* states develop mutually beneficial institutional solutions for competing factions over the long term.

(2) When <u>networks are narrow</u> and <u>uncertainty is low</u>. In this context, political elites dominate economic elites. The resulting *patronage* states award selective benefits to allies on a case-by-case basis.

(3) When <u>networks are narrow</u> and <u>uncertainty is high</u>. In this context, economic elites dominate political elites. This combination of features gives rise to *captured* states, which are colonized by and helpless in the face of strong societal actors.

(4) When <u>networks are broad</u> and <u>uncertainty is low</u>. This combination describes an *embedded corporatist* state in which groups of well-established political elites do not face the disciplining effects of uncertainty and they co-opt business through broad networks. Although this type is logically possible, the combination of low uncertainty and broad networks does not appear among the cases covered here and is unlikely in contexts with competitive elections.[4]

The different dynamics that took hold between business, parties, and the state are brought to life in the statements of business leaders and officials. A Polish businessperson described the relationship as one driven by *"wspolny interes,"* mutual interests: "Mutual interests are the basis of interaction with parties and the state. It is not about the general interest but self-interest so it would be difficult to say that politicians are on the side of business or anyone else. They each solve their own problems." Business leaders also spoke of this relationship as a collaborative one, however, looking to the state as a partner "with which you can do something together." This combination of self-interest and partnership defined the Polish dynamic, and contrasts sharply with the other two cases.

Noting the influence of narrow interests, a Romanian business leader said, "The biggest challenge for Romanian big business today is the bureaucracy, but not just the bureaucracy but the input of special interests into this bureaucracy. And the relations and sweet deals that come out of it." These relations developed in the context of top-down party–business relationships in which parties held the upper hand; as another business leader pointed out, "The idea of party leaders running around to gather money is wrong. There is more money available in the grey and black economy than can be spent." And, as

---

[4] This combination, in fact, most closely describes the case of South Korea, as discussed by Kang (2002). Kang calls the tightly linked political and economic elites in South Korea "mutual hostages" because of the stalemate that exists between them.

will be discussed later in this book, numerous interviewees noted the absence of any coherent business community.

In Bulgaria, the opposite dynamic took hold. Remarking on the inability of the state to govern business and the consequent explosion of corruption, an official said, "There were too many sharks in too small a lake, which the state cannot cope with." Describing the power and reach of business over the state as an unofficial lobby, another offical observed, "The lobby that these business groups own involves not only senior people but also lower levels of the state."

CONCLUSION

This chapter has advanced an argument that is distinct from much of the literature on the political economy of institutional development. Existing scholarship focuses on the extent of democratization and popular opposition, the speed of reform, and the role of legacies. I take a different view: that institutional development is essentially a collective dilemma facing political and economic elites. To this end, the developmental state and varieties of capitalism literatures both offer insights into the way that these two sets of elites view economic institutions and the process by which these two groups can work toward socially beneficial outcomes. I draw on both lines of scholarship to construct a theory that also incorporates the untreated variables of networks and political uncertainty. Bringing political competition over economic resources to the fore, I extend and develop both literatures to contexts that are democratic but not in the advanced industrialized world. The result is a theory that conceptualizes the moves of political and economic elites and their success in realizing mutually beneficial outcomes.

PART II

THE ROLE OF NETWORKS

2

When broad networks increase cooperation

Firms are the basic unit of capitalism, yet political science has only begun to study the role of firm governance on the construction of institutions in emergent capitalist economies, such as corporate governance law, contract and transaction law, property rights, financial institutions and access to credit, tax codes, and trading structures. Individual firms each have their own means and goals, but rarely do they have sufficient influence to choose policies alone.

My argument is that the extent to which firms can coordinate their actions to achieve political goals has a strong effect on the trajectory of institutional development. Part III situates business collective action within varying levels of political uncertainty. First, however, Part II seeks to understand what shapes the incentives of firms to act together instead of trying to pursue political preferences alone. This requires the mapping of both incentives for and obstacles to joint political action. Following on the previous chapter, my view is that firm collective action depends on the ability of firms and their directors to overcome problems, establish trust and frame common goals. Focusing on the networks of ownership ties between firms, I show here that the likelihood of collective action rises when networks are broad because shared ownership among firms is a basis for credible commitments among firms on issues, such as political action, on which contracting agreements is impossible (Williamson 1985: 166).

The interactions of economic and political elites likely have one broad goal: all actors seek influence in order to shape regulatory and bureaucratic decisions, and choices regarding the development of institutions, in their own favor. A long-standing body of work argues, in line with Olson's seminal point, that entrenched, wealthy insiders pursue rent-seeking activities to preserve the status quo (Olson 1963; Krueger 1974; Olson 1982; Veblen 1994 [1899]; Morck, Strangeland, and Yeung 2000; Olson 2000; Rajan and Zingales 2003). My argument, to the contrary, is that firms do not have a single set of interests. Instead, firm preferences and demands depend heavily on the network structure

55

of a particular economy. I show that, when the ownership structure is broad, more collective action ensues than when a narrow ownership structure is present.

Ownership structure is a key variable in this argument because different forms of ownership are matched by different opportunities for owners to exert influence and control (Kogut 2012: 12–15, 20–23) (Windolf 1998). Hence, whether ownership is broad or narrow will have a determining effect on the emergence of joint action. The types of actors that inhabit important positions in a given network determine the dominant structure of ownership that emerges. To take just two examples, as is explained below, banks and institutional investors are more likely to create broader, more horizontal structures, while industrial and family firms favor the opposite.

Other networks – personnel ties between firms, overlapping career paths, and joint membership in organizations – also have an important impact on the ability of individuals and their respective organizations to engage in collective action. While ownership networks provide a structural view of polity–economy ties, career networks provide the individual-level perspective and are analyzed in later chapters. At the structural level, ownership networks are the key ties that link firms and structure the payoffs of collaboration between firms. Ownership networks are often seen as the basis under which credible commitments among firms are possible in conditions in which formal contracting of agreements is unavailable.[1] Williamson (1985: 167) defines credible commitments as "reciprocal acts designed to safeguard a relationship" involving "irreversible, specialized investments." Moreover, ownership networks create the basis for other forms of connection, such as the sharing of directors on boards.

It is also important to note that firms that exercise influence on political actors are neither exceptional nor limited to state-owned firms that are unable to adapt to the new rigors of the market economy. According to the EBRD's "Business environment and enterprise performance survey" (BEEPS) (EBRD 2005b) of firms across the Baltics, central and southern Europe, and the Commonwealth of Independent States, firm involvement with the state is much more common than what may be expected in what are frequently believed to be competitive markets that have passed through two decades of reform and are populated by mostly privatized firms. The transformation of socialist economies is often believed to have separated the economy from politics. Instead, survey data show that the economy continues to be deeply enmeshed in politics, but the nature of this connection varies across countries.

In the extreme version, firms seek to engage in direct one-to-one influence of state actors, known as state capture. The dynamics of state capture run counter to the usual expectation that weak uncompetitive firms seek influence to

---

[1] For example, it is well known that Japanese firms exchange their own shares as a form of credible commitment to joint decisions because of the difficulty of repeatedly writing contracts to govern supplier and customer relations (Gerlach 1992).

compensate for their inability to compete in the marketplace. To the contrary, survey evidence finds that larger firms often attempt to influence policy and also engage in state capture – when vested interests exert an excessive influence on the state – more than do small firms (EBRD 2005a: 90). This is also true of foreign-owned and exporting firms, which are often believed to be less interested in domestic politics and regulatory decisions and less involved in seeking influence. Moreover, firms operating in competitive markets have been more active in attempting to intervene than monopolists, suggesting that it is precisely the pressure of competition that leads firms to seek political influence. Finally, firms with higher investment rates tend to be more likely to engage in state capture (EBRD 2005a: 90), countering the belief that only the uncompetitive behemoths of state socialism still rely on protection and influence. The EBRD *Transition Report 2005* indicates that attempts at state capture tend to originate from better-performing firms, rather than firms struggling to survive. And these better-performing firms have a significant impact on the constraints facing other firms, with the strongest effect in the area of tax administration (EBRD 2005a: 90–1).

How, then, do the structures of ownership create opportunities for firms to cooperate in designing the trajectory of institutional development and mitigate the temptation for firms to exercise direct influence? This chapter answers the question by drawing on a broad literature on corporate governance that discusses the opportunities and agency problems that arise for firms with various forms of ownership. My argument is that broad networks of ownership raise the likelihood of collective action because they promote firm cooperation. The network structure of ownership reflects the distribution of control over firms in the economy.

The classic problem of corporate governance has been formulated by Berle and Means (1991) as the separation of ownership and control. When ownership and control are separated, owners suddenly face a problem of agency. The "agency problem" refers to the difficulty that financiers have in monitoring and influencing how their funds are used. Not only do they face classic principal–agent monitoring problems, but they also face voting constraints if they are minority stakeholders. In other words, as large shareholders who are able to alienate minority shareholders become more prominent in a given economy, agency problems become more pronounced. Scholarship interested in the separation of ownership and control has typically focused on the challenges of governance generated within a firm. If firms are also considered political actors, however, then these agency problems can be scaled up to the level of market governance. Agency problems aggregated to the national level make it possible for a small group to be influential because of its control rights of capital, despite the ownership rights held by others who are in a minority in each firm. Building on this intuition, the agency problem defined by Berle and Means provides a foundation on which to construct an understanding of firms' political action.

This approach departs from existing studies of firm political preferences, which have focused on variables that capture the macro-distribution of actors in an economy: asset specificity, the size of the export sector, employer coordination, the tradition of guilds, and employer–worker relations (Frieden 1988; Rogowski 1989; Crouch and Brown 1993; Milner 1997; Mares 2003; Thelen 2004). Instead, I consider ownership structure as the lever by which coordination for political purposes can take place among firms, and in so doing I draw on insights from the literature on corporate governance to complement existing studies of business sectoral negotiation over policy choice that tend to focus mostly on sectoral (import versus export) or class (employers versus unions) conflicts rather than on the level of the individual firm.

Not surprisingly, forms of capitalism vary widely in how ownership and control are configured. They also differ sharply on what types of firms are most prominent. For example, in industrial capitalism, commodity-producing firms are the key owners of other firms. In institutional or financial capitalism, in which financial firms predominantly own other firms and the commodity-producing firm is in itself a commodity, large institutions are the key power holders (Windolf 1998). Pension funds and investment banks hold key positions in the framework of economic power and have different interests and goals from industrial firms. In yet another variant, managerial capitalism, the power of managers rests on the underlying wide distribution of ownership. In each variant, shares of control over firms are distributed differently. The next sections discuss the interests of different types of firms. Following these sections, a framework is developed to link firm types to the various problems of coordination that emerge when networks include homogeneous versus heterogeneous firms.

ACTORS AND INTERESTS

Olson and others have made the argument that greater control of economic resources translates into greater political power, which can be used to shape institutions in the future toward the goals of those in power. This link thus presents, they argue, an economic incumbency effect (Olson 2000; Morck and Yeung 2004; Acemoglu, Johnson, and Robinson 2005). The authority structure of a firm decides who can lay claim to the cash flow. Hence, corporate governance affects wealth creation and distribution, the fate of suppliers and distributors, the fortunes of pension funds and retirees, and the endowments of charitable institutions (Gourevitch and Shinn 2005). And the distribution of political resources via lobbying affects who wins elections and what policy options are chosen. Further, "the players in the firm, as they turn to politics to get the regulations they prefer, have to appeal to a broad set of external stakeholders" through the system of political institutions (Gourevitch and Shinn 2005: 10). The size of this external stakeholder group will differ as the ratio of small shareholders to large shareholders changes.

When broad networks increase cooperation

TABLE 2.1 *Ownership concentration, 2000*

Country	Average number of largest shareholders
Bulgaria	2
Romania	1.55
Poland	5.56

Source: EBRD (2005b).

Whether small or large shareholders dominate will affect the choice of political institutions. For example, the concentration of ownership and control are related to the basic features of a country's legal system, and in particular to the choice of minority shareholder protections (LaPorta, Lopez-de-Silanes, and Shleifer 1999). In other words, other scholars have identified how ownership distribution and corporate governance are critical components shaping the political economy and the link between firms and political outcomes.

Table 2.1 shows variation in ownership concentration by comparing the average number of largest shareholders in a firm in each country under examination. Firms were asked to report the number of shareholders holding the largest packet of shares. Poland has the highest number, indicating that ownership is spread across a relatively high number of stakeholders. Bulgaria is significantly lower, and Romania has the lowest value. In the latter, larger shareholders dominate. The variation here is sufficient to lead us to expect very different types of coalition forming among firms.

The prominence of small and large shareholders is not the only factor that affects the macro-structure of ownership. Owners in a firm vary also by how likely they are to hold shares in only a single other firm, in a set of firms in a particular sector of the economy, or in a broad assortment of firms. For example, banks and financial firms are more likely to have an interest in many different types of firms as part of a portfolio of diverse investments. Industrial or family firms tend to hold stakes in fewer firms and will often vertically integrate other firms in supply chains. Thus, when banks are prominent, networks will be broader, and this raises the likelihood of collective action. Because banks and financial firms have an ownership interest in a much more diverse group of firms, I hypothesize that banks are more likely to lobby for broadly conceived rather than narrowly distributive institutions.

The cases analyzed later in this chapter therefore examine the form of owner (or combination of owners) that dominates: bank, institutional investor, state, industrial, or family. Broad and narrow networks each impart a different flavor to the broader behavior of firms in a particular political economy, as each owner type can perform a different characteristic function. These are shown in Table 2.2 and explained in more detail below. Broad ownership indicates that there are many smaller shareholders and firms widely connected to each other. Narrow ownership means that large block holders dominate.

60   *The Role of Networks*

TABLE 2.2 *Owners, ownership structures, and resulting functions*

	Dominant owner	Ownership structure	Characteristic function
Horizontal	Banks	Broad	Monitoring, information brokerage
	Business groups	Broad	Alliance, reduction of contracting costs
	Institutional investors	Broad	"Super"-monitoring (agents watching agents [Black 1992]), information brokerage
Hierarchical	Industrial pyramids	Narrow	Control and risk sharing
	Family firms	Narrow	Insider privilege

As shown in Table 2.2, owner types can be divided into two categories: those that promote a horizontal structure by virtue of their direct ownership of many firms (see Figure 2.1a) and those that promote a hierarchical structure, such as family groups and business pyramids (see Figures 2.1b and 2.1c). Banks and institutional investors, for example, will tend to acquire stakes across sectors to spread risk across a portfolio. These firms will sometimes seek input in firm governance but are less likely to own controlling shares. By contrast, owners that promote a hierarchical structure will tend to value control.

Table 2.2 also illustrates how each type performs a different characteristic function. Banks and institutional investors serve as information conduits and facilitate monitoring (Useem 1984; Mintz and Schwartz 1985; Davis and Mizruchi 1999). Business groups reduce contracting costs and facilitate alliances (Gilson and Roe 1993). In contrast, the two hierarchical types that create narrow networks protect and retain control for insiders while facilitating risk sharing with minority shareholders (Rajan and Zingales 2003).

Each form affects how control votes of firms are aggregated in the economy and spreads risk differently at the macro level of the economy. Family pyramids, for example, tend and often seek to alienate small shareholders while benefiting from the use of their capital. Institutional investors, by contrast, promote the interests of diffuse shareholders as intermediaries by virtue of the fact that, when these investors are prominent, they mediate between a large economy of shareholders and the firms that are the target of their investment.

What are the advantages of each form? Each structure provides a different solution to the problem of ownership and control in contexts in which risk is high and financial resources are scarce. The pure hierarchical structure (Figure 2.1b) joins both ownership and control: those possessing funds have full control of the firm(s). The pyramidal structure (Figure 2.1c) separates minority owners from control of the firm. A range of intermediate outcomes are possible, for example when multiple, cross-cutting ties link firms

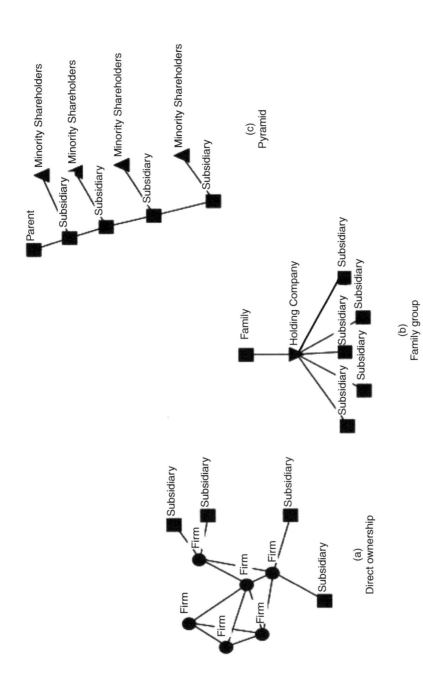

FIGURE 2.1 Ownership structures

(Figure 2.1a), with the possibility of reciprocal holdings of shares among a group of firms such that mutual ownership blurs the lines of ownership and control but can reinforce alliances between firms (Gerlach 1992). This last type can be either loosely or tightly connected.

The question of ownership and control in its classic form has focused on management issues that arise when managers are separated from owners. Different structures of ownership also offer owners different access to the resources of firms in a group, however (Perotti and Gelfer 2001). Whether a business group will add a firm in a pyramidal or direct (horizontal) fashion depends on the business environment. Loose horizontal ties are viable when coalition governance is possible and trust is high. In periods of financial distress, instead, collective action can become more difficult. As coalition-enforced threats become less credible, hierarchical control is preferred (Berglof and Perotti 1994).

Different structures also allow owners to benefit to varying extents from the cash flow of the firm. Ownership in a structure in which the family takes on direct ownership of the new firm (as in Figure 2.1b) is preferred when the controlling shareholder does not wish to share any of the cash flow rights of any firm in the group with other shareholders, as it would in the pyramidal structure. The drawback is that, in creating new firms, the controlling shareholder has access only to its retained cash flow in the original firm but receives all the benefits and costs from the new firm (Almeida and Wolfenzon 2006). By contrast, pyramids allow the already established firms in the group to finance the acquisition or creation of new firms with capital belonging to minority shareholders higher up in the pyramid.

Hence, network structure is a direct reflection of the level of cooperation that is possible among holders of capital. More hierarchical structures make collective action among firms less likely, while more dispersed structures raise the likelihood that firms can collectively agree on the structure of institutions.

One feature that determines the structure of ownership in the economy is the identity of owners. Some owners will tend to promote certain kinds of structures. For example, if financial institutions dominate, then the structure of the economy will tend to be more horizontal, as funds and banks invest in firms and in each other. When families dominate, a more hierarchical structure will tend to emerge. The next sections explain how the identities of owners impact the macroeconomy by tracing the incentives generated by different types of horizontal and vertical owners. Based on an analysis of these types, I argue that horizontal structures raise the likelihood of collective action among firms.

HORIZONTAL

Three types of horizontal owners – banks, business groups, and institutional investors – raise the likelihood of collective action.

Banks

How does the presence of prominent banks in the ownership structure influence governance? Banks facilitate finance, information sharing, contracting, bargaining, and political cohesion among firms.

Bank prominence in networks of ownership channels capital and anchors the social organization of business (Mintz and Schwartz 1981; Mintz and Schwartz 1983; Davis and Mizruchi 1999). Although in the US case banks own a large share of US firms, they rarely seem to have used their power to control management directly. Banks are able to influence firms broadly, however, because of their control of funds and access to short-term loans (Mintz and Schwartz 1983), particularly in hard times when capital is in short supply (Davis and Mizruchi 1999). Banks can particularly constrain the behavior of firms during contraction periods and thus affect the direction an economy takes toward the next upswing (Davis and Mizruchi 1999). Firms that have a director of a financial institution on their board are much more likely to borrow than those without such ties (Stearns and Mizruchi 1993; Mizruchi and Stearns 2001). Moreover, firms with a banker on their board are more likely to engage in short-term borrowing, while firms with an investment banker on the board are more likely to issue bonds (Stearns and Mizruchi 1993). Firms with bank ties also gain access to what Useem has called "business scan": they have an unparalleled view of the economy, because banks have privileged access to information about firms, are invited to sit on boards, and are better at recruiting directors from heavily interlocked firms to sit on their own boards (Useem 1984; Mintz and Schwartz 1985; Davis and Mizruchi 1999).

Bank prominence thus favors governance and political cohesion among a corporate elite (Davis and Mizruchi 1999). In the United States, for example, firms in economically interdependent industries, and particularly those connected through the same banks, contribute to similar political candidates (Mizruchi 1992). Thus, banks not only provide access to information and monitoring but also, in their role as gatekeepers to short-term finance, structure political action in a way that other types of ties do not. Bank prominence also supports other functions: in the case of Japanese *keiretsu*, the system of banks with extensive investment in industry (and industry with extensive cross-ownership of shares) existed not only to organize relationships among firms, their shareholders, and senior managers but also "to facilitate productive efficiency." Thus, banks existed not only to resolve the Berle and Means problem of monitoring – and hence address the central problem of corporate governance – but also to implement what they call "contractual governance": monitoring suppliers or customers for cooperation when it would be impossible or impractical to write contracts (Gilson and Roe 1993). Finally, in the context of business groups, when banks are in control they act much as an internal financial market, transferring assets toward better investment opportunities when compared with industrial groups (Perotti and Gelfer 2001).

Broad business groups

Contractual governance is a core characteristic of cross-ownership and generates large advantages in creating coalitions by facilitating monitoring and bargaining. Such cross-ownership among nonfinancial firms helps to reduce opportunism in long-term relationships and maintains internal discipline and monitoring among managers due to the ability of coalitions to threaten managers with removal from control (Berglof and Perotti 1994). Cross-ownership networks thus can lead to the development of reputational mechanisms over time as firms exert their voice, monitor each other, and join together to exert influence. The diversification that results from cross-ownership means that institutional actors have many points of contact (the firms in which they have stakes), raising the value of reputation. In turn, this creates economies of scale in monitoring (Black 1992). Such business groups are also a substitute for missing or inefficient markets (for example, financial markets) and thus serve to facilitate the sourcing of finance (Leff 1978, cited by Almeida and Wolfenzon 2006; Khanna and Palepu 1997; Khanna and Palepu 1999; Khanna 2000; Ghatak and Kali 2001; Kim 2004).

Gilson and Roe (1993: 874) understand such groups as solutions to long-term production problems that would otherwise require a complex series of contracts among a number of parties. This same logic extends to the complex political problems that accompany production. In other words, I consider institutional bargains among interests as much a part of the production problem as the long-term relationships among suppliers, creditors, and customers who require just-in-time delivery, quality standards, joint investment in procedures and new products, and the costly tailoring and specialization needed to create complex products. Firms are trying to solve a series of institutional problems in order to make and/or raise profits: they require institutions tailored to their interests, labor laws that make their work possible, product standards of a certain form and stringency, public contracting laws, subsidies, tariffs, and a host of other institutional goods. Thus, contractual governance is the business equivalent of collective action – with cross-ownership being the commitment mechanism that reduces the risk of opportunistic behavior among allies. The parallel can be extended, and is reinforced by the fact that pacts of political action among firms cannot be formalized in the way that contracts can be written to mitigate risk among suppliers and customers.[2]

Moreover, just as long-term relationships between two hierarchically integrated firms are fraught with risk for both purchaser and supplier, so is the decision to undertake coordinated political action. In both cases, firms must make commitments that are difficult to reverse and that leave them vulnerable to exploitation. Just as large investments tailored to a particular customer limit

---

[2] It is worth noting that in most cases even business contracts cannot address in a practical manner the universe of possible contingencies in a complex transaction. Instead, mechanisms are devised to allow parties to address actual contingencies as they arise (Williamson 1985).

When broad networks increase cooperation 65

firms' flexibility, so firms burn their bridges when allying with a particular political party in order to achieve their goals. Similar to the Japanese *keiretsu*, in politically allied firms, cross-ownership provides a credible commitment mechanism in high-risk situations. Diversified ownership also leads firms to focus on structure and process rather than firm-specific concerns (Black 1992). Thus, when cross-ownership and diversified ownership are present, firms will tend to focus on broad procedural and structural issues rather than the concerns of any one specific firm or sector.

Institutional investors

The hallmarks of the so-called fiduciary capitalism brought about by the dominance of institutional investors are dispersed ownership and long time horizons (Hawley and Williams 1997). The term "fiduciary" alludes to the duty of institutions to act in the interest of their beneficiary. When legal provisions and norms may not be so well developed and market integrity is low (Pistor, Raiser, and Gelfer 2000), as in the post-socialist world, the presence of institutional investors implies wide stakeholdings and longer time horizons. In the United States, fiduciary duty has unexpectedly reinforced the link between ownership and control by engaging funds in the management of firms (Hawley and Williams 1997). As a result, institutional investors provide a horizontal link between corporations and function as powerful collective actors usually representing a diverse array of firms. Hence, they perform many of the same functions as banks.

HIERARCHICAL

Family firms and individually owned industrial groups or pyramids are two hierarchical forms of ownership that lower the likelihood of collective action.

Family firms and industrial pyramids

Family or individually controlled firms, which have become common and visible players in the post-socialist environment, are characterized by the dominance of control over ownership. Such firms thus have different configurations of agency, with the key features of family dominance over other shareholders and the capture of professional management by the family (Morck and Yeung 2003). It has been argued that family firms experience better governance because they have concentrated ownership and thus more focused decision making (Jensen and Meckling 1976 and Shleifer and Vishny 1997, both cited by Morck and Yeung 2003). As Morck and Yeung point out, however, it is important to distinguish between different types of family firms. Those in which family control is highly concentrated or absolute naturally have very low agency problems, because ownership and control rest with the same individuals (barring intrafamily conflicts, which are beyond the current focus). In firms in which a pyramidal structure is used, the family owns a group of firms, and outside investors are brought in to provide capital but are never allowed to acquire a majority of votes in these firms. In terms of corporate governance, the resulting agency problem emerges because managers serve the interest of the family while neglecting other shareholders (Morck and Yeung 2003). Moreover, because of the pyramid structure, the family firm bears a decreasing share of the costs and risks in firms lower in the pyramid.[3] As a result, the family can retain a controlling stake in a large number of firms, benefiting from the capital of public shareholders while bearing increasingly small shares of the risk as the pyramid grows.

What are the interests of such groups? One argument, akin to an incumbency argument, is that family firms have an incentive to prevent innovative upstarts from eroding the value of "old money." In other words, it is in the direct interest of established firms to prevent the emergence of new competition (Morck and Yeung 2004). Supporting this view, Rajan and Zingales (2003) have shown how the wealthy elite, having used existing financial institutions to become wealthy, redesign those same institutions to lock in their position and protect their profits. Therefore, as pyramids become more extensive, their interest in subverting and their ability to subvert economic institutions to their own purposes grows, and they gather clout in what are effectively a series of predetermined majoritarian contests to control capital, and thus influence. As a result of this influence, old families do extremely well in political lobbying because of lobbying's dependence on networks and money (Morck, Strangeland, and Yeung 2000; Rajan and Zingales 2003; Morck and Yeung 2004). On the basis of this ability, old families erect barriers to discourage competition and subvert institutions. Thus, family firms correlate with more interventionist governments, less developed financial markets, more onerous bureaucratic obstacles, price controls, and a lack of shareholder rights protection (Fogel 2006). In other words, economies with a significant presence of family firms are likely to have institutions that discourage new entrants and protect family business interests. Family firms thus protect their own profits while functioning in market environments that are not efficient. Their success and emphasis on self-preservation seriously decrease the likelihood of coalitions, and, even when brief coalitions among family firms may emerge, these are likely to seek to halt institutional development.

Arguments applying to family pyramids can also be extended to industrial pyramids – groupings of firms owned by a parent industrial firm with a few shareholders. The difference in political behavior will depend on the extent to

---

[3] For example, the family owns the family firm outright. In turn, the family firm owns 51 percent of firm A, which owns 51 percent of firm B, which owns 51 percent of firm C. In this example, the family has only an actual 25.5 percent stake in the profits of firm B, and a 12.5 percent stake in the profits (or costs) of firm C. See Morck and Yeung (2003) for more detail.

When broad networks increase cooperation 67

which industrial pyramids are the result of vertical integration into a supply chain, and unite firms in closely related sectors.

FIRM COLLECTIVE ACTION

As the previous sections show, firms that tend to promote a more horizontal structure raise the likelihood of collective action by facilitating information flow, monitoring, and credible commitments. Firms that promote hierarchical structures are better placed to defend the status quo and narrow elite interests, and thus they lower the likelihood of broad collective action.

Having introduced these different incentives for different types of firms, it is possible to construct a framework for business political action in terms of the factors that shape the extent of firm cooperation. Two key features governing the emergence of coordinated political action are (1) agency problems (if owners and managers are the same person, their interests overlap; if owners and managers are different people, agency conflicts are likely) and (2) the diversity of assets, which reflects the breadth of ownership networks.

What are the expected outcomes as these two features vary? High asset diversity, meaning that firms across different sectors of the economy have links through common owners, raises the likelihood of coordination, because common ownership interests trump asset-specific interests. This is the case because common ownership of firms in different sectors will tilt collective action toward non-sector-specific preferences, rather than industry-specific demands. As a result, firms will be likely to find joint ground on which to broadly coordinate their political demands. High levels of the agency problem (found under concentrated ownership) instead lower the likelihood of firms coordinating their political demands, because high levels of this problem allow controlling owners to separate minority shareholders from control of their investments, making credible commitments to broad coalitions difficult. This relationship is summarized in Table 2.3.

Why does concentrated ownership lower and dispersed ownership raise the likelihood of collective action? Concentrated ownership is a sign of low levels of underlying social trust and increases the influence of a small and established elite that seeks to sustain the status quo. This elite also faces incentives to exercise political pressure in order to sustain the status quo. According to

TABLE 2.3 *Agency problems, asset diversity, and the likelihood of collective action*

		Diversity of assets	
		Low	High
Ownership concentration	High	Low	Moderate
	Low	Moderate	High

Morck and Yeung (2004: 392), close ties "between members of a small elite magnif[y] the returns to political rent seeking by this elite." Investors hold concentrated shares only in order to exercise control and gain a strategic input into the management of the firm (this block need not be a majority stake, because small shareholders often do not vote). If investors are not concerned with control, according to portfolio theory, passive portfolios should be diversified across industries and countries to reduce risk.

Owners are often concerned with control when they are faced with conditions in which passivity equates with risk. In other words, the ownership structure is in some ways a reflection of the extent to which there is social trust and elites expect to be able to cooperate. Dispersed ownership is possible in contexts in which the expectation is high, while concentrated ownership exists when common ventures among strangers cannot easily be sustained.

One example of concentrated ownership – family firms – illustrates how it undermines collective action. Concentrated ownership in family firms lowers the likelihood of collective action because, in order to maintain their competitive edge and prevent the erosion of their wealth, they operate in ways that are less socially responsible than nonfamily firms (Chrisman, Steier, and Chua 2006). The owners of old wealth and corporate assets are the most likely funders of innovation, but they prefer to withhold investments in anything that threatens the status quo. In fact, economies with more family-owned assets spend less on research and development (R&D) and file fewer patents. Family firms also spend less on R&D than comparable nonfamily-owned firms (Morck and Yeung 2004). Concentrated ownership supports cooperation between a narrow elite of managers, capital and/or oligarchic families, and political elites who are likely to support the status quo or their own narrow interests at the expense of the broader political economy (Morck and Yeung 2004). In fact, higher levels of family control are associated with inferior quality in terms of bureaucracy, higher barriers to entry (making the entry of innovators more difficult), and more extensive regulatory burdens (Fogel 2006). Although it is possible that family firms are just more adept at dealing with such obstacles and do not push for institutional reforms, it seems more likely, based on agency theory and incumbency, that these firms are using their power to affect government policy and block competition (Fogel 2006). For example, financial markets in economies dominated by family firms are likely to be intentionally less advanced because corporate elites favor a weakened financial system to maintain the position of already powerful firms (Rajan and Zingales 2003). Further, when ownership is concentrated, politicians tend to emerge from families that control the largest firms in an attempt to reinforce economic power with political power (Faccio 2006). Concentrated ownership thus bolsters the influence of a small and established elite seeking to reinforce its status through both the economic and political arenas.

In contrast, Morck and Yeung argue that dispersed ownership is related to a broad and dispersed elite. Dispersed elites have incentives to put their capital to the best use possible and seek the highest returns available by investing in innovative practices. Countries with this structure sustain high rates of growth because assets are used in a more efficient manner and are directed toward innovation (Morck and Yeung 2004). Because dispersed owners obtain economic benefits from innovation instead of by exercising pressure to obtain rents, defending the status quo, and creating barriers for new entrants in the marketplace, they are more likely to support political projects that improve market-supporting institutions.

These observations support the view that, when agency problems are high or asset diversity is low, firms will tend toward industry-specific demands but have a difficult time pursuing them because of the small space within which they are able to define goals. This dynamic may be reversed at the highest levels of ownership concentration, however. It is possible, if the principal shareholders are sufficiently large and sufficiently few in number, that they may be able to coordinate despite the presence of agency problems and regardless of the level of asset diversity. In other words, ownership concentration in such cases may trump asset diversity. Apart from these extremes, however, higher asset diversity and lower levels of the agency problem (i.e. lower ownership concentration) will raise the likelihood of coordination among firms.

The next section applies these arguments to empirical data. Scholarship that attempts to understand how economic structure affects politics has focused on ownership concentration (mean shareholder size) or the role of banks in ownership (because banks tend to hold smaller shares on average). Below, I use these two types of data as proxies for the level of agency problems (through ownership concentration) and the level of asset diversity (by considering the role of financial firms and public ownership, because both are more likely than other types of investors to spread their investments across sectors in order to mitigate risk).

FIRMS IN CENTRAL AND EASTERN EUROPE

The remaining sections focus on patterns of business collective action in post-communist Europe. The argument thus far has been that the structure of networks between firms, which depends on the size of the average shareholder (ownership concentration) and the extent to which common owners link different sectors, shapes the window of opportunity for business to act collectively. In the next two sections I present two kinds of evidence. First, I use comparative data for Bulgaria, Romania, and Poland to show that decreasing ownership concentration and rising asset diversity are associated with an increase in business collective action. Second, I conduct case studies of business organizations in these countries to show how collective action organizations developed in Poland around broad and diverse coalitions of businesses. By contrast, Romanian organizations tended to be personal political vehicles. In Bulgaria, organizations were largely irrelevant and unable to organize business as a group.

Figure 2.2 compares the role of financial firms in Bulgaria, Romania, and Poland in 2005. The level of ownership by financial firms varies even across the more advanced economies; for example, banks are much less present as owners in Hungary than in Poland. This situation developed because banks and industrial firms were promoted into different roles by the policies of privatization pursued in each country. Thus, the absence of banks in Bulgaria and Romania is not the result of poor economic development or financial failures so much as the product of a conscious policy of promoting industrial firms as owners. In Poland, banks came to be owners of other firms not because they were flush with cash but because the state pursued a strategy of swapping debt for the equity of indebted firms and concentrating the debt in banks while recapitalizing firms. The banks were later partly, and then fully, privatized. This was a very different strategy from that pursued even by Poland's neighbors. In the Czech Republic, for example, firms were privatized via a voucher system, which only later generated a concentration of ownership as shares came to be publicly traded and gradually landed in the hands of larger owners.

Table 2.4 shows the level of ownership concentration and asset diversity (from Table 2.1 and Figure 2.2, respectively) plotted against each other. To remind the reader, higher levels of ownership concentration are expected to reduce business collective action. Asset diversity is expected to have a positive effect on business collective action because, when the owners are financial firms, they are likely to also own other, dissimilar assets.

In fact, Poland has high levels of asset diversity and low levels of ownership concentration. Romania and Bulgaria, by contrast, have high levels of ownership concentration and low asset diversity. The effect of these two factors leads to sparse networks for Romania and Bulgaria and broad networks for Poland. While Romania and Bulgaria share sparse networks, their institutional development differs as a result of differing levels of uncertainty, as will be examined in Part III of this book.

Business collective action

How do these features affect the emergence of collective action among firms in practice? There are numerous challenges to assessing firm collective action in emerging markets. First, official organizations are often status organizations with little impact. In post-communist countries, many firms continued to be members of such organizations simply because they had always been members. Secondly, much firm collective action takes place informally. For example, numerous informal business councils were created in Bulgaria for the purpose of coordinating lobbying and business alliances. There are, however, ways to try to understand the extent of business collective action using survey data on firms. One available avenue is to examine perceptions of owners and chief executives regarding the extent to which collective firm associations matter and are able to impact politics. Firm CEOs are at the front line of interactions

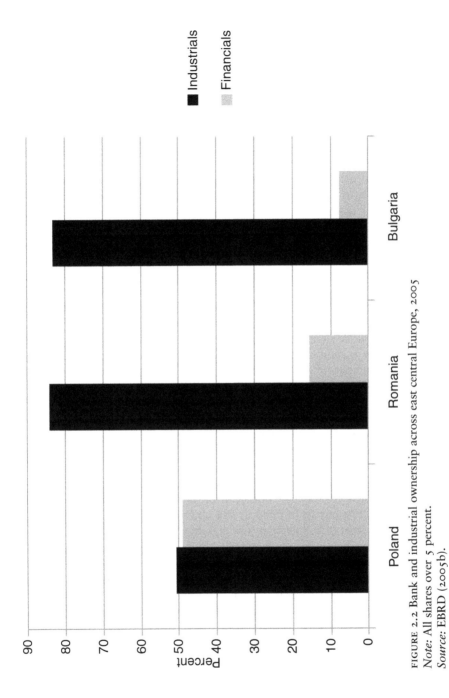

FIGURE 2.2 Bank and industrial ownership across east central Europe, 2005
Note: All shares over 5 percent.
Source: EBRD (2005b).

TABLE 2.4 *Ownership concentration and asset diversity*

		Diversity of assets	
		Low	High
Ownership concentration	High	Romania, Bulgaria	
	Low		Poland

with the state and are consequently one of the best sources of information about practices prevalent among firms.

I begin with membership in business associations – a poor indicator on its own, because firms can be members of such organizations for the purpose of status, in order to have access to information, or simply because the marginal cost of membership does not justify withdrawal. Nevertheless, Figure 2.3 shows that at least 40 percent of all medium- and large-sized firms are members of such organizations. On the basis of this evidence alone, we can conclude that a significant number of firms pay membership dues in the belief that membership might help and probably does not carry any negative consequences. As expected, membership is highest in Poland, where more than twice as many firms are members as are not members. In Romania, the majority of firms are not members, while slightly more Bulgarian firms are members than not. This is in line with the outcomes expected as a result of ownership concentration and the diversity of assets.

BEEPS (EBRD 2005b) makes it possible to also assess firms' views of the value of business association or chamber of commerce membership and the impact that firms can have as a group, which is the outcome of interest here. Figure 2.4 shows how medium- and large-sized firms assess the value of business associations in resolving disputes with other firms, workers, and officials.

As expected, associations are seen to have the greatest relevance in the country with low ownership concentration and high asset diversity: Poland. They have the least impact in Bulgaria, the country with the lowest level of asset diversity. The level of influence is also significantly lower in Romania than in Poland. Further, because only a minority of Romanian firms are members of associations, a much narrower grouping answered this question than in either of the other two countries. Thus, Polish associations are much more likely to promote cooperation among firms than associations in either of the other two countries. According to the same question on the EBRD survey (EBRD 2005b), this holds for the role of such associations in performing other functions, such as distributing information about regulations: Polish firms find the most value, while Bulgarian firms detect the least value.

BEEPS (EBRD 2005b) asks a further question about the value of associations in lobbying. Polish firms find such associations less valuable when it comes to

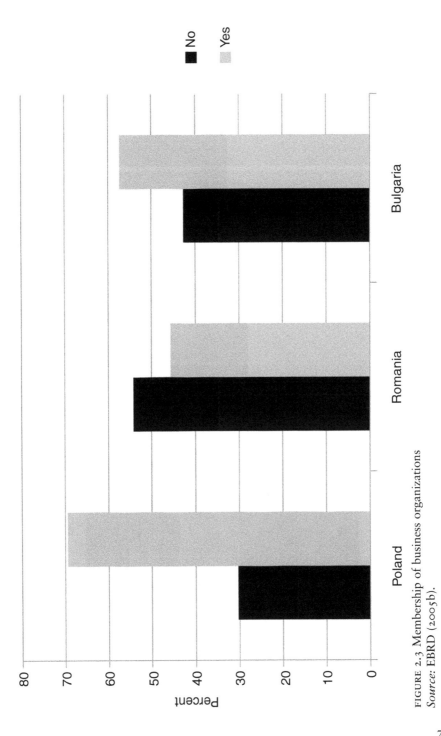

FIGURE 2.3 Membership of business organizations
Source: EBRD (2005b).

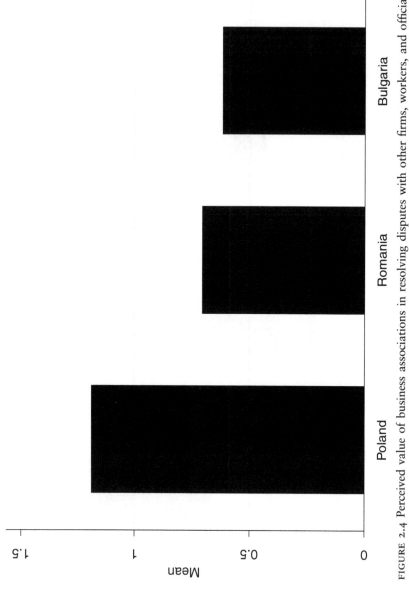

FIGURE 2.4 Perceived value of business associations in resolving disputes with other firms, workers, and officials
Note: Means of ordinal scale responses, higher values indicating greater impact.
Source: EBRD (2005b).

FIGURE 2.5 Value of business associations in lobbying government
Note: Means of ordinal scale responses, higher values indicating greater impact.
Source: EBRD (2005b).

direct lobbying than do Bulgarian firms (see Figure 2.5). This result is also consistent with the argument, as it reflects the perception that associations do not serve the direct interests of firms. Further, because so many Polish firms are members of business associations (see Figure 2.3), when associations lobby they do so on behalf of a broad group. The opposite is true for Bulgarian firms. While they generally see little value in such associations along dimensions that foster group collective action, Bulgarian firms find them more valuable for lobbying. This lobbying takes place on behalf of a narrower set of firms, however. As we shall see in the case study of Bulgarian business associations, this is to be expected in a country where narrow groupings of elite firms have created their own powerful associations to pursue specific goals. In Romania, few firms are members, and they receive relatively little in the way of representation.

INSTITUTIONAL FACTORS

Any discussion of collective action needs to also address the institutional context and how it may promote collective action. Do the countries that achieve high levels of business collective action benefit from institutional structures that promote it? Some institutions designed precisely to represent business as a collective actor are present in central eastern Europe and the Balkans. The foremost examples across the post-communist area are collective bargaining arrangements, which bring together employers and employees.

Building on legacies of worker representation in socialist factories, tripartite arrangements linking employers, unions, and the state were developed in most post-communist countries. These were seen as a way to emulate western European arrangements and thus to establish what was understood to be an institutional precondition for acceptance into the community of European welfare states. Although worker–employer negotiations were commonplace, countries varied in the extent to which these negotiations were formalized. For example, in Poland, the law establishing the tripartite commission was passed in 2001.

Despite their widespread presence, the general consensus is that such institutions have little impact. With the exception of Slovenia, where collective bargaining covers over 90 percent of all employees, institutional arrangements linking unions, the state, and employers have declined in importance over time and do not cover enough firms to make collective bargaining a meaningful forum within which business interests are brought to bear on government. Crowley (2004) surveys east European countries and finds that only 44 percent of employees on average are covered by such agreements (this drops to 33 percent if the outlier, Slovenia, is excluded). The form that these arrangements take further reduces the credibility of joint employer–state–union action. Across the region, employer–worker negotiations often do not take place in a centralized fashion, even when they cover a significant number of workers. For example, in

When broad networks increase cooperation 77

Hungary a relatively low coverage of 51 percent is rendered even less meaningful because 80 percent of such agreements are made at the individual firm level instead of the sectoral or central level (Crowley 2004).

Thus, tripartite arrangements are unlikely to serve as a platform on which business collective action can develop. Moreover, with the exception of Slovenia, there is scant evidence that variation in collective action outcomes is determined by the extent of corporatist arrangements in the post-communist context. In that country, high levels of collective action are probably the result of formal tripartite structures. Enthusiasm about the importance of such arrangements in other countries that emerged in the early 1990s has since faded. In the majority of cases, corporatist institutions in post-communist countries have been characterized as weak (Rutland 1993; Ost 2000; Crowley 2004), and essentially a "political shell for a neo-liberal economic strategy" (Pollert 1999, quoted by Crowley 2004: 409).

Another approach to exploring firms' collective action would be to relate it to privatization strategy. Yet the loose relationship between early privatization outcomes and subsequent ownership structures is itself a testament to the fact that post-communist trajectories create legacies, but that these legacies do not prevent countries from changing the path on which they initially embarked. Said another way, the development of ownership subsequent to and often independent of privatization outcomes is a sign that these countries have entered a phase of post-post-communist development. Hence, in order to understand the forms of capitalism that are developing there, we must look well beyond the initial trajectories of privatization. Take, for example, the case of the Czech Republic, where voucher privatization was used to distribute shares of state-owned enterprises to the public. Within a few years these shares had moved their way into concentrated holdings, with the result that the Czech Republic has ened up with the highest average shareholder size in the region. This is not to say that the legacies of early privatization and related policies do not continue to affect ownership structure. The widespread use of debt-for-equity swaps in Poland, for example, made banks into important shareholders. Subsequent exchanges of shares in all countries altered the initial paths, however, in ways that were often discontinuous with the policy choices of the early 1990s.

THREE CASES: POLAND, ROMANIA, AND BULGARIA

The remainder of this chapter focuses on a discussion of the role of business associations and gives qualitative confirmation of the patterns seen in the data above. It also establishes a link between the preceding analysis and the following chapters, which focus on detailed within-country data, process tracing, and interview-based research conducted in Poland, Romania, and Bulgaria. The subsequent pages show how the organizational sphere that represents business developed differently in each country on the basis of the characteristics of the prominent actors. This discussion seeks to highlight the characteristics of the organizational landscape in each country, not to explain why the countries followed such different paths, beyond the brief discussion that may be useful to the reader here.

In Poland, the variety of firms that were bound together by common interests led to the development of broad organizations that were consequently able to assemble significant lobbying power. By contrast, in Romania, firm owners joined organizations that were led by business leaders who already had political power. These organizations were largely personal vehicles for their founders and reflected a tendency toward the formation of narrow clique groups. They were able to extract benefits and exert influence, but this ability depended heavily on the personalities of group leaders and their ties to state actors and political parties. Finally, in Bulgaria, the tendency toward self-interest undermined projects of building collective organizations and left a barren associational landscape.

Each of the major Polish business organizations united firms across sectors. Common owners also often joined firms across sectors. Ownership stakes tended to be lower than in other countries, reflecting a tendency among firms to take stakes in other firms. This was reinforced by the prominence of financial firms in the economy, which acquired stakes across sectors because of the common strategy of swapping debt for equity and concentrating this equity in what were initially state-owned banks that were then partly privatized. As a result, the organizations that became powerful in post-socialist Poland were broad rather than sectoral.

The major Polish organizations included the following.

- The Polish Business Roundtable (Polska Rada Biznesu: PRB), an elite grouping of the owners and CEOs of the most prosperous private and foreign firms present in Poland, created in 1992. Its presidents have been the owners and CEOs of the largest Polish firms. It was formed to represent business interests and sits on the tripartite commission. Headquartered in a lavish villa in central Warsaw, it also acts as a social club for those holding vast wealth.
- The Polish Confederation of Private Employers Leviathan (Polskiej Konfederacji Pracodawców Prywatnych Lewiatan: PKPP), an organization of private employers that was established in 1998 to represent the interest of the private economy. Henryka Bochniarz, a strongly pro-market figure who served as minister of industry in the government of Jan Bielecki, has led the PKPP. In 2001 it joined the newly formed tripartite commission. It is also the only Polish member of BUSINESSEUROPE, the main business association at the EU level.
- Employers of Poland (Pracodawcy Rzeczypospolitej Polskiej: Pracodawcy RP; before 2010 the Konfederacja Pracodawcow Polskich: KPP), an association, created in 1989, that represents mostly state-owned firms and was

seen by members of Leviathan as an organization that emerged from the planned economy and exists to protect the state sector. The Pracodawcy RP is also represented on the tripartite commission. It is led by Andrzej Malinowski, a peasant party activist before 1989 and MP for the Polish Peasant Party (PSL).

- The Business Centre Club, which represented the interests of a much larger number of medium-sized firms, as well as some large firms. It was established in 1991. It was created and led by Marek Goliszewksi, a journalist before 1989 and one of the early initiators of the negotiations that led to the roundtable talks.

Although these organizations are broad and diverse, cleavages still exist between groups. They developed around the principle cleavages in the early post-socialist economy: the emergent division between state and private industry, as well as an early division between managers of state-owned enterprises and private entrepreneurs. In other words, organizations tended to unite firms around a broader political struggle. Exceptions to the rule existed, but Polish business organizations tended to have their own political identities related to the post-communist/anti-communist cleavage.

By contrast, the Romanian business organization scene is much less developed. The role of business interest groups and associations in Romania is insignificant. By their own admission, business associations find it very difficult to even collect dues from members, not because member firms lack funds but because they simply do not see the value of group representation. Hence, it is nearly impossible to convince members that it is important for the business community to lobby the state in unison, even for issues on which there is no conflict of interest between firms. According to directors of all influential business organizations, wealthy firms refuse to contribute funds to joint lobbying campaigns or to fund political campaigns by the associations. The leader of one organization lamented the failure of multiple attempts to organize, commenting to me that "there were several attempts to form a consolidated group of firms but they failed."

A critical question is whether this is in response to a perception that such a business organization cannot be effective because of Romania's political structure. Or do firms simply prefer direct exchanges? When probed, the directors of the business organizations all attribute the situation to the preference of business to engage in direct exchanges of campaign funds for personal political goods. In an interview, the head of one organization attributed the difficulty of collectively organizing firms to the outlook of firm owners: "Owners don't have the right formation to address their problems collectively and continue to use methods from before 1989; in other words, they work through political channels to address their problems. These owners have relationships directly with political parties, not through associations."

The business organizations that do exist in Romania are symbols of failed attempts to build effective representative organizations. They are often "prestige groups," or personal showcases for single entrepreneurs who are trying to further their political careers. Their other members are firms that would like to benefit from group representation but have not succeeded in causing such an organization to emerge.

The main organizations are as follows.

- The Businessman's Association of Romania (Asociatia Oamenilor de Afaceri din Romania: AOAR), which is largely a personal vehicle for a major businessman who allegedly managed Romanian firms and hard currency funds in Cyprus before 1989. Whereas many members are clearly committed to what they see as the only possible future for Romanian business, the organization is largely a status symbol for Dan Voiculescu's political and business ambitions.
- The General Union of Romanian Industrialists (Uniunea Generală a Industriaşilor din România: UGIR), which was largely associated with the Paunescu family and served as a personal status vehicle.
- The General Union of Romanian Industrialists 1903 (Uniunea Generală a Industriaşilor din România 1903: UGIR-1903), a rival organization to UGIR that established itself as the legitimate heir to the original organization after a lengthy court battle.

These bodies are very different in character from those present in Poland. Businesspeople such as the Paunescus, who were closely connected to the Romanian Social Democratic Party, did not need formal organizations for any purpose other than the status attached to the organization itself. This status was considerable; a business organization called UGIR had been created in 1903 and operated to represent the interests of pre-war industrialists. This group was of particular interest because the Paunescus and many of their peers had allegedly emerged from Romania's security apparatus and sought to deflect calls for investigation of their dealings by assuming the outward appearance of conventional businesspeople. For interest representation, however, they opted for a one-to-one strategy by using their links to the PSDR, which held power without interruption until 1996 and regained power in 2000 from an ineffectual opposition coalition. Interviewees thus repeatedly argued that the Paunescus do not need such an organization for lobbying purposes.

The desire for status organizations led to a bizarre conflict, however, over who the rightful heir was to the original UGIR. Multiple groups of businesspeople sought control of the name of a new organization that was to resume the activities of a powerful pre-war organization. The Paunescus and their allies eventually decided on a new name, UGIR-1903, to emphasize their claim as the continuation of the original UGIR. UGIR-1903 became less active after 1996 because the Paunescu family relocated to the United States in order to avoid prosecution once the Romanian democratic opposition came to power.

When broad networks increase cooperation 81

AOAR had a similar link to Voiculescu, one of the wealthiest new business-people of the 1990s. His dealings were the subject of much discussion because of this alleged links to businesses and accounts belonging to the Ceausescu regime abroad. Again, it became a vehicle through which a coalition of businesspeople sought to acquire a legitimate image.

The two organizations that undertook most lobbying on behalf of business, organize executive and entrepreneurial education, and provide a location within which to network were the alternative UGIR and the Romanian Chamber of Commerce (CCIR). These organizations have had very little actual impact on policy, however.

Overall, Romanian organizations formed around and worked to further the interests of particular powerful business groups, and thus they sustained a certain level of cooperation among their members, who probably sought to attach their fortunes to the individuals and firms that anchored each particular organization.

By contrast, the Bulgarian organizational scene was a barren landscape. Three large organizations were divided according to the historical identities of the firms they represent. These were as follows.

- The Bulgarian Industrial Association (Българска стопанска камара), which was established in 1980 and retains an organizational structure that recalls socialist industrial organization. It continues to represent industrial "branches" and coordinates the organization of branch associations. Moreover, individuals who rose through the socialist industrial hierarchy staff it and sit on its management board. Since 1990 most of those who retain a management role have served as directors of state-owned enterprises or formed firms that have strong ties to the state sector.
- The Bulgarian Industrial Capital Association (Асоциацията на индустриалния капитал в България), which was created in 1996 as a union of privatization funds and brings together high-profile managers from the state sector.
- The Bulgarian Investors Business Association (BIBA), which was formed in 1992 to represent the interests of foreign investors in Bulgaria against some of the early attempts to keep foreign direct investment (FDI) at a disadvantage.

These groups have negligible influence, however, and were not able to make progress in formalizing the process of affecting the policy-making process. Describing the general approach to lobbying, even the leader of one association said in an interview, "Foreigners come here and tell us that we should paint in these colors. But we have our own colors. Why should a lobbying law be an important institution for us?" Another business organization leader added, "Business has no interest in investing in the main organizations." Recounting how the business community was divided, a business owner said, "In Bulgaria, the different organizations that were created could not carry through their vision because each organization was working for its own survival and met with lots of opposition." Summing up the actual interaction between parties and firms, one politician said simply, "The moral of the story is that they all interact behind the scenes."

Not surprisingly, several additional, informal groups were formed in Bulgaria, whose members carried somewhat more influence than the above-mentioned organizations. These were the groups that formed around business clusters. The first of these was known as the "Group of Thirteen" (G-13), which emerged as a lobbying vehicle in 1993 and dominated the private sector until 1995 (Synovitz 1996). This group, including subsidiaries, consisted of the owners of the largest banks, insurance companies, stock exchanges, large trading companies, newspapers, and private security firms. The group was formed with the intention of protecting Bulgaria from the entrance of foreign firms. Member firms aimed to work together in order to obtain preferences, licenses, and other preferential benefits from the state. The group even created its own business organization, the Confederation of Bulgarian Industrialists. Divisions began to appear among the members quite early, however, as individual firms had differing interests. Some of these divisions were driven by the narrow interests of business owners, most of whom focused on various primary activities ranging from telecommunications to banking. Some realized that they could benefit from doing business with foreign firms, while others benefited from protection, which clashed with the stated purpose of the organization. Even the identities of the individual business groups that made up the G-13 was grounds for disagreement beyond single policy areas; this disagreement reflected the inability of firms to elaborate preferences as a group. Thus, as firms tried to diversify their holdings, individuals also came into conflict around privatization deals. The one-to-one manner in which preferences were awarded to firms in such deals meant that the organization could not offset the divisions arising from them. Faced with conflicts, firms fell back on a dyadic logic.

BIBA also accused the group of supporting economically nationalist policies that might have served the interests of domestic private business but were in conflict with those of foreign investors. Those firms interested in joint ventures with foreign firms sought closer ties to BIBA, making the institutional landscape unstable. Finally, the firms of the G-13 began to lose their political protection as economic pressure on Bulgaria mounted.

As the Confederation of Bulgarian Industrialists crumbled and many of its member firms – the early winners of the transformation – failed or faced significant economic difficulties, it was replaced by other groups with new political protectors. These shifts in business coalitions are discussed in more detail in the following chapters. Their significance here is to underline the unstable nature of the organizational landscape in Bulgaria. In contrast to the Romanian organizational landscape, these organizations were undermined by the excessively individualistic nature of negotiation and interest expression.

When broad networks increase cooperation 83

In other words, interests were conceptualized in such an individualistic fashion that they precluded the successful expression of joint aims.

The striking difference between these three countries is that state–business relations were conducted on fundamentally different bases. In Romania, individual leaders were able to form personal organizations that attained a measure of stability, accounting for a higher level of impact among business organizations. In sharp contrast, the Bulgarian business leaders were unable to make any significant progress in creating organizations (with the exception of BIBA, which owes its prominence to support by foreign investors). Instead, individual business owners and CEOs used their influence over political actors to control both the content of policy and individual decisions. Although attempts to form groups were made, they were doomed from the outset, undermined by the strong dyadic alternative available to those seeking influence in politics.

CONCLUSION

These three cases complement the survey data presented earlier to make the broader point that horizontally networked and heterogeneous groups are more likely to have success in articulating group goals than narrow groups or groups wherein individualistic ties interfere with the elaboration of group objectives. There is a middle range in which narrow groups can be held together by leadership, and the Romanian case is precisely a case of the latter – individuals who exerted enough authority were able to create lasting groups – but these organizations depend on individual personalities for their cohesion, and, although they are stable, their performance is very modest. Poland, by contrast, is a case in which heterogeneity and networks in a period of uncertainty and political conflict raised the incentives for firms to collaborate. Bulgaria represents the other extreme, where the lack of network ties among firms and a strong tendency toward dyadic relations undermined efforts to elaborate group goals.

This chapter has argued that there is a link between ownership structures and the development of firm collective action, drawing on a literature that focuses on the macro-effects of corporate governance. I have shown how broad networks raised the likelihood of collective action. More precisely, two dimensions of networks – (1) the diversity of assets and (2) agency problems in the management of the firm – predict when firms have an incentive and the ability to act collectively. Data on the average size of shareholders and the prominence of firms that tend to hold heterogeneous assets, together with survey data on membership in business organizations and the value that firms obtain from those organizations, illustrated the effect of these two dimensions on business collective action.

3

Tracing ownership networks

Having explained the determinants of collective political action among firms, this chapter examines the emergence of dominant stakeholders in three transition countries, with two goals. First, it observes the historical process by which business networks were created. Second, it explores how the process in each country generated three strikingly different relationships between business networks and political actors. In Poland, the relationship was one of joint problem solving leading to the emergence of a *concertation state*. In Bulgaria, economic elites used their power in a barren organizational landscape to dominate state institutions and bring about a *captured state*. In Romania, the lack of strong networks among firms left them at the mercy of strong political actors, who held the reins of what I label the *patronage state*.

Privatization was an important initial part of the process of creating stakeholders. Yet in seeking to understand what might be called "post-post-socialism" – the period beyond the first phase of economic and political transformation, when markets were already in operation – this chapter goes beyond privatization policy. Ownership changes subsequent to privatization often dramatically altered the initial ownership distribution effects of privatization and promoted a different set of owners from the early stakeholders. Both these moments must be considered in order to understand the development of networks of firms, and thus the different trajectories of institutional development identified in the previous section.

Much research has been conducted on the politicization of the privatization and transformation process in the 1990s. Little is known, however, about the political bases of institution building that have emerged in post-socialist countries. After the political and economic transformations began, various patterns of interaction between political and economic stakeholders took shape that affected the trajectory of the institutional transformation begun after 1989. These patterns of interaction have not been widely explored as a causal factor in the nature of institutional development. Chapter 2 showed that banks and

84

financial firms contribute to broader networks, while industrial and family firms tend to create narrower networks. Narrow networks reduce the likelihood of collective action, while broad networks increase it. This chapter builds on this finding to show the causal processes through which the interaction of networks of owners with political actors shaped institutional development.

The chapter proceeds as follows. The next section identifies the mechanisms by which networks of ownership affect institutional development. The following section shows how different kinds of owners emerged in each of the three country cases – Poland, Romania, and Bulgaria. It then explores the development of firm networks in each country using ownership networks data. In each country, state ownership remained quite prominent until the early 2000s. What differed was the non-state actor chosen as the key vehicle in the transition to the private economy.

I show that banks became the anchors of a network of ownership that joined the 200 largest firms in Poland. Beyond this, political actors encouraged an array of hybrid ownership forms not seen elsewhere. For example, several banks were partially privatized to foreign investors, with the state retaining important shares. These banks held shares in a multitude of firms. In turn, many firms held shares in other firms and banks, creating a web of crossing alliances.

A very different dynamic took hold in Romania. In the first decade state privatization funds remained prominent as owners until they were displaced by domestic industrial firms and individual owners. This strategy generated far less new capital, as it did not produce the financialization of the new private sector that took place in Poland. It succeeded only in attracting foreign capital well into the second decade of transition, when foreign industrial firms acquired stakes in Romanian firms. Few firms created cross-ownership ties. Private individual investors were also key figures. Moreover, the early choice of management/employee buyout as a privatization strategy left many firms isolated, without consolidated leadership, and put them at the mercy of a relatively well consolidated political elite. The resulting narrow networks provided little support for firms maneuvering in a context in which a single political party dominated much of the first two decades of transformation.

In Bulgaria, a third approach to private sector development promoted industrial firms – among which were many state-owned holding companies – and private individuals as owners. The hostile business environment in Bulgaria discouraged foreign firms from taking much of an interest, and Bulgaria remained an unattractive destination for FDI. For different reasons, the resulting network of owners was also narrow.

As I have argued throughout, these three different network structures shaped the preferences and possibilities of elites with regard to the development of fundamental market institutions. That network structure was the cause and not the result of institutional development is also clear from the process tracing carried out in this chapter. The seeds of each network

86 *The Role of Networks*

structure took shape early after 1989, well before the large differences in institutional trajectory took shape.

OWNERSHIP NETWORKS AS MAPS OF POLITICS–BUSINESS RELATIONS

Ownership matters because modern states derive a considerable portion of their power from the economic assets that they control directly and indirectly, as well as the assets that they regulate. States build this power by coordinating and promoting sectors and particular groups of firms. In other words, the configuration of ownership ties among firms is a key component of the politics of economic development.

In making this argument, I follow a tradition that has recognized the impact of the configuration of accumulated assets on state capacity and regime type (Moore 1967). For Moore, where ownership lies, how it is configured, and the participation of landed and peasant classes explain the transformation of agrarian societies into either democratic or authoritarian (fascist or communist) ones. Moore's focus is on class conflict, but similar arguments have been used to explain the development of institutions without such a focus on class. The point is that the configuration of assets structures conflict between classes and determines the trajectory of political development.

Carruthers (1996) makes a similar point: that elite cooperation on state-building projects is often based on exchanges between elite groups. Thus, as political elites are trying to resolve state-building dilemmas by soliciting support from powerful societal interests, the latter are also seeking to resolve their own institutional dilemmas. These projects can be complementary if the different parties involved are able to make credible commitments, although that itself is a complicated problem of political innovation. Carruthers details how the Crown in seventeenth-century Britain essentially invented the possibility of state borrowing from the public in order to push forward with the project of centralizing and expanding state power. The fundamental puzzle that the Crown overcame was to find a way that the sovereign could credibly commit to the repayment of loans obtained from its subjects. Economic linkages not only solved a financial problem but also served as the glue for a broad exchange of loyalty between different social groups. This resolved a dilemma for both parties by unleashing stocks of capital for productive use in early bond markets and generating desperately needed resources for state projects. What economic actors saw as a struggle to shape the rules of the economic game, the state and its political leaders viewed as the search for extractive capacity and control (Carruthers 1996).

The British Crown's success in developing financial markets was not just a result of collaborative bargains between economic and political elites. The period is interesting because the financial revolution was taking place just as political parties were created in the British parliament. Carruthers shows that

Tracing ownership networks 87

the new parties, the Whigs and Tories, used the economy for political ends and imposed a political logic on the economy that shaped institutional outcomes such as the development of competitive and efficient capital markets.[1]

Within these struggles, networks were deployed to offset uncertainty. Stark and Bruszt (1998), McDermott (2007), and Stark and Vedres (2012) have shown that early post-communist ownership reconfigurations were often geared toward achieving political ends, or attempts to recombine elements into new valuable property or to provide protection from external pressures. Network reconfigurations also served as an adjustment mechanism that helped firms cope with changing external conditions, because networks reorganize in reaction to external stimuli such as globalization or economic liberalization (Hamilton and Biggart 1988; Hall and Soskice 2001; Kogut and Walker 2001; Stark and Vedres 2006). These networks also provide support to firms in difficult times. In other words, networks – whether they are based on ownership, membership of boards of directors, or even friendship – are strategic assets, and ties are deployed as a part of the profit-making efforts of individual firms. Whether banks are allowed to merge with each other, and which firms are allowed or encouraged to acquire stakes in other firms, are similarly political decisions.

This chapter observes how ties of ownership between companies took form between 1990 and 2005. Decisions to configure or reconfigure the economy in a particular way and create joint links – to create ownership ties between two firms – are all reflections of the political organization of the economy (Mizruchi 1992; Davis and Mizruchi 1999; Uzzi 1999). As decisions over economic policy were made in the early 1990s, banks, foreign investors, single large private owners, investment funds, holding companies, or large industrial firms began to emerge as more or less prominent stakeholders. These actors acquired different roles in each context. These early decisions, in turn, generated pressure for certain policies that favored the dominant type of stakeholder and thus reverberated through the process of institution building.

The ownership structure is one way of assessing the configuration of interests and their potential for constructive interaction (concertation). Economic transactions took place against the background of a political contest that instrumentalized firms for the sake of gaining an edge in politics. This dynamic

---

[1] Other authors have dealt with this question. Lachmann (2000) argues that, in medieval Europe, conflict between elite groups, rather than class configurations, was the primary determinant of the state form that emerged. Similarly, Waldner (1999) looks at cases in the Middle East and Asia during the late 1800s to argue that more intense conflicts between elites made it more likely that they would support the project of state building. Kang (2002) makes yet another related argument: that a deadlock between economic and political elites in South Korea was what led to effective state function, differentiating it from the Philippines, where the economic and political elite were united and able to effectively collude and derail economic planning for short-term private interest. The common element among these arguments is that inter-elite tensions created an incentive for these elites to develop stable institutions and look to the long term, when they faced a viable opposition.

88 *The Role of Networks*

also reproduced itself within the market, however, where competitive pressures rose in accordance with the needs of political actors. Firms also were pushed to perform in order to generate profits that were partly used to buy much-needed political capital. Said another way, when political competition was sharp, firms went from being the spoils to generating the spoils for political actors. Market institutions thus served and were shaped by political struggles. In some cases, as in Poland, these conflicts were sufficiently deadlocked to push elites toward the development of more stable rules of interaction. When elites were less balanced, as in the other two cases examined here, institutional outcomes were significantly poorer.

OWNERSHIP DEVELOPMENT IN POLAND, ROMANIA, AND BULGARIA

To understand the development of different state–business relationships, two types of data are considered in addition to a historical analysis of business networks: (1) data on the top owners and the number of stakes they hold in the top 200 firms (ranked by revenue); and (2) data on the characteristics of the networks among the top 200 firms themselves.

The following questions are posed with regard to the data. What types of owners have emerged in each country? How did privatization reshape firm networks? What subsequent changes restructured those networks? Are the networks between firms broad or deep? Are cross-holdings between firms common? Do they extend across business sectors? Do these networks include the state? What kinds of actors are the most central owners in the economy? Are institutional investors, banks, industrial groups, or family firms prominent?

Comparing data on firm ownership networks across countries shows the starkly different paths followed by each country in the political process of creating marketized economies.[2] This difference is based not only on the speed of privatization or the persistence of state ownership in particular sectors. In each country, different structural shifts took place across the economy, transferring ownership stakes from the state to different dominant types of actors. The following sections present data on the types of key owners emerging in each country. Table 3.1 shows the changes in the ownership structure of the 200 largest firms by revenue between 1995 and 2005 for each of the three largest categories (by number of ties) in any given year and country. It is compared to the status of the same owner type in the other countries to show how sharply different paths were taken. Examining the ties between the 200 largest firms by revenue and their owners captures the control structure of the powerhouses of economic activity in each country and effectively delivers

---

[2] I use the term "marketized" to indicate that these economies mix markets with nonmarket forms of economic interaction.

Tracing ownership networks

TABLE 3.1 *Top owners by type and their ties, 1995, 2000, 2005*

	Poland	Romania	Bulgaria
		1995	
N	276	828	184
MEBOs and mass privatization investment funds	0	40.14	0
Individual investors	4.35	13.44	16.30
State	55.80	23.52	76.09
Total industrial firms (percentage foreign)	19.20 (39.62)	19.76 (37.00)	7.61 (50.00)
Total financial firms (percentage foreign)	20.65 (36.84)	2.96 (80.00)	0 (0)
		2000	
N	395	1,102	405
MEBOs and mass privatization investment funds	1.52	21.22	6.91
Individual investors	2.28	23.77	31.85
State	24.56	14.71	18.02
Total industrial firms (percentage foreign)	36.71 (56.25)	31.97 (25.5)	38.77 (31.21)
Total financial firms (percentage foreign)	26.58 (58.1)	8.35 (53.98)	4.44 (55.56)
		2005	
N	4,921	703	2,966
MEBOs and mass privatization investment funds	0.02	2.56	9.13
Individual investors	13.62	37.70	42.41
State	4.79	3.7	4.15
Total industrial firms (percentage foreign)	31.46 (35.48)	45.66 (73.10)	36.31 (36.81)
Total financial firms (percentage foreign)	49.73 (88.96)	8.4 (74.65)	7.86 (63.13)

Note: Percentage of ties held by each type of owner.

a picture of the choices about restructuring that each government took. These paths were not the reflection of an unintended choice but largely conscious decisions on the part of policy makers and their allies in the economy. They reflect the dominant alliance between political and economic stakeholders.[3]

---

[3] The results were obtained by counting the number of firms by category that are present among the owners and the number of ownership ties each category has to the top 200 firms.

As the table shows, state ownership – unsurprisingly – declined between 1995 and 2005 as a result of privatization but remained a prominent feature in each country until 2000. Partial privatization was a common strategy in the transition economies and was driven by the desire to retain some political control on the part of the state, inadequate capital on the part of new investors, and the division of risk between private investors and the state (Maw 2002). The gradual pace of privatization in transition economies was an avenue for states to signal commitment, a logical way of showing that the government was willing to retain a share of the residual risk – that is, "a signal that it does not intend to redistribute value through a future shift in policy" (Perotti 1995). This is particularly important to potential private stakeholders in periods of future policy uncertainty that have the potential to bring about reversals that would reduce the future value of the privatized firm. Such uncertainty could come from the possibility that the party in power could change or simply because an insufficient amount of time has passed to allow investors to gauge the government's longer-term intentions. All these factors were present in the transition economies, and thus it is not surprising that partial privatization persisted for such a long time.

Although privatization as a broad goal was common to all transition countries, they chose different paths in addressing uncertainty. Comparing the three countries shown in Table 3.1, it is quite apparent that privatization strategies and subsequent policy decisions privileged some potential owners over others, and different types of owners emerged as the largest stakeholders in each country. As early as 1995 state-owned banks were being pushed forward as stakeholders in the Polish network of large firms. By 2000 Poland's ownership structure was heavily influenced by foreign banks and investment funds. Strikingly, four large banks linked the state to foreign capital, while one linked the state with private domestic capital. By 2005 foreign firms were heavily in control of assets in the Polish economy. This injection of foreign capital was, at least in part, a fruit of the early strategy of placing banks in control of industrial firms as part of the process of restructuring.

Throughout the Polish transformation, financial firms were key owners. The data show that the politics of industrial restructuring privileged the shifting of ownership to state-owned banks, even when these were partially privatized to foreigners, and resisted the transfer of industrial firms to other industrial firms. Later sections of this chapter show that banks held ownership ties both to other banks and to industrial firms. The network position of banks thus made them the decision-making centers for the management of the economy and rendered them influential in the operative decisions of a wide range of nonfinancial firms. Comparison with Bulgaria and Romania shows that this financialization of the economy was a quite peculiar characteristic of the Polish approach and distinguished it from other countries, which chose mass privatization, employee participation, or the creation of industrial groups by sector as their preferred strategies. Instead, the Polish path

Tracing ownership networks

postponed the transfer of ownership rights in a significant way even to industrial firms until quite late – between 2000 and 2005. Only in 2005 did industrial firms appear as significant stakeholders there.

By contrast, in Romania, management and employee buyouts (MEBOs) and mass privatization funds were the key emergent ownership form until 2000, when industrial companies displaced them. In place of Polish banks, Romanian private owners and family groups, representing the very prominent new economic elite, ranked highly but were not in the top three. Foreign financial firms were present in 2000, but the lack of domestic financial firms meant that the overall presence of finance as an owner was much smaller. Instead, the overwhelming characteristic of Romanian ownership networks was that of direct individual or group ownership of assets. By 2005 private individual investors were the second largest owner type in Romania. Some of these were small stakeholders, but the majority held large stakes in the top firms.

A different strategy was pursued in Bulgaria – perhaps even one that can be defined as the opposite of the Polish strategy. Instead of financializing ownership by transferring debt in exchange for equity to state-owned banks, the Bulgarian state focused on giants in each sector to conduct restructuring. The hope was that agglomerating firms in the same sector under single holding companies would make the assets easier to restructure and more attractive for privatization down the line. Hence, in Bulgaria, state-owned firms actually increased their profile as owners, reflecting this transfer of ownership from the state to state-owned holding companies that took place during the first decade of transformation. The move effected an informal decentralization of power and loss of control of state-owned assets by putting large numbers of firms under the control of holding company managers instead of subjecting each firm to ministerial supervision. Consistent with this trend, management buyouts and mass privatization dominated, together with state ownership until a later period, when individual investors began to emerge.

Consider the contrast with the Polish case. In this, an alliance of financial capital with the state slowly transformed into a union of financial and industrial capital. In Bulgaria, a decentralization of ownership stakes to state-owned firms and employee privatizations transformed into an economy governed by individual stakeholders and industrial firms. Unsurprisingly, these groups had dramatically different interests and time horizons. Polish financial firms and the links they promoted between firms led the network structure of ties to be much more horizontal. As a result, firms were locked into a web of mutual interest with other firms by debt and equity holdings. These allowed information to flow and bound firms into ongoing relationships. They also generated a distributed interest in the performance of each firm. Bulgarian firms had no such ties, and individuals in charge of both state and private property had only their immediate self-interest in view in a highly uncertain political context that offered few incentives to invest in the long term.

To give more texture to this argument that owner types and their networks influence management style, the following sections discuss in more detail the development of the network of firms in each country.

POLAND'S PATH TO PRIVATIZATION: BANKS PROMOTE BROAD NETWORKS

In Poland, two features were distinctive in the first period of the transformation. First, banks were a critical part of the post-1989 capitalist development, emerging at the center of clusters of firms. Banks became involved in a series of debt/equity swaps that created broad networks of cross-ownership because of a government preference for workouts. Under the workout procedure, banks could negotiate workout agreements with problem debtors and force them on creditors. This put banks in a position to focus on long-term value and the development of a broad network of firms connected by ownership ties. Second, the facilitation of debt/equity swaps was part of a distinct policy that avoided or delayed the foreign purchase of many attractive firms. This policy delayed the transition of nearly a half of all ownership shares in financial firms until after 2000 and caused the majority of shares in industrial firms to remain in domestic hands. As a result, in the second stage, private entrepreneurs found it difficult to dominate national economic – and hence political – activity. The new Polish magnates were certainly important in Polish politics, but they were as much dependent on political parties as the parties were dependent on them. When asked why his firm had such extensive ties to parties and the state, one business leader commented, "Because the political sphere is so present – in ownership transformation, in regulation. It's like in business: in the early phase, you look for a partner with whom you can do something together." The level of political competition raised the stakes for both sets of elites. As a result, a broad horizontal network of ownership emerged in Poland that was distinct from the other countries under comparison.

The initial step in the distribution of ownership stakes was the process of privatization. The most common methods of privatization were: (1) the restitution of property to former owners (this applies only to property existing before nationalization); (2) direct sales of state property, either to domestic or foreign owners; (3) MEBOs; (4) free distribution through a voucher system; or (5) a combination of these strategies (Andreff 2005). Poland largely chose direct sales, with some voucher privatization to legitimate the process (Stark and Bruszt 1998), the creation of national investment funds to inject capital (Błaszczyk et al. 2003), and some MEBOs (Svejnar 2002).

Moreover, privatization proceeded slowly. Indeed, despite being hailed as an example of the success of neoliberal reform, Poland actually proceeded more slowly with regard to the overall reduction of the state sector than did countries such as the Czech Republic (Stark and Bruszt 1998). It even lagged behind Hungary, often cited as an example of gradualism, as late as 2000. Progress was halting and largely marred by political infighting and the consciousness that privatized property would be valuable in future political contests. Privatization in Poland, as elsewhere, was also marked by political manipulation. Great lengths were taken by Polish state officials to create politicized spheres of property: firms were privatized to domestic business groups in exchange for future benefits in the form of campaign contributions to political parties. As a former minister of privatization, Janusz Lewandowski, said, "The government has frequently used words like 'national' or 'Polish' in consolidating state assets in the sugar, power or shipbuilding industries. In the end, however, 'national' often turns out to mean 'partisan'" (Polish News Bulletin 2004). Businesspeople also spoke of the need to shield national entrepreneurs from foreign pressure – a discourse that resonated with broad nationalist sentiments already in the first decade of transition. For example, one business leader, asked to identify priorities for economic policy, stated, "The government needs a system of supporting business – a system of financing, a system of supporting *Polish* owners [emphasis added]."

Bank restructurings in particular were subject to politicization because of the emphasis on workouts rather than liquidation, as described by McDermott (2007), and the rejection of bank sale by distributing vouchers to the general public (Balcerowicz and Bratkowski 2001). At the same time, large privatizations were used as a means of plugging holes in the budget and reducing liabilities for the state. Addressing budgetary shortfalls is a common element of most privatization processes, but the combination of workouts, domestic favoritism, gradual pace, and political competition created ample opportunities for the entrance of politics into the process in Poland.

The system of corporate governance further enforced these trends. Poland adopted a two-level system of corporate governance. This structure was chosen because supervisory boards would act as state agents, doing what was known in Poland as "sanitizing" (bringing to a healthy state) firms without political interference. In practice, this process was heavily politicized (Jarosz 2001: 47), with the supervisory boards often staffed by political insiders loyal to the then minister of the Treasury (Grzeszak *et al.* 1999).

Finally, Poland's early governments were reluctant to accept foreign ownership, to the point that one early privatization minister stated that he had created as many obstacles as possible to foreign purchases of Polish companies in order to encourage a class of domestic owners (Stark and Bruszt 1998; Schoenman 2005). This last position reinforced the politicization of Polish business.

Altogether, the Polish government's policy of economic transformation amounted to an attempt to manage the slow combination of private market forces with state intervention in order to retain both political and policy influence. After 1997 economic pressures led governments to look increasingly to foreign investors for injections of capital, but these were still managed and cautious attempts to attract investment without relinquishing control over economic development policy. Throughout, these moves increased the breadth of the network of ownership.

Banks

Banks and funds were a central part of the Polish transformation, due both to the level of state involvement and restructuring that took place instead of liquidation and to their role as anchors of the broader process of property transformation. In transition economies, the short supply of capital and the exigencies of rapid growth placed banks in a particularly important position. In Poland, however, it was debt/equity swaps that drove the initial ties with banks, rather than firm borrowing through credit.

As banks became key owners, they attracted foreign investment through the privatization process. In addition, Poland's privatization policy established fifteen closed-ended national investment funds (NFIs in Polish), which became publicly listed companies. Ownership of these funds was transferred to the public through vouchers that were convertible into shares, with the NFIs accounting for 60 percent of the shares of 500 state-owned firms slated for privatization (Dzierzanowski and Tamowicz 2003).[4]

In Poland, the banking system privatization began in 1992. At the same time, before 1995, a number of small private banks appeared as a result of a liberal licensing regime that came into effect with the banking law of 1989. Many of these ended in failure, with some generating spectacular scandals. As a result, the Polish government changed the licensing policy in 1992 and ended the period when solely domestic banks were being founded (Balcerowicz and Bratkowski 2001: 13). The state also chose to privatize some large state-owned banks to Western firms (Svejnar 2002: 7). The Polish process was eclectic, however, shifting over time between initial public offerings (IPOs), minority stakes, and tender offerings from strategic investors (Bonin and Wachtel 1999).

The privatization of banks can be divided into two periods. The first, lasting from 1992 to 1997, was a period of halting progress. In March 1991 the initial program of bank privatization was approved. This foresaw a period in which nine commercial banks would be "commercialized," meaning that their legal form would change from that of state bank to joint-stock company, thus preparing them for privatization. The intention was to privatize these nine commercial banks quickly, with the goal of two to three per year until 1996 (Balcerowicz and Bratkowski 2001). Banks with specialized functions, such as Bank Handlowy SA, PKO BP, and PEKAO SA, would be held for privatization after 1996.

The privatization process did not start properly until 1993. This delay was caused by the poor financial condition of these state-owned banks. In 1991 the government decided to postpone the privatization and to deal with banks' bad debt portfolios first. In order to do so, some foreign investment was permitted

---

[4] The reader should recall that the sample used in Table 4.1 includes the top 200 privately *and* publicly owned firms, whereas the statistic cited by Dzierzanowski and Tamowicz (2003) applies to SOEs that remained outside the public market.

Tracing ownership networks

under the condition that it be used to restructure existing small banks in distress. In total, fourteen banks were granted such licenses from 1993 to 1997. Simultaneously, large banks faced a mounting crisis, as their holdings of unrecoverable credits rose from 9 percent to 20 percent in 1990, and by June 1992 they accounted for between 24 and 68 percent of all bank loans (Balcerowicz and Bratkowski 2001). Against international advice about how to deal with this problem, Poland also undertook a decentralized approach to restructuring both banks and enterprises, with the former leading the way (Kawalec 1994; Balcerowicz and Bratkowski 2001). Largely, this was done because of skepticism about the ability of a centralized restructuring agency to resist political pressure, and a belief that bad debt workouts would be most effective if they were initiated and negotiated by the banks themselves. As a result, the "Enterprise and Bank Financial Restructuring Program," approved by the Polish parliament in 1993, set up a system of incentives so that recapitalized state-owned banks could write off unrecoverable loans and take action against bad debtors. The banks themselves were recapitalized with an issue of state Treasury bonds that obliged restructuring. The argument in favor of this policy maintained that it would simultaneously lead the restructuring of debtor firms and encourage privatization via debt/equity swaps (Belka and Krajewska 1997), transforming banks into key national holders of firm equity. This move established banks as the hubs (owners) of large networks of firms, promoting the emergence of broad firm networks.

In April 1993 Wielkopolski Bank Kredytowy (WBK) was privatized, followed by Bank Slaski (BSK) in early 1994. Both banks were sold via IPO, and in both cases a foreign strategic investor became a shareholder (the EBRD and ING, respectively). Yet the strategic investors' share in stock was limited to 28.5 percent in the former and 25.9 percent in the latter, and the state Treasury retained a vast share in equity (44.3 percent in WBK, 33.16 percent in BSK). As a result, the privatization of these two banks was far from complete, but the initial goal – injecting foreign capital without relinquishing control to foreigners – had been achieved.

In January 1995 a third commercial bank, Bank Przemyslowo-Handlowy (BPH), was sold via a public offering. Because of limited demand, however, the EBRD took over 15.06 percent of the shares according to an underwriting contract, and more than 48 percent of the shares remained with the state Treasury. In December 1995 the fourth commercial bank, Bank Gdanski, was privatized via IPO. Another domestic bank, Bank Inicjatyw Gospodarczych (BIG) (established in 1989 with the former Polish president, Aleksander Kwasniewski, as one of three partners), turned out to be the biggest investor. Together with its subsidiaries, BIG purchased 26.75 percent of the shares. Another 25.1 percent of shares were sold to foreign investors. In the case of Bank Gdanski, 39.94 percent of shares remained with the state Treasury. Thus, by the end of 1995, only four banks had been partially privatized.

Between 1995 and 1997 a period of bank reform took over the push to privatize, driven by the idea that Polish banks were too small and too weak to be competitive. Hence, it was argued, they should be reformed and strengthened through mergers, and only afterward privatized (Sikora 1996; Balcerowicz and Bratkowski 2001). As mentioned above, the shift in philosophy also reflected a strong dislike of foreign capital by some political parties and a desire to keep banks in national hands (Balcerowicz and Bratkowski 2001). It was this approach to workouts that sustained many of the state-owned banks (McDermott 2007). At the same time, this route led to a dispersed ownership structure that privileged insiders in the management of the firm after privatization.

While a plan to reorganize and strengthen banks was being developed, two banks, Powszechny Bank Kredytowy (PBK) (one of the nine state-owned commercial banks) and Bank Handlowy, worked out their own privatization plans and successfully pressed for their acceptance by the government. In the first half of 1997 both plans were realized. In the former, the state retained over 50 percent of the shares, operating largely as a passive owner, with the bank management playing the ownership role. Bank Handlowy was privatized to three foreign investors (26 percent), with the remaining shares sold via IPO (59 percent) and the state retaining 28 percent of shares but only 8 percent of votes. According to Balcerowicz and Bratkowski (2001), this was an even more sophisticated form of insider privatization, after which the state Treasury had little power, the ownership was dispersed, and bank management governed the bank.

Throughout these initial phases of transformation, the dominant concern was to improve the condition of banks, establish them as key holders of capital, and resist the loss of control to foreigners. The return to power in 1997 of the right-wing coalition of parties affiliated with Solidarity, the Solidarity Electoral Action (AWS), brought about yet another shift in bank privatization, with the minister of the Treasury proposing sale to foreign investors and speeding up the pace of privatization. Despite broad opposition in parliament, and even from within the governing coalition, to the strategy, the remaining state-owned commercial banks and two other large banks were privatized (Balcerowicz and Bratkowski 2001: 27). Three state-owned commercial banks (BDK, PBG, PBKS) and PEKAO were merged in 1998. Fifteen percent of the resulting Bank PEKAO was sold by IPO in that year, and a 52 percent stake was sold to Allianz Capital and Unicredito Italiano in 1999. The latter was the largest capital transaction in the history of Polish privatization (Dzierwa 1999). During the same year 80 percent of the last state-owned commercial bank, Bank Zachodni, was sold to Allied Irish Bank.

At this point, only two large fully state-owned banks remained, and they would soon also come up for sale. In 2001 40 percent of the ailing PKO BP was sold via the stock market to domestic institutional investors (13.2 percent), 8.5 percent to foreign institutions, and 16 percent to domestic individuals, with

Tracing ownership networks

51.5 percent remaining in state hands. Lastly, 40 percent of the cooperative bank BGZ was sold to a private Polish bank, leaving 43 percent in the hands of the state Treasury.

Although this last phase shifted away from the initial focus of privatization strategy, the overall approach did much more than simply heed external pressure to privatize. An innovative approach to privatization and ownership restructuring established banks as key owners, held by a combination of the state, domestic private investors, and foreign stakeholders in an uneasy strategic alliance. In other words, successive Polish governments did not simply heed the external injunction to privatize at all costs. By navigating this complicated path of banking sector restructuring, banks came to occupy a defining place in the emergent Polish market economy. Through debt/equity swaps and restructuring, banks became major shareholders among the largest firms in the Polish economy, creating a broad web of cross-holdings that persisted long after privatization. Moreover, because of the strategy of gradual privatization, an emphasis on restructuring, and a program of avoiding sale to foreign investors, many banks retained a significant share of state ownership, creating still-prominent finance-based links between industrial firms and the state. Such ties serve to reassure firms that governments will maintain their commitment to a particular policy, because the latter signal that they are willing to retain residual risk (Perotti 1995: 848). The strategy of developing ties between banks, the state, and other firms allowed Polish governments to make a credible commitment to investors about the direction of future policy choice. These ties also aligned interests to the extent possible among such diverse stakeholders.

Business groups

Alongside banks, Polish industrial groups formed early in the process of transition, often the creations of emergent large entrepreneurs such as Aleksander Gudzowaty, Zygmunt Solorz-Zak, and Jan Kulczyk. As in much of the post-socialist world, these businesspeople were responding to opportunities in the privatization process, and they tended not to focus on a particular sector, but they were closely allied to a political party. For example, the group of firms belonging to Gudzowaty, who vied for the title of wealthiest man in Poland, developed out of an opportunity to control and obtain a mediation fee on the transit and import of natural gas to Poland. The group later developed, however, to include a joint insurance venture with CIGNA, develop biofuels that were subject to government subsidy, and build a high-speed telecommunications backbone.

Gudzowaty was closely allied to the left-wing SLD and suffered when the right-wing post-Solidarity coalitions came to power. He was similarly threatened when the Law and Justice Party emerged to take power in 2005. Although it is commonly believed that many socialist-era managers and bureaucrats became wealthy by taking advantage of long-standing contacts with

98 *The Role of Networks*

the leftist politicians elected after 1989, in Poland politicians on the right also took advantage of ties to business and cultivated a coterie of closely allied businesspeople. For example, Solorz-Zak, the owner of a satellite television network, was closely tied to center-right coalitions and was able to obtain broadcasting licenses through political contacts. Kulczyk had been involved in the import of German automobiles to Poland since the 1980s, and he controls a group of firms that has been involved in the building of highways across Poland. He was also similarly seen as close to the post-Solidarity coalition. McMenamin and Schoenman (2007) find that these businesspeople tended to have relationships with either one or the other political option over time. In fact, throughout the 1990s and until 2005 two loose business coalitions existed, alternating in power and jockeying for advantages when their political allies were in office. The fact that businesspeople tended to hold ties to one side of the political spectrum set up a complex structure that allowed business and political actors to develop long-term relationships.

ROMANIA'S PATH TO PRIVATIZATION: A REDISTRIBUTION OF ASSETS TO POLITICAL CLIENTS

The Romanian case offers a second path. Here, ownership networks were narrow, and uncertainty was low. Firms had no way to coordinate, as they did not have the broad links that Polish firms could use to share information and mobilize for cooperation. Early post-1989 governments in Romania delayed reform questions, opting in favor of a gradualist approach that was preferred by managers and in the interest of the new political class. Although they began to put the infrastructure of privatization in place by 1991 with the passage of the first mass privatization law, only 260 companies were privatized by 1993, and 92 percent of these were small firms (those with fewer than fifty employees). Only two of the 708 larger companies on a 1990 list of firms to be privatized were actually sold by the end of 1993 (Roper 2000: 95). This was a very small number compared to the overall task of privatization. More importantly, the National Salvation Front – a broad coalition of caretakers dominated by transformed members of the Communist Party elite emerging from the second circle around the former dictator, Nicolae Ceausescu – was firmly in control of government.

Hence, privatization took on the form of redistribution to constituents and insiders. Highlighting the flaws of the process in an interview, one official concluded, "It was a fake process of wealth creation by spoiling state property." The majority of firms that were privatized were actually transformed into joint-stock companies by distributing 70 percent of their capital to state ownership funds and the remaining 30 percent to the private ownership funds that were, formally, owned by the public (Roper 2000: 91; Earle and Telegdy 2002: 661; Grahovac 2004: 28, 68). The public received certificates that could be used to purchase the tranche owned by the private ownership funds, thus linking private shareholders with state ownership. This is important in terms of the creation of the network of ownership, because it diluted ownership, granting public participation to a limited extent but without bringing about privatization in any meaningful way (Grahovac 2004: 28). Further, according to Earle and Telegdy (2002: 661), the private ownership funds remained state-governed, with government-appointed directors who were approved by parliament, and effectively no way for the public to exercise control.

Moreover, all other state-owned enterprises (SOEs) were turned into so-called *regies autonomes* (RAs), which remained under state ownership and were overseen by the Ministry of Finance. The 450 companies that became RAs were utilities, natural monopolies, or other companies of sufficient interest or importance that they could be deemed "strategic." The precise motives for placing companies into this group is unclear (Earle and Telegdy 1998a). With 450 companies in this group, however, it seems likely that the strategic nature of some firms was largely a function of the number of jobs they provided or the income they generated for political interests. Thus, the strategic discourse became an excuse to shield companies from privatization until an unspecified later date. Within this context, the privatization program began under a dark cloud. The state ownership funds rarely offered shares in the best companies, and those that represented politically powerful constituencies were sheltered from privatization and allowed to continue operating under a deficit (Ahrend and Oliveira Martins 2003: 333).

By 1992, after numerous splits within the NSF that brought a faction known as the Party of Social Democracy of Romania to power, the government recognized that the economic situation required a reorientation in economic policy and enacted a strategy of price liberalization, wage stabilization, and austerity combined with increased export concessions. The hope of the government of Theodor Stolojan, who replaced Petre Roman as prime minister, was that industries would be able to increase their exports and reduce the large trade deficit, offsetting the difficulties associated with austerity measures. The companies that were encouraged to export did not produce goods that could be sold on the world market, however, and required increasing energy imports, which the government subsidized (Roper 2000: 92; Ahrend and Oliveira Martins 2003: 337). The move was also meant to redirect trade from former Council for Mutual Economic Assistance countries toward the European Union. Although EU trade increased, imports from Europe also rose drastically. According to Daniel Daianu, former minister of the economy, the weak results of the election that brought Stolojan to power over factional rivals prevented the government from pursuing real export-led growth tactics (Roper 2000: 93).

Reform continued but took on a stop-go character. In 1995 new measures were introduced to limit inflation, then rescinded after several months, largely as a result of complaints from political constituencies. Government subsidies to the industrial sector persisted. By 1995 only 25 percent of commercial companies identified in 1990, and only 8 percent of large SOEs, had been privatized (Economist Intelligence Unit [EIU] 2001).

Serious economic problems ensued, leading to the creation of another mass privatization program (MPP) in mid-1995. Vouchers were again distributed to the public, but it took until May 1996 for 93 percent of the vouchers to be exchanged for shares. Moreover, this method introduced no new capital into the industries, and none of the important RAs were part of the second MPP. This move also made the network even more disconnected (Earle and Telegdy 1998b).

The victory of the opposition leader Victor Ciorbea, head of the Christian Democratic National Peasants' Party, in 1996 – an isolated instance of protest voting against the poor economic policies of Stolojan – created the chance for a new era of Romanian economic reform. The government passed a set of reforms that gained the confidence of the International Monetary Fund (IMF) and secured a new loan package. The other members of the new Romanian Democratic Convention (CDR) coalition, however, the Union of Social Democrats (USD) and the Democratic Party (PD), opposed many of the reforms promised in the IMF agreements. For example, the USD and PD were closely allied with business interests that rejected the elimination of subsidies to industry (Roper 2006). It would also have been difficult to interrupt the supply of credits to industry by banks, a sector that had not begun to privatize. The entrenched interests in the banks and ministries worked to prevent the government from making any progress on the restructuring of firms (Roper 2000: 92).

In the end, the Ciorbea government was unable to maintain the pace of reform. Many SOEs were placed on the closure list and then never closed (Roper 2000: 102). The same was true of companies slated for privatization. Disagreements continued between Ciorbea and Roman's USD. The narrowly constructed economic networks allied with the opposition helped prevent any progress in the construction of a new economic framework during this brief window of opportunity. The failure of this potential new force in Romanian politics paved the way for an end to Ciorbea's short and ineffective disruption of one-party dominance.

The conflicts that had existed during the Ciorbea government continued with the successor government of Radu Vasile, organized under the umbrella of a political alternative. Roman and his political allies from the previous era had little interest in promoting economic reform because of pressure from interest groups allied with the USD. The miners, a potent force that could be brought in to riot in Bucharest, also continued to play a role in Romanian politics. After several violent outbreaks, Vasile's government came to an undisclosed agreement with the miners' union, which allegedly postponed or revoked the closure of two mines and brought financial benefits to the miners. Even in such devastated sectors, reform seemed nearly impossible. Ultimately, Vasile's government was short-lived. Ion Iliescu, the leader of the NSF/PDSR (now renamed the PSD), returned to power by capitalizing on the failures of the Ciorbea government – failures that were largely a consequence of PDSR obstruction.

Business groups

In this context of stalled reform and the lack of a clear political break with the past, two groups came to dominate: industrial state-owned firms, which had preferential access to resources and the state budget, as well as the ability to influence legislation; and an emerging wealthy elite that was drawn mostly from

Tracing ownership networks

the ranks of the military and the former security service, the Securitate. Both set about creating a hierarchical ownership structure that was well adapted to Romanian politics.

Many currently prominent businesspeople allegedly owe their success to their experiences abroad before 1989 and access to bank accounts belonging to the Ceausescus. Given these political ties, their firms sought the protection of and links to the NSF/PSD. The dominance of the PSD, however, meant that these alliances failed to provide the security that firms sought, because business owners depended more on the PSD than it depended on them. The Paunescu brothers, among the wealthiest Romanians and allies of the PSD, were forced to move their business abroad in order to avoid investigation with regard to a banking scandal under the PSD. They were forced to leave Romania themselves during the period of the CDR government for fear of prosecution. Emblematic of the dominant position of the PSD and the insecurity it brought to wealthy businesspeople, the extremely wealthy formed their own small parties that acted in coalition with the PSD in order to provide the degree of security that comes with political prominence. For example, Dan Voiculescu, president of the Grivco group, is also the founder of the Humanist Party, which was a member of the ruling PSD coalition. Gigi Becali, a beneficiary of insider land deals with the Romanian army, founded the ultra-nationalist New Generation party for the same reason.

Even those businesspeople whose success was allegedly tied to the CDR, such as Ioan Niculae, were ultimately forced to negotiate better relations with the PSD. Niculae's business began acquisitions during the CDR government, particularly in the period 1996 to 1998. Predictably, Niculae was faced with a series of investigations when the PSD returned to power in 2001, related to various acquisitions of privatized property that occurred under the CDR. According to insiders, after some negotiations he managed to improve his relations with the PSD leadership and, in particular, with the influential PSD minister of privatization, Ovidiu Musetescu, and he obtained a majority share in the tobacco company SN Tutunul Romanesc.

In the absence of noteworthy political opposition, firms did not create deep and stable ties with the PSD. Business and the Social Democrats exchanged goods when opportune, rather than operating as identified clients. Thus, none of my informants felt comfortable identifying more than very few firms as "clients of the Social Democrats" or any other party. Pasti (1997) describes the situation: "Ties with the state are retained through managerial links with high-placed government officials and the prominence of governmental privat-ization agencies in shareholding. The network between ministries, central departments and large enterprise managers has also reproduced itself. The laws seeking to undo these ties were constantly opposed by ministries and enterprise managers." A Cabinet member summed this up when he stated that Romania's leaders "do not want privatization – they want assets for themselves so they can supply their parties with money" (Pasti 1997, cited by Stan 2003: 15).

This was a dramatically different and much more direct approach compared to the way that politicians formed relations with firms in Poland.

This result reflects the general failure of the government to outline a decisive privatization plan: "Instead of creating the new bourgeoisie, privatization allowed the *nomenklatura* to obtain *de jure* ownership rights of assets it already *de facto* controlled" (Stan 2003: 13; italics in original). In other words, it did little to broaden connections between economic actors while doing much to strengthen the narrow, hierarchical nature of ties between the Social Democrats and firms, often by establishing direct party control of firms.

BULGARIA'S PATH TO PRIVATIZATION: THE STATE STRUGGLES TO CONTROL FIRMS

In Bulgaria, ownership networks developed quite differently from how they did in Poland and Romania. First, because of political infighting, there was an inability to commit to a policy of privatization. In this context of political chaos, and because of it, groups of insiders became institutionalized as economic stakeholders and gained an inordinate amount of influence. These insiders even attempted to coordinate so as to prevent the entrance of foreign business. Although banks were politically prominent initially, the spectacular bank failures during the financial crisis of the late 1990s – itself caused by insider dealings – removed them as a viable organizing pole. The network of firms that developed was ultimately narrow in structure.

Privatization in Bulgaria took place under a mix of direct privatizations and voucher privatization. The latter, like most voucher programs, was intended to speed up the process and attract local participation (Prohaski 1998). The Bulgarian state lost control of the process of economic transformation soon after Decree 56, passed in 1989, allowed for the limited creation of private firms and gave SOEs some autonomy. These were the basic preconditions for the emergence of a private sector that had parasitic relations with the now more autonomous SOEs, given the political context. Radical decentralization of the state banking sector, in combination with liberal licensing policies for private banks, assisted the emergence of large conglomerates of questionable origin.

Efforts at limiting these trends produced weak results. Attempts in 1991 by the then finance minister, Ivan Kostov, failed to reel in the more influential economic agents, who continued to enjoy access to credit. The Privatization Act was passed by the Bulgarian parliament in 1992, allowing privatization of state-owned enterprises to move forward. After February 1993, when the first SOE was privatized, privatization gradually gained momentum.

Proponents of privatization faced serious opposition from entrenched groups, such as SOE managers, government officials, and large banks. State officials, not surprisingly, were generally unwilling to give up their ability to

Tracing ownership networks

reap personal rewards from the situation. Thus, until 1996 only small privatizations were successful, and practically no progress was made on the privatization of large industry. The situation of enlarged bad debt finally led to massive bank failures in 1996 and stricter conditionality from the IMF, to the point that it became the main factor in the collapse of Zhan Videnov's socialist government in 1997. A currency board was subsequently put in place, effectively eliminating the possibility of central bank lending.

Bulgaria was also the first country in which the socialists were re-elected to power, in 1994, and it was not until 1997 that a full mandate was given to nonsocialists. The re-election of the Bulgarian Socialist Party (BSP) was taken as a U-turn away from the transition. This gives a sense of the political and ideological tension that emerged in Bulgaria after 1989. In addition, there were widespread allegations of clientele-favoring behavior against the center-right Union of Democratic Forces (UDF) (Stanchev 1999). Even during the center-right UDF government of Kostov (1997–2001), often assessed as the first government committed to making difficult but unpopular policy choices associated with economic reform, preferential privatizations continued to take place (Stanchev 1999). An official noted in an interview that this was the product of a broader vision and tolerance for political wealth creation: "There was a popular slogan at the beginning among UDF members: we want to create the blue [right-wing] bourgeoisie, not the red [left-wing] bourgeoisie. But when this happens only by corruption, it creates a corrupt bourgeoisie. It's very much the official policy of the party and it was defended as appropriate because the Socialists also created their bourgeoisie."

Throughout the transition period, Bulgarian politics has been marked by the strong influence of economic interests – a dynamic that did not fail to attract the ire of the electorate. Bulgarian frustration with the lack of state capacity and the influence of powerful figures in the economy created a window of opportunity for the return of the former tsar Simeon II, who had been in exile since 1946. Having left Bulgaria as a young boy and worked in finance in Spain, Simeon was seen as a political outsider who would, it was hoped, be able to bring together a group of young professionals with foreign work experience and few ties to the existing networks.

Even Simeon's government had difficulty sidestepping existing social structures, however. According to political scientist Ognyan Minchev, speaking on Radio Free Europe/Radio Liberty on April 3, 2002, the government of the former tsar (2001–2005) and the new party he created for the 2001 election, the National Movement Simeon II (SNM), faced the problem of legislators who did not "work in the interest of the state, but act[ed] as lobbyists for business interests or even on behalf of business groups linked to organized crime, which flourishes under a fragile, powerless government." In an interview, an official observed, "Big business is happy under SNM because, even though they started as thieves, the new government does not interfere. We cannot get rid of the criminals."

Business groups and insiders

Business groups and insiders have been a key group of economic actors in Bulgaria since 1989. Until the economic collapse in Bulgaria, semi-criminal business groups with names such as VIS-2, SIC, and 777 dominated the country, struggling to take control of industry, banks, and tourist infrastructure along the Black Sea coast. They represented a dynamic of entrepreneurship that privileged those with access to coercion. In a slow and often brutal process, these groups began to consolidate their hold on regions and certain industries. After gaining regional power, they sought to link regional groups into national players. VIS-2 was one such group, involved in the selling of car insurance and private security; it also controlled a large number of car thieves. Over time, VIS-2 and its leader, Vasil Iliev, managed to co-opt regional groups, and it became the first national-level "business group" that straddled the boundary between legal and illegal activities. The emergence of such large players eventually created a demand for business organizations to attempt to influence politics and obtain preferential policy. The first of these, known as the "Group of Thirteen," emerged as a lobbying organization in 1993 and dominated the private sector until 1995 (Synovitz 1996). This group, including subsidiaries, consisted of the largest banks, insurance companies, stock exchanges, large trading companies, newspapers, and private security firms. An official pointed out, however, "Within the G-13 there is no clean businessman because it was generated in a period of semi-chaotic economic rules. For example, one of the most influential, Orel Corporation, he is a wrestler [sic] and was connected to the counterintelligence." Another official noted, "If you start to investigate the way that those people got their wealth, you simply would not find information about it. These barons are like a parallel state." The group was formed to protect Bulgaria from the entrance of foreign firms so that member firms could position themselves for big profits. The G-13 did not collaborate with political actors, as firms and business organizations in Poland sought to do.

The lack of an alliance between business leaders and political actors was due partly to the internal dynamic of the group and partly to the difficulty of identifying viable partners for cooperation. The G-13 operated through its own business organization, the Confederation of Bulgarian Industrialists. In 1994 this grouping began to fracture when the chairman, Emil Kyulev (assassinated in 2006), criticized the most powerful company in the group, Multigroup (its chairman, Ilya Pavlov, a former wrestler, was assassinated in 2001), for "aggressive and non-market expansion using the Confederation as a cover" (*Finance East Europe* 1994). Kyulev's bank, Tourist Sports Bank, left the confederation, and he was dismissed as its chairman when the meeting ended. The powerful group TRON and its president, Krassimir Stoichev, also left at this time. It was more likely, however, that the conflict was over competing bids that group members had made for the purchase of debts owed by Kremikovtsi, Bulgaria's largest steel and iron works, and Chimco, Bulgaria's largest producer of urea, to Bulgargas.

Another force that was tearing apart the G-13 was the growing interest of some of its members in conducting business with foreign investors in Bulgaria. This was in conflict with the central purpose of the confederation, which was to obstruct the entry of foreign investors. In fact, the Bulgarian Investors Business Association (BIBA), an organization formed in 1992 to represent the interests of foreign investors, accused the confederation of supporting economically nationalist policies. A clear illustration of the inability of Bulgarian business to collaborate is offered by the duplicitous behavior of Stoichev and his group TRON, which was engaged in a Mobiltel venture that included Siemens and US West as foreign partners. Stoichev was thus going counter to the platform of his organization, G-13, and he approached BIBA. Such individual defections reflected the inability of business to develop and implement a larger framework and longer-term goals, as achieved by its Polish counterpart.

In addition to these dynamics, the Russian financial crisis had a strong effect on the Bulgarian economy. By late 1996 the nine largest banks in Bulgaria had become insolvent. The initial collapse began because the lynchpins of the system, oligarch banks, were failing due to mounting bad debt, which landed some of the directors of the large conglomerates in jail. The grouping of early business leaders that effectively functioned as a parallel state was under siege, and the early winners were rapidly becoming losers because their overindulgent greediness prevented the accumulation of lasting benefits. This first stage of rapid accumulation and then bankruptcy occurred because these firms had inside access to power brokers. The critical choice that many of the leaders of these groups made, responding to political volatility in Bulgaria, was to focus on short-term profits and asset stripping instead of building an organization based on synergies with state leaders.

In fact, the political influence that the G-13 did enjoy ended with the election of Zhan Videnov as prime minister in January 1995, partly because Videnov allegedly wanted to create his own group of firms using contacts in a group called Orion. Commenting on Videnov's approach, an official observed, "Zhan Videnov ended up complaining publicly about the absolute egoism of business leaders. And he was disappointed by the so-called 'red bourgeoisie' because it didn't support him at all. They just made their business at the expense of the state and carried it out without consideration of the political interests. The so-called allegiance of business to parties did not materialize." His consequent attempt to create a new elite established a conflict between the G-13 group, particularly Pavlov and Multigroup, and Videnov's government. In 1996 the downfall of the oligarchs "left Bulgaria in shambles," with "little national wealth, virtually no middle class and no entrepreneurial elite – only 'a mafia network thirsty for new victims' and an impoverished population that questions the merits of democracy" (Synovitz 1996).

National investment funds

At the same time as the oligarchs were facing their first stumble in 1996, Videnov's socialist government embarked on a privatization plan that aimed to shift away from domination of the oligarchs and promote the return of political actors. In contrast to the popular Czech model, the Bulgarian government decided to create a series of investment companies that would function as funds for mass privatization (Prohaska 2002: 3). The intention of this program was to prepare particular sectors for privatization by gathering companies related by sector under one umbrella corporation in the form of a physical or legal person. The method was to create investment funds that functioned in a semi-autonomous fashion. This differed from the Polish and Romanian models, in which the state retained the leading role in the guidance of funds. The main purpose of the funds was to act as an intermediary between enterprises and the investing public. The funds themselves were similar to holding companies, except that they were created with the intention of operating as investment funds. This created a strange hybrid structure, with serious implications for the power structure within the economy.

The move to privatize began in 1996, when eighty-one privatization funds out of 141 applicants obtained licenses from the Securities and Stock Exchange Commission (Prohaska 2002). The majority of the funds directed their investment strategy toward a specific enterprise or sector, while about thirty of the funds were regional. This was a contradiction in logic of the goal of reducing the risk of these investments, but it led to the hierarchical integration of firms within a particular industry. The initiative for setting up such funds came from the managers of the enterprises on the mass privatization list or from the joint initiative of local government representatives and local business elites.

Once the UDF had returned to power in 1997 under Kostov, the situation changed dramatically. Interviews indicate that the socialists did not manage to profit from the experience of voucher privatization because they had little influence over who ended up acquiring the vouchers and because they presided over the process for too short a time once it started. Once the UDF had gained control of the government, however, it began to privatize companies that were performing well to investors allied with the party. These privatizations were allegedly reserved for investors who made donations to party-allied foundations. One such foundation, the Future of Bulgaria, was headed by Elena Kostova, the wife of the prime minister (*Standart* 2001).

Once the mass privatization program was in place, the UDF deployed another scheme, to introduce management–worker partnerships (known as RMDs) in the remaining companies. The UDF government managed to change the directorates of a large number of companies. The newly installed directors were party allies or top members of the party, and often these firms were sold to the RMDs. According to an analyst, this further entrenched corruption in Bulgaria: "The UDF was selling to the local UDF members, who were privileged

Tracing ownership networks

in buying. This was a form of appropriation of state assets for funny money. When nothing happened to the leaders and this was the main scheme of privatization, political corruption became the model." Many of these firms faced bankruptcy after the UDF lost power, and were not converted into a long-term source of income. Thus, although the process of privatization was politicized, it failed to convert firms into sources of political revenue or to connect political and economic actors in mutually beneficial exchanges.

Struggles for direct control: Bulgartabac, Bulgargas, and the National Electric Company

How these struggles played out is illustrated in the case of Bulgartabac, which highlights the difficulty of establishing networked alliances that link political and economic actors. One alternative in Bulgaria was for political actors to try to retain direct control of property, although this reached an absurd extreme with cases of management by the prime minister, who feared the dangers of delegation. The emergence of the monopolist group Bulgartabac represents the implementation of a broad strategy of firm development by the Bulgarian state. It is reportedly the largest tobacco company in central and eastern Europe, created by the linking of twenty-three subsidiary companies. The structure of the holding includes companies for tobacco buying and processing, the leaf trade, the manufacturing and export of cigarettes, and research and development. It is also a monopolist on the domestic market and the largest taxpayer in Bulgaria. Bulgartabac Holding was of significant structural importance for the Bulgarian economy, generating about 4 percent of budget revenues.

When formed in 1993, the holding had a 30 percent share in twenty-two factories, while the Ministry of Trade and Tourism held the remaining shares. The holding company did not interfere in the operation of the companies but functioned as a trading company, largely in conformity with the socialist model. This lasted until 1997, when it was argued that centralization of the tobacco industry would reduce internal competition and allow for better coordination of the constituent companies (*Banker Daily* 1997). Such a move was expected to increase the overall performance of the constituent companies, and the scheme was suggested by Bulgartabac's supervisory board (Bulgarian News Agency [BTA] 1997).

Thus, on December 6, 1997, the state swapped its stake in the subsidiaries for an increased stake in the holding. This added a degree of separation between the state and day-to-day control of the subsidiaries, which now belonged to Bulgartabac Holding but reinforced the state's control over Bulgartabac Holding.

This approach was seen as reducing the likelihood that the constituent companies would be sold off individually. In fact, the chairman of the supervisory board, Dako Michailov, strongly favored privatization through a foreign stock exchange (*Banker Daily* 1997). The strategy was widely seen as problematic, because only two of the twenty-two daughter companies, Sofia and Blagoevgrad, had attracted strong investor interest (*Capital Weekly* 1998b). By May 1998 any agreement on the strategy of privatization was still far off.

This was not only a move to restructure and strengthen the production and marketing capabilities of the tobacco industry. Until mid-1997 several companies, operating through two cigarette distributor associations that they had established, concluded preferential contracts with individual cigarette companies. One such company belonging to Multigroup, BT MG, had negotiated a sole distributorship with the former Bulgartabac bosses and the Blagoevgrad Bulgartabac factory. The two associations claimed to control 80 percent and 50 percent of the market, respectively (*Capital Weekly* 1998a). Thus, although the subsidiaries of Bulgartabac remained the property of the state, these firms were already operating together with the private sector for the benefit of the latter. This state–private partnership was different from the synergistic forms that emerged in Poland, however, and was more akin to asset stripping.

In this context, the new UDF government that took power in 1998 began to fight for control of Bulgartabac at general shareholder meetings (Mancheva 1998). The new executive director of the Privatization Agency, Zakhari Zhelyazkov, announced his privatization strategy for 1999 and highlighted Bulgartabac as one of the key companies to be privatized, on a list that included the top companies in the country (BTA 1998c).

This was taken as a sign of a significant turnaround, and there was already talk of a "Bulgarian miracle" based on the UDF's attempts to take on corruption and tackle the hyperinflation that had wrecked the economy (*Emerging European Markets* 1998). The UDF's successes led to statements by the deputy prime minister and minister of industry, Aleksandur Bozhkov, that privatization would be complete by 1999 or 2000 (BTA 1998a; BTA 1998b). By May 1998, however, problems began to arise for the privatization process. In particular, there was widespread disagreement about the choice of an agent for the sale (BTA 1998a). Simultaneously, there was disagreement about whether shares should be sold in the holding company only or in the individual daughter companies. The leader of the Euroleft party, Alexander Tomov, strongly contested the latter strategy because he felt that it would destroy the strength of the sector in Bulgaria (*Pari Daily* 1998).

A further problem arose when the general meetings of shareholders in seventeen of the twenty-two daughter companies were suspended on May 8, 1998. Soon afterward the boards of directors were dismissed on the orders of the prime minister, Kostov, signaling a conflict between the government and the firms, which were insubordinate to the state (Viktorova 1998).

This dynamic of insubordination illustrates the centrifugal forces working to disconnect state and firms in Bulgaria, and is in sharp contrast to the deployment of state bureaucrats and party faithful to corporate boards in Poland as a way of propagating policy preferences and keeping firms within the party

Tracing ownership networks 109

system. In Bulgaria, the crackdown was an attempt by the government to consolidate a year of achievements in economic reform (Alexandrova 1998), and was accompanied by a host of other dismissals in leading state sector companies such as the National Electric Company (NEC) and Balkan Airlines. Among others, Georgi Kostov, the CEO of the Blagoevgrad Bulgartabac factory, which held 50 percent of the domestic market, was dismissed. Kostov had been appointed as a courtesy to Euroleft. As the conflict between Kostov, the prime minister (no relation), and Tomov, the Euroleft leader, developed, Georgi Kostov was removed, demonstrating the importance of controlling economic assets to political coalitions (Ilieva 1998).

Throughout his tenure as CEO, Kostov remained in the executive leadership of Euroleft, and his dismissal consolidated the UDF's hold over the powerful tobacco company. It also paved the way for Bulgartabac Holding's plans to remove private distributors from the market and create a monopoly cigarette distribution company while simultaneously introducing a licensing regime to control wholesalers.

Herein the contrast with the Polish strategy, which relied on network ties for governance, can be seen. Alliances were so fragile in Bulgaria that, even at the level of prime minister, delegation was being undone in favor of direct control. This is an indicator of the extent to which alliances around even state property could not be forged. According to *Capital Weekly*, this particular sacking fit the pattern followed by all prime ministers: "In the beginning, they delegate powers to their [ministerial] teams. Then, frightened by the minister's affinity for individual games, [they] start to concentrate power more and more in themselves. A good example is the management of monopoly companies. After two years Bulgaria is back to the 'Prime minister-head of company model'" (Alexandrova 1998). Ivan Kostov himself said, "Officially, this model is explained with the need for the prime minister to personally control the management of individual commercial companies to make them more efficient and to halt corruption and shady dealings. The idea is to make it possible for the Cabinet to directly participate in the management of commercial companies and the distribution of the resources of key industries" (Alexandrova 1998). In a related move, in the summer of 1998 Kostov announced that he would take charge of the power industry, meaning that he would supervise the NEC, Bulgargas, coal mining, and the central heating supply companies.

This was not a dynamic established just during Kostov's government. After taking office in February 1995, the socialist prime minister, Videnov, took over the state monopoly structures in the petroleum and gas delivery industries. When he encountered obstacles to the removal of the energy minister, Georgi Stoilov, because of opposition from coalition partners, he transformed the whole ministry into a government committee, allowing for staff changes without the approval of the parliament. Once this had been accomplished, Videnov put the NEC under the direct control of Ivan Shilyashki. One year later he decided to isolate Shilyashki and the deputy prime minister in charge of the power industry, Evgeni Bakurdzhiev, in order to establish direct control of the energy firms.

As these examples make clear, struggles in Bulgaria among elite political actors were focused on the direct control of firms instead of the creation of broad alliances among firms and political organizations. This reflected a broader pattern of an inability to create relationships with potential allies in the economy.

NETWORKS

The strong point of network analysis is not just in identifying the most connected members of a group but also in considering the structural position of a particular member of the network in relation to other members. Although the early discussion in this chapter makes it clear that three very different alliances emerged to support marketization in Poland, Romania, and Bulgaria, the tools of network analysis can add a great deal of depth to this picture. The previous discussion of the development of state–business ties in each country shows the radically different forms of this relationship that can sustain the transition to markets. This background allows us to return to a macro-view of each of these variants.

The most striking feature in the transformation of ownership networks in Poland is consistent with the development of private firms discussed above. In 1995, despite the beginnings of privatization, Poland's ownership network retained some of the features it had had in 1989. Most notably, the state still was the main owner in the economy. As a result of partial privatizations and the generally slow pace of change, more than 50 percent of the largest firms were still wholly or partly state-owned at this time. The resulting network had a star shape, created by firms owned mostly or wholly by the state, as seen in Figure 3.1. In other words, partial privatization accentuated the central role of the state by linking private firms to the state through jointly owned state and private businesses.

By 2000 more of such shared ties with private owners had developed, as seen in Figure 3.2. This was the result of the privatization strategy discussed above, which used debt/equity swaps and created opportunities for private investors to purchase partial shares of state-owned firms. Such hybrid forms of property ownership – neither public nor private – limited the ability of policy makers to take autonomous decisions by aligning the economic interests of firms with the state. It thus added to the security of firms (Perotti 1995; Stark 1996)

A more significant shift occurred in these five years than the increase in number of such ties, however. In 1995 there were few connections linking the private actors among themselves, as the initially desirable move for new private firms was to create joint ventures with the state by taking ownership in state-owned firms that were being partially privatized. Between 1995 and 2000 the ownership position of the state in the network did not become much less

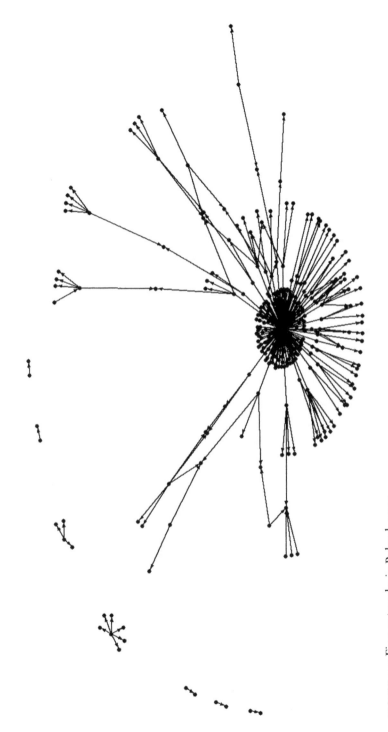

FIGURE 3.1 Firm networks in Poland, 1995
Note: Arrows point to owners.

111

FIGURE 3.2 Firm networks in Poland, 2000
Note: Arrows point to owners.

Tracing ownership networks

TABLE 3.2 *Mean degree and normalized mean degree, 1995, 2000, 2005*

	Bulgaria	Romania	Poland
Mean degree and normalized mean degree (in parentheses) 1995	0.902 (0.212)	1.039 (0.033)	0.987 (0.164)
Mean degree and normalized mean degree (in parentheses) 2000	1.133 (0.054)	1.063 (0.034)	1.018 (0.114)
Mean degree and normalized mean degree (in parentheses) 2005	0.754 (0.026)	0.886 (0.037)	1.805 (0.055)

significant, contrary to what one might expect given the prominence and international pressure for economic reform during that period. A new feature, however, was that the ownership network changed from one highly centralized around the state to one in which firms also held numerous ownership ties in other firms. These ties between firms also served to cement alliances between firms. Such swapping of ownership ties is a common practice in Japanese capitalism (Gerlach 1992).

The sheer number of ties that resulted from this ownership transformation was a distinctive feature of the Polish economy. The number of ties maintained by an average firm when compared with other countries can be seen in Table 3.2. The table shows the mean degree – the number of network ties maintained by an average member – and a normalized value that can be compared across networks of different sizes.[5]

In 1995 Poland did not have the highest level of connection among countries. Instead, the Bulgarian network of firms was the most connected, reflecting the persistently high level of state ownership. As a result of the slow pace of privatization, few firms had disconnected from the key owner, the state. Hence, the mean degree was high, by virtue of firms' ownership tie to the state. Nevertheless, the Polish network was only slightly less connected.

Over time, the density of network ties dropped in both Bulgaria and Poland, as privatization took place, more firms entered the network as owners, and firms became disconnected from one another as they lost their tie to the state. A falling mean degree is to be expected as the network grows. This change happened much more slowly in Poland, however, as firms replaced their ties to the state with direct ties to other firms and indirect ties to the state through banks. Although the average Polish firm maintained a decreasing number of ties over time, the network of firms was much more connected through the first decade, and Poland remained the most connected of the three countries by 2005.

---

[5] "Normalized degree" expresses the actual connectedness of a network as a percentage of connections that are maximally possible if the network were complete – i.e. all network members were connected to all other members.

As the early parts of this chapter began to show, a distinguishing characteristic of the Polish case was not just that the network was more tightly connected throughout the first fifteen years of transformation but that certain types of firms held the most ties in the network. Which were the most connected firms in the Polish ownership network? Was a specific type of actor privileged in the Polish case, subsequently influencing the way that the Polish economy and institutions developed? These can be identified by looking at the most "central" firms at each point in time – those that are most connected by ownership ties and are the centers of larger groups of less connected actors. These firms were leading the broader reorganization of the economy and placing themselves at the center of a wide web of ownership relations, because their ownership rights granted control rights over many other firms. Thus, more connected firms are frequently able to impose their policy preferences in the governance of firms in which they hold a significant stake.

By calculating the degree of each firm, the number of connections it shares with other firms, one can identify these "most linked" firms, as shown in Table 3.3 for 2005. In 1995 the state was the largest owner, with direct connections to seventy-five other firms among the sample used here. Four foreign financial institutions (the EBRD as an international lender, ING, Barings, and Creditanstalt) and three foreign financial groups (two Finnish and one US investment fund) also appeared in the top twenty. The remaining top owners were nine Polish banks, one pension fund, an import-export company, and the electrical parts company Elektrim. Thus, a ranking of the top twenty most connected firms reflects the policy decision to push banks and financial firms forward as principal owners of other firms in the process of restructuring.

In 2000, after a decade of reform, the same trend can be observed. Apart from the state, which then had 104 direct connections to other firms among the top 200, two foreign banks were present (Bank of Austria and Bank of New York) and the investment firm Franklin Resources. The remaining owners were fourteen Polish privately managed investment funds of state capital (NFIs), banks and financial services companies, and the oil and gas giant PKN Orlen.

That largely "bank groups" and a few "industrial groups" dominated the ranking of powerful firms by 1995 and in 2000 highlights a particular development process under way in Poland. In the Polish development strategy, groups that were organized primarily around domestic financial services companies came to occupy strategic positions within the network of successful firms. The owners in the process of acquiring strategic positions in the economy were largely Polish banks and, in the latter half of the 1990s, domestic investment funds. These banks and investment funds stood between the state and the long chains of connected firms and were the centers of groups of firms. In this way, they were able to channel capital to subsidiary firms for the initial period of reform. A second key part of the strategy, however, involved the integration of foreign capital. By 2005 the situation had changed dramatically, in that

TABLE 3.3 *Top twenty most connected firms, 2005*[6]

Rank	Poland	Ties	Romania	Ties	Bulgaria	Ties
1	Polish state	121	Romanian state	28	Bulgarian state	40
2	Unicredito (finance)	50	Lukoil Downstream	8	Sofia municipality	4
3	ING (finance)	46	Rompetrol Downstream	7	Valeri Georgiev Nikolov	4
4	BPH TFI (finance)	44	Rompetrol Group	6	Chimimport	4
5	Credit Suisse (finance)	44	Oltenia (state investment fund)	5	Stara Planina Holding	3
6	Allianz (finance)	43	Vodafone Europe	5	Industrialen Kapital Holding	3
7	Aviva (finance)	43	East Capital Asset Management (finance)	4	Vats Medyna Group Holding	3
8	Skandinaviska Enskilda Banken (finance)	43	Muntenia (state investment fund)	4	National Electric Company	3
9	Nordea (finance)	37	Canton of St. Gallen	4	Bulgartabac Holding	3
10	BNP Paribas (finance)	35	British American Tobacco Germany	4	Berenberg Bank (finance)	3
11	Dimensional Fund Advisors (finance)	34	Mechel Trading	4	Sparky Bulgaria	3
12	BZ WBK AIB Asset Management (finance)	32	Arcelor Mittal	3	Telso	3
13	Generali (finance)	32	Tenaris Financial Services (finance)	3	Favorit Holding	3
14	Deutsche Bank (finance)	31	Zareba Holdings	3	Julius Baer Holding (finance)	3
15	Union Asset Management (finance)	31	Julius Baer Holding (finance)	3	Krasimir Kirilov Sineverski	2
16	AIG (finance)	30	Mittal Steel Company	3	Unicredit Bulbank (finance)	2
17	Pocztylion – ARKA Pension Fund (finance)	29	Interbrew Central European Holdings	3	CEZ AS	2
18	Banco Comercial Portugues (finance)	29	Lafarge	3	Gustavia Holding	2
19	Aegon (finance)	29	Renault	2	Bulgarian Telecommunication Company	2
20	Legg Mason (finance)	28	Natuzzi Netherlands Holding	2	Bulgarian Eko Projects	2

[6]Multiple centrality measures were compared, including Bonacich power, k-step reach, and betweenness. All measures delivered a similar list of most connected owners and support the same conclusion.

Polish firms had switched places with foreign firms among the key financial companies. The list of top twenty most connected firms in 2005 had only three Polish financial firms and sixteen foreign financial groups, showcasing a virtual "Who's who?" of the financial world, headed by the likes of Unicredito, ING, and Credit Suisse. The state still dominated the list, however, with 121 connections. Comparison against the other two cases explored in Table 3.3 points to the distinctiveness of this strategy.

The comparison between the three countries, even just in 2005, displays fundamentally different types of entity as the most connected owners and shows how the top firms in Poland maintained dramatically more ties to other firms in absolute terms than firms in both Romania and Bulgaria (the top twenty firm owners in Poland averaged 40.55 connections, while in Romania they averaged 5.2 and in Bulgaria 4.7). As noted earlier, the most connected firms in Poland were almost exclusively foreign financial firms by 2005, while in both Bulgaria and Romania they remained mostly industrial firms.

Firm networks in Poland

When compared to Romania and Bulgaria, the novelty of the Polish strategy is noticeable. The decline of state ownership was slower in Poland than in the other two cases. In 1995 the state was still the largest owner by far, but already many partial privatizations were visible (see Figure 3.1).

This trend continued in the latter half of the 1990s, so that many firms were partially state-owned and partially privately owned. When compared to the other network graphs, the Polish network in 2000 (Figure 3.2) is distinct for the number of firms that were partially in the private sector and partially in the public sector. Even more striking is the presence of state-owned firms with shares in other firms. Thus, there are horizontal ties within both the state sector and the public sector. As discussed above, these ties often led to banks, which came to be the focal points of ownership in the economy.

Turning to Figure 3.3, we see that, by 2005, state–firm ownership networks were still extensive, particularly when compared to the other two countries, where state ownership was reduced dramatically by fiscal burdens and international pressure that drove those countries to speed up privatization. The trend that began early in Poland – the emergence of banks already in 1995 as key owners of other firms – was fully cemented by 2005. Although the state continued to play an important role, the state–bank alliance of the early 1990s was replaced by an alliance between industrial and financial firms, as seen in Table 3.1. While the majority of industrial owners were domestic, the vast majority of the financial capital by 2005 was foreign. As discussed above, however, a key component of the Polish path was to delay this move as political and economic elites both sought ways to retain a domestic presence in industry and finance alike and hold off foreign competition. The network graph here

FIGURE 3.3 Firm networks in Poland, 2005
Note: Arrows point to owners.

also shows that, despite its decline as a shareholder, the state was structurally still vital.

Bank centrality – the quality of banks as firms with particularly many ties to other firms – can be seen more clearly by examining the network ties of a single bank (Figure 3.4). Bank Handlowy in 2000 was representative of the network ties maintained by banks in Poland. The bank was by then partially owned by Citibank and by the state, and had ownership stakes in a number of other industrial firms, including some firms that were also partially owned by the state Treasury. The state maintained its position, and in fact grew in relevance, in contrast with Romania and Bulgaria.

This mixed nature of financial institutions so late in the transition process reflected a central choice of policy makers to mix state intervention and non-market forms of interaction with market signals. Although in all the cases discussed above we can find some co-mingling of state and private ownership, the mixed nature of the economy here was not just a case of partial privatization. The financial sector in Poland took on forms of governance that reflected a decision to retain nonmarket forms of activity and the persistence of practices, such as the maintenance of ties to other firms and the state, that promoted the development of alliances between the industrial and financial sectors (Williamson 1985: 20).

Firm networks in Romania

The situation in Romania was quite different. Looking at the whole network in 1995 in Figure 3.5, we see again a sparsely connected network of inter-firm ownership. The star at the bottom shows the group of firms connected to the state. There are a number of chains of firms extending away from the state, representing the early privatization deals struck by that time. There is a second ring of owners around the state, representing shares held by employees and manager groups, and not shares sold via privatization to other firms.

In Figure 3.6, we can see how the network had developed by 2000. Keeping in mind that the second ring of owners around the state (cluster on right) are actually employees and managers, inter-firm ownership ties played a much less significant role than in the other cases under study. Romanian firms did not seek to create bonds of ownership with other firms as actively as their counterparts in Poland and Bulgaria.

As in Bulgaria, once privatization had advanced and state ownership (the state is the cluster at the bottom center) had receded, the main cohesive element linking firms to each other disappeared, with nothing new coming in its place. By 2005 the Romanian ownership network was made up of narrowly connected firms and their owners (see Figure 3.7). The identities of these owners was similar to that in Bulgaria: Romanian capitalism is underpinned by an alliance of domestic individual owners, many of them closely tied to the Social Democratic Party, and mostly industrial firms.

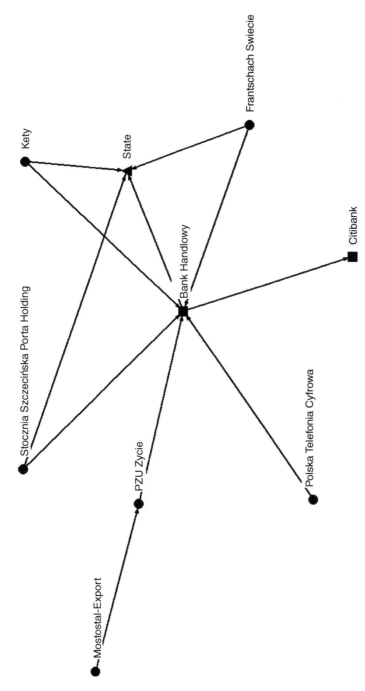

FIGURE 3.4 Ownership network of Bank Handlowy, 2000
Note: Arrows point to owners.

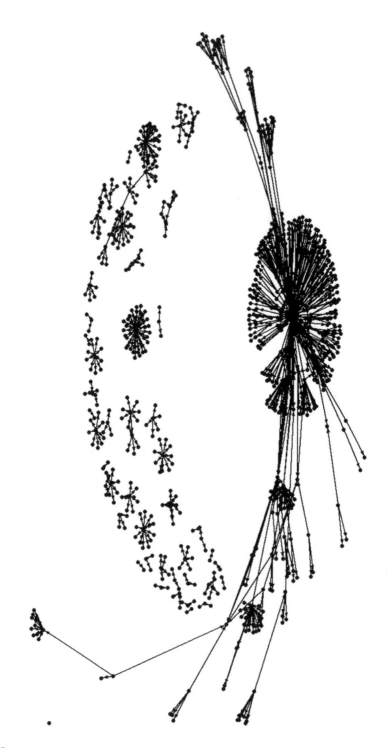

FIGURE 3.5 Romanian ownership network, 1995
Note: Arrows point to owners.

FIGURE 3.6 Romanian ownership network, 2000
Note: Arrows point to owners.

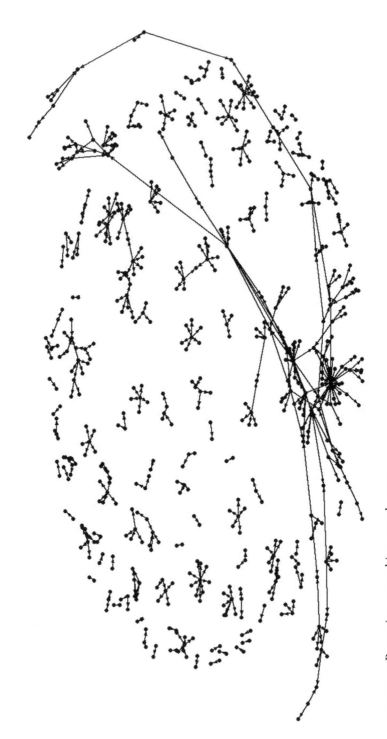

FIGURE 3.7 Romanian ownership network, 2005
Note: Arrows point to owners.

Firm networks in Bulgaria

The firm network in Bulgaria looks strikingly different from the initial discussion above of the Polish network. In 1995 (Figure 3.8) it consisted of a core of state-owned firms (cluster at the right) that were directly linked to the state (with only three partial privatizations), as well as a non-state sector made up of many small business groups and firms with many small owners.

By 2000 the network structure had changed quite radically, as seen in Figure 3.9. The most connected firms were industrial companies in the chemical and gas industries. Among the owners, new key actors had emerged since 1995, but these were also of a strikingly different character from those in Poland. Three main types of industrial owners were present. The first were holding companies that integrated firms within a single industrial sector, such as the tobacco and pharmaceutical industries. These were holding companies established by state actors under a plan to consolidate control over firms in a single sector under one corporate structure in preparation for future privatization. A second type were holding companies established by private industrial owners. Third were privatization funds, such as the Neftochim fund and the Petrol fund, set up by the managements of stable large companies that were also strategically important. This last form was conceived as a substitute for management privatization. They were also seen as a viable way of transferring ownership of these companies in the absence of investors and in light of the difficulties of financing privatizations with credits from Bulgarian banks (Prohaska 2002).

In addition to these industrial holding companies, a second distinguishing feature in Bulgaria was the prominence of individual owners in possession of ownership shares greater than 5 percent. From early in the transition, individual owners were a key component of the ownership transformation. By 2000 individuals held nearly the same share of the ownership of the largest corporations as industrial firms, and by 2005 individuals exceeded the share held by the industry.

Apart from the state (the cluster at the bottom), the most connected firms were companies such as Bulgartabac Holding, or private actors trying to gain a hold on large industrial firms. These new groups (such as Albena Invest Holding and Aktioner Holding) emerged alongside already powerful holding groups such as MG Elite (the renamed Multigroup) that were well established in the early 1990s.

Some horizontal ties among firms are visible. Across the network, however, the average number of ties that a particular owner maintained was much lower in 2000, as is confirmed by the data in Table 3.2. In other words, although there were many actors, each of these had few ties to other actors. This suggests a much narrower type of embeddedness of owners: firms were connected to the state but not so much to one another. Another key feature adds to the distinctiveness of the Bulgarian model: the broad use of holding companies put firms at an arm's length from the state while nevertheless providing opportunities for

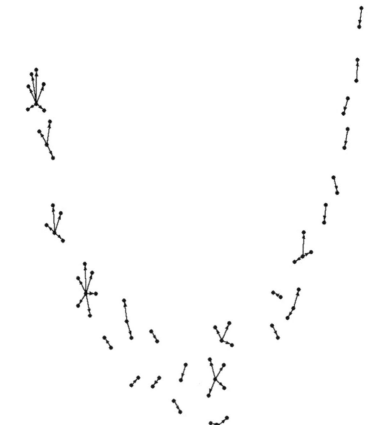

FIGURE 3.8 Bulgarian ownership network, 1995
Note: Arrows point to owners.

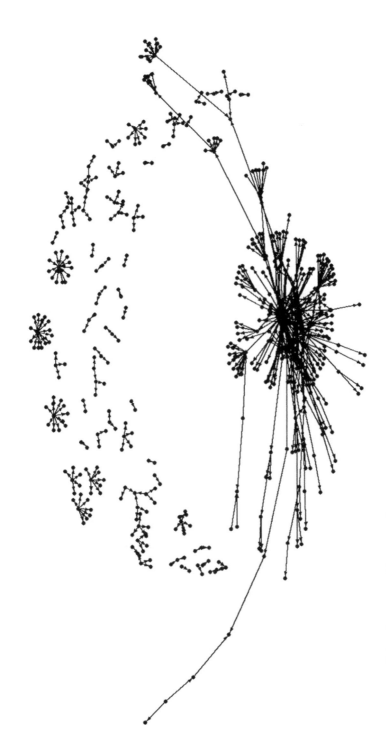

FIGURE 3.9 Bulgarian ownership network, 2000
Note: Arrows point to owners.

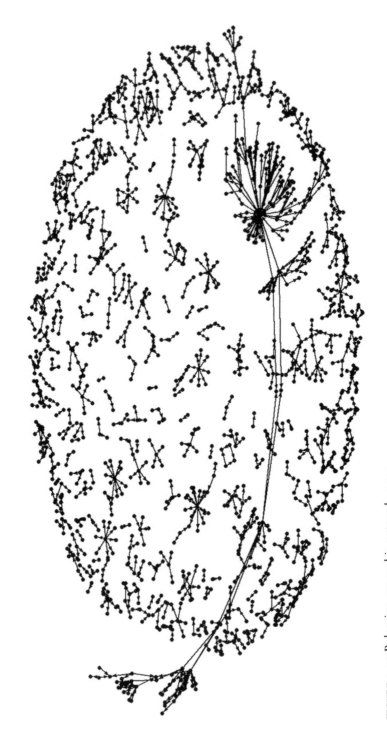

FIGURE 3.10 Bulgarian ownership network, 2005
Note: Arrows point to owners.

Tracing ownership networks

interference, as the example of Bulgartabac above illustrated. Consider the contrast to the Polish approach, in which the government used swaps to broadly restructure the economy while retaining political access to the firms. In Bulgaria, state officials found themselves struggling to control and restructure assets that they had themselves distanced but that were still a burden on the state budget.

By 2005 the Bulgarian path of market building was solidly founded on the alliance between individual stakeholders and largely domestic industrial firms, toward which it had been trending for the previous fifteen years. As can be seen in Figure 3.10, networks between firms had become much sparser with the retreat of the state (the cluster at the bottom right). This removed the state as a source of joint ownership ties and thus a possible source of cohesion and alliance among firms. Firms themselves did not, and perhaps were not able to, create networks with other firms on their own. The overall picture, therefore, is one of individual firms connected to owners but with few ties to other firms through those owners. In other words, the majority of firms are detached from other firms except their direct owners.

CONCLUSION

The mixed nature of the economy in Poland – the combination of market forms with the deliberate persistence of state ownership – also brought with it hybrid institutional forms. These mixed ownership forms in turn supported hybrid forms of market behavior. Activities such as bank lending were not fully marketized, but neither did they take place fully on the basis of social networks. Instead, market signals operated within and were supported by network structures. This distinguishes the Polish path from that of the other two countries examined, in which network forms distorted market outcomes in a way that altered their macroeconomic trajectories.

Business networks developed in a broad fashion in Poland, organized around banks that exchanged debt for equity and developed a broad network of stakeholders. This breadth also empowered and integrated domestic private investors and created opportunities for foreign firms. By contrast, networks of ownership were much more hierarchically organized in Bulgaria. They also developed around a different set of actors: holding companies formed by the state, which often created ownership ties with private holding companies and business groups. By the end of the period under study, the Bulgarian economy was dominated by a mix of individual investors (many with unscrupulous business methods) and ungainly industrial firms. Finally, in Romania, networks retained strong hierarchal features and linked a vast number of passive shareholders, state ownership funds, and large industrial firms – a structure that ultimately empowered a small group of state insiders. Although the effects were not as dramatic as those in Bulgaria, Romania was hardly a robust example of economic development in post-communist Europe.

The question posed at the outset of this chapter was: what role did these different network configurations have in setting the broader political path that each country has followed? With the evidence above, I have argued that both the composition and the structure of business networks shaped the pattern of state–economy interactions. Thus, the prominence of banks with state participation and broad, horizontal business networks in Poland created a context in which much of the leading business sector was part of a network of joint obligation, distributed risk and access to credit, information, and political action.

Bulgaria's ownership network linked a much narrower group of firms, and from an early stage put an emphasis on linking firms along sectoral lines. This move was intended partly to facilitate political control of assets, but, ironically, it failed both to retain strict hierarchical control and to establish a set of distributed stakeholders across the economy. Thus, owners had a different impact from the one they had in the Polish case. As the examples discussed above suggest, this network structure facilitated the parasitic relations that took hold in Bulgaria.

Finally, the strong hierarchical nature of ownership ties in Romania reinforced the position of insiders against the weak participation of largely passive outsiders, and explains much of the battle of interests against legislative and regulatory reform.

PART III

THE ROLE OF UNCERTAINTY

4

When uncertainty increases cooperation

We can observe collective action or a lack of collective action between firms and parties depending on the breadth of networks and the level of uncertainty. I now explore this argument through party finance, because a major form of collective action between firms and parties takes place when firms finance party political campaigns in exchange for support.

Parties and firms both have reasons to pursue financing arrangements. Parties seek to maximize financial support to increase their political advantage. Firms' financing of campaigns constitutes an investment geared toward obtaining favors from the winner. A firm's decision to finance depends on (1) the likelihood of identifying the winner (which in turn depends on the degree of electoral uncertainty) and (2) the likelihood that the receiving party, if it wins, will actually deliver on the promise of favors once in office. The mechanism behind the second condition brings in the role of network density. The winner is compelled to deliver on a promise of assistance to the firm that supported the campaign if shirking can easily be detected and punishment ensues. Network density favors this outcome, because information flows rapidly, reputation mechanisms can operate, and a collective response can mobilize. Broad networks, in other words, make the informal and often hidden contracts behind party financing more enforceable. Firms feel more confident about supporting parties, and parties pay back by delivering favorable policies in order to maintain future streams of support.

When broad networks are combined with high uncertainty, as happens in Poland, the result is a virtuous form of collective action, which I call "concertation," and we observe the winning party exercising responsiveness to its supporters through broad distributive policies. Concertation sustains cooperation between parties and firms by facilitating the enforcement of agreements. In particular, political uncertainty presents parties with the threat of losing at the polls, and thus provides an incentive to pay back firms once elected or risk losing in the following election. Broad networks

131

provide an effective flow of information among firms, which are therefore more able to avoid parties that shirk on their campaign promises. The two factors together mean that pre-election agreements are secured by both the threat of noncompliance and the monitoring allowed by effective information sharing.

The result of this cooperation over time is the development of broad distributive policies, for two reasons that are also related to political uncertainty and broad networks. The first focuses on the supply side. Political uncertainty means that parties will seek financial support from an ever larger number of firms as they face the costs of sharp competition. As the number of supporters increases, parties have an incentive to provide their payback not in the form of innumerable selective handouts but in generalized, business-friendly regulation that will appease a broad constituency. This solution is more cost-effective and more defensible at the polls. The second reason why broad policies emerge from this configuration rests on the demand side. As examined in earlier chapters, broad networks in Poland (with a heavy presence of financial actors) imply that firms have cross-sectoral stakes and, therefore, preferences. Hence, regulation that is generally business-friendly is in demand by firms in this configuration.

The workings of political uncertainty are different when networks are narrow. When elections are uncertain but networks are narrow, the winning party cannot credibly commit to campaign promises, because defection will go undetected or unpunished by supporters. This is the situation in Bulgaria. The result is the impossibility of cooperation between firms and parties.

Finally, when political uncertainty is low and networks are narrow, as in Romania, the dominant party wins election after election and there is low expectation of a turnover of power. Because networks are weak, the dominant party is in an extremely strong position, as firms lack not only the incentive but also the means to coordinate any leverage against it. Hence, the dominant party exploits them for financial support, and firms are in a position of subjugation: they know that they need to support the dominant party if they are to hope to receive support and if they wish to avoid punishment, and the result is a clientelistic relation between parties and firms, and a patronage state.

WHAT BINDS PARTIES AND FIRMS?

Poland: stable party–business alliances

The case of Poland shows how high uncertainty and broad networks promote cooperation. Because uncertainty in Poland meant political alternation, the left and the right competed for supporters. The result was that both political sides developed a network of powerful and loyal contributors. In the short run, the arrangement required significant and individualized handouts to key supporters

When uncertainty increases cooperation

when each party was in power. In the long run, however, as more and more firms in the country picked one side with which to align, the result was two increasingly broad and dense networks. Hence, over time, dynamic governing-party–firm relations moved from a prevalence of individual handouts to a prevalence of broad distributive institutions better suited to sustainably addressing the claims of the respective widening support coalitions. It is precisely the "arms race" derived by political uncertainty that promotes the alignment of increasing numbers of firms to one of the two political sides. The analysis of the Polish case below focuses on the early phase of individualized handouts to large backers. Evidence of the progressively higher rates of broadly distributive institutions is presented in Chapter 6, which discusses the impact of state types on governance.

The pitched competition between post-communist and anti-communist forces shaped the nature of political financing and reinforced the dynamic of strong links between political and economic actors that began to take shape right after 1989. It is still widely believed that the former Communist Party elites who seized economic assets as they transformed themselves into post-communist politicians were largely responsible for the promotion of insiders to prominent places in the business world (Solnick 1998; Gustafson 1999; Staniszkis 2000). Poland provides new evidence against this view, as parties that emerged out of the Solidarity movement were also repeatedly involved in scandals related to contacts with business. In fact, influenced by the sheer number of scandals, the public believed in 2000 that post-Solidarity politicians were far more corrupt than the post-communists. During the government of Jerzy Buzek (1997–2001) an unrivaled twenty-two ministers were dismissed, many as a consequence of corruption.

As this suggests, politicians in post-communist Poland have frequently attempted to exert influence over public and private assets. Their interest in these assets stems from a need for financing in order to retain power. Critical packets of extra money originated from political allies in large business in the form of a-legal donations (known as *cegiełki*, or "bricks") and free business services. Although these contributions were clandestine, available evidence confirms the importance and magnitude of covert contributions by firms and how the process of undocumented party finance was supported by a deficient legal framework governing party finances and poor monitoring and enforcement (Walecki 2000). Walecki (2005) offers an excellent discussion of the shortcomings of the laws regulating political parties and the bureaucracies charged with monitoring them. Walecki (2005) and (2007) highlights the role of plutocratic funding, the failure of parties to provide election expense returns, and the lack of adequate policing throughout the 1990s and early 2000s.

Few factors seem as important as personal ties in explaining which firms contribute to which party. This can partly be attributed to the fact that the programmatic differences on economic policy between the leftist SLD and the rightist AWS were narrow (Brada 1996).[1] On industrial policy, political views had little meaning, since the room for fiscal expenditures was thin and budgetary demands pushed privatization and restructuring to the top of the policy agenda. Conversely, some issues were too prickly for discussion by either end of the political spectrum. For example, in 2000 no political faction would have dared to privatize Polish sugar. Even the last AWS and strongly pro-privatization minister of the treasury, Aldona Kamela-Sowińska (known as the "Iron Dame"), backed down from this proposal in the Council of Ministers.

In the context of intense competition and a long-inadequate system of official financing for parties, alternative strategies of campaign finance became commonplace shortly after 1989, when parties had access to assets that came from unofficial sources. For example, the Centrum Alliance (PC) was formed in 1990, and its source of financing was to be a newly registered company called Telegraf. The firm's worth grew many times over, and this contributed to the PC's subsequent development into one of the three large Polish parties (Walecki 2000; Paradowska 2001). The Kaczynski brothers, who reshaped Polish politics in the 2000s, were early activists in the PC.

Once in place, the situation proved hard to reform. It persisted partly because regulations failed to provide adequate means to stamp it out, and parties have not found it in their interest to design a more stringent framework for oversight. The Law on Campaign Financing of 1997 provided no means of supervising party financing other than declarations submitted after elections.[2] These are so general that it is hard to verify the size of donations. No disclosure was required of political donors, and only parties are required to provide reports summarizing their finances. Furthermore, no sanction is specified for violating the law (Walecki 2000: 86). This created a broad system of financing parties through firms, including state-owned firms (Walecki 2000: 113). The situation changed somewhat after 2000, when a system of broad public financing was introduced. It did not address the issue of the disclosure and monitoring of party finances, however. It simply added another layer of financial inflows that exists in parallel to illicit financing. Instead of decreasing the competition for funds, it has left Poland with a situation that Ikstens, Smilov, and Walecki (2001) describe as a party finance "arms race." According to Szczerbiak (2006), electoral finance appears in the form of the direct financial support and indirect state subsidies that parties receive, but both types are supplemented by forms of patronage through the appointment

---

[1] Despite the narrow differences in policy, these parties were organized around a sharp post-communist versus anti-communist ideological cleavage.

[2] In 2000 campaign financing regulations restricted the types of contributions that could be accepted. Restricted sources of funding for presidential campaigns were defined in the law of May 25, 2000 (Dziennik Ustaw nr 43, poz. 488). Parliamentary campaigns were reformed on May 16, 2002 (Dziennik Ustaw nr 46, poz. 499). Political party financing was reformed in the law of July 31, 2001 (Dziennik Ustaw nr 79, poz. 857).

When uncertainty increases cooperation 135

of party loyalists to state and quasi-state bodies, such as state-owned or partially privatized firms.

In this context, the left political parties assisted in the formation of a group of entrepreneurs who have been their strong supporters for much of the post-communist period. These ties brought financing to the left, but were openly portrayed as a political effort to create a domestic class of entrepreneurs in the face of intense foreign competition. This group included men such as Gudzowaty, who became a billionaire in dollars for his role as an intermediary in the import of natural gas to Poland.[3] In exchange, Gudzowaty received vital support to expand his firms beyond gas supply. Rightist political parties perceived him as a stable ally of the left. According to his allegations, right coalitions in government were aggressive in their attempts to intimidate and dislodge him, allegedly even using the secret police.[4]

Other businesspeople also developed strong contacts with leftist parties that were vital to the success of their business. Among these was Piotr Bykowski, a rising member of the Communist Party until 1983, when he declined a job in the central committee of the Poznan region and left the party as an "unreformable organization" in order to become a capitalist (Gabryel and Zieleniewski 1998). His banking empire was created with the support of left parties. In keeping with Bykowski's idea that "state bureaucrats are obligated in helping to create new economic solutions, which will serve society" (Gabryel and Zieleniewski 1998: 168), Bykowski placed many former government officials on his supervisory board. As an aide to Waldemar Pawlak, the socialist prime minister from 1993 to 1995, he worked closely with two ministers of foreign economic cooperation and persuaded the government to establish an institution granting export credits and supporting trade with the West. Effectively, this was an attempt to have the SLD–PSL government build a financial empire with government capital. The program was halted later by Włodzimierz Cimoszewicz when he was prime minister (1996–7). Bykowski's Bank Staropolski declared bankruptcy in 2000 after Bykowski was arrested for allegedly transferring $500 million of the bank's funds abroad.

The left was not alone in creating and promoting a group of loyal entrepreneurs. The post-Solidarity groupings also had their protégé businesspeople. Like the SLD, the right attempted to cast the behavior of the political class toward firms as being not purely about economic gains. The interest in and need to create ties to the economy was critical in light of the sharp political struggle with the SLD. The support of domestic entrepreneurs also became an integral part of the discourse of economic development proposed

---

[3] Although Gudzowaty has been a strong, open supporter of left politicians, he was also a major contributor to Wałesa's political campaigns. Gudzowaty insists that his support for Wałesa was an indication of his enthusiasm for a man who brought about the end of communism in Poland.

[4] Gudzowaty discussed the aggressiveness of right governments in an interview cited earlier.

by the right, however. One of the most visible individuals involved in this policy was Jan Kulczyk.

In 1993 Kulczyk, vice-president of the Polish Business Roundtable, the most elite business organization, suggested that Polish entrepreneurs should be able to buy SOEs with payment plans extended over many years. Upon receiving an entrepreneur's award in 1992, Kulczyk said, "I believe that Polish firms should remain in our hands. Instead, selling domestic capital to foreign firms should be a way of filling out privatizations" (Gabryel and Zieleniewski 1998). Again, the comments of the Democratic Union (UD) minister of privatization at the time, Janusz Lewandowski, testify to the concern with domestic development: "We decided on preferences, for example, payment in parts over time. This was a conscious choice against the best offer. Western groups have a tremendous advantage over us. Privatization created an opportunity for the rise of domestic groups" (Gabryel and Zieleniewski 1998). Hence, when Lewandowski put 40 percent of Lech Breweries on sale, he announced that only Polish business could take part. Kulczyk won the tender through his firm Euro Agro Centrum, and thus established his relations with the center-right coalition then in power. All Kulczyk's major deals – Lech and Tyskie Breweries, TPSA, Autostrada Wielkopolska – were concluded under right-leaning governments. He had such access that some transformed his name from Kulczyk to *kluczyk*, the Polish word meaning "key" (Solska 2012). Later that year the post-communist SLD returned to power and decided, through the Ministry of the Treasury, to raise the capital of the firm. Subsequently, the Treasury decided not to buy any new shares. Kulczyk, lacking capital, was forced to find an outside investor (South African Breweries). Thus, the SLD government succeeded in undermining Kulczyk's control of the company (punishing him for his affiliation with center-right parties) and limiting the distributional consequences of the deal.

Individual businesspeople who cultivated relations with political elites held massive fortunes but accounted for only a portion of business support. The privatization process, which often only partially privatized firms, enabled the political appointment of selected directors and managers to newly private companies. These directors and board members, often selected from the ranks of poorly paid but politically faithful bureaucrats, became loyal backers of their political sponsors. Banks also became a critical chip in the Polish post-1989 game of wealth accumulation by political actors. The struggle over their control and the involvement of national political figures, including the second Polish president, Aleksander Kwasniewski, illustrate the centrality of the struggle to control property and its connection to the political struggle between the communist successor parties and the Solidarity/post-Solidarity coalitions. Simultaneously, the race to appropriate assets for the national political contest also created the major banking institutions in Poland.

Throughout these moves, parties and firms became tightly allied partners in the struggle to increase revenue on both sides. There is an important distinction to be made between the race to control assets and the attempt to manage them,

When uncertainty increases cooperation 137

however. Parties did attempt to politicize firms but they did not seek to interfere in their management. Describing the interaction with parties in an interview, one businessperson used the phrase "They govern but they don't manage" (*Rzadza ale nie zarzadzaja*) to express the perception that parties did not have a coherent plan of firm development. What they sought was a reliable stream of revenue as part of a mutual exchange. This outcome was strikingly different from that of Romania and Bulgaria.

Romania: the state against firms

Romania displays low uncertainty and narrow networks, a combination that results in a patronage state. Party finance in Romania offers a potent and contrasting example of how the level of party competition structures the ability of parties to extract funds, and shapes firm incentives to finance political parties. Whereas parties in Poland were engaged in a sharp conflict between alternative ends of the political spectrum, Romania's post-transition political history can be summed up as a period of rule by a group of elites emerging around the Romanian dictator Nicolae Ceausescu. These elites founded the National Salvation Front, which underwent several splits into competing factions. One of these factions, the Party of Social Democracy of Romania, eventually became the Social Democratic Party in 2001. President Iliescu and the PDSR/PSD dominated Romanian politics until the Romanian Democratic Convention was elected in 1996 – the first time that an opposition party was able to form a democratic government following success at the polls. The CDR was voted out of office after one term, however. Although there have been numerous splits and recompositions of individual political parties, the range of alternation is without question much narrower than in Poland or Bulgaria. In this context, the general situation of Romanian party financing leaves much to be desired. Regulations demand that a list of persons who have donated more than the equivalent of ten times the minimum wage must be published. This regulation is not enforced, however, and some parties, such as the Party of Social Democracy of Romania, never published such a list despite numerous scandals about illegal financing. The Liberal Party also never published these financial statements (Ikstens, Smilov, and Walecki 2001).

With such lax monitoring, Romanian political parties are able to aggressively seek out donations. In fact, in an interview one party official argued that "the main problem of party finance is to begin to apply the laws of party finance, not to create new ones." In Romania, flaws in party finance laws are also intensely exploited by parties to receive funds from the state and private donors. These included the awarding of lavish public contracts to campaign sponsors and large-scale patronage to reward important donors (Gherghina, Chiru, and Casal Bértoa 2011: 22) According to Roper, Moraru, and Iorga (2008: 150), "The lack of transparency has led in certain cases to the transformation of the party's finances into a private business. This mechanism starts

138

with the charging of 'fees' for candidates that are not reported, the obtaining of contributions that remain undeclared and the conclusion of contracts with companies owned by party members." Matichescu and Protsyk (2011) argue that business elites are prominent on party lists as part of a system of clientelistic exchanges that provides parties with electoral funds and businesspeople with protection of their interests and, potentially, immunity from prosecution. They also point out that this dynamic has become stronger over time. The percentage of parliamentarians with a business background steadily increased in the period from 1990 to 2004 (Protsyk and Matichescu 2011: 214). The use of a closed-list proportional representation system until 2008 reinforced the ability of political party organizations to use positions on the party list to obtain campaign funds (Matichescu and Protsyk 2011). While we might expect an electoral reform to disrupt the ability of parties to trade seats in parliament for funds, the introduction of single-member districts had a minimal impact on the power of party leaders (Coman 2012).

To illustrate the Romanian dynamic of party finance, consider the following example: on November 15, 2003, PSD secretary-general Dan Matei Agathon announced in Botosani that the party had just 20 percent of the funds it needed to finance its upcoming electoral campaigns, according to the dailies *Adevarul, Evenimentul Zilei,* and *Romania Libera* (reported on November 17). Agathon said that party officials who wished to retain their current posts should immediately embark on securing the needed funds, keeping in mind that they would be judged by their performance. He added that prospective candidates had to contribute to the PSD's electoral funds. Those candidates would have to raise campaign funds from private companies, to which they were to make clear that they could not finance other political parties at the same time.

Romania thus followed a quite different path, and firms there occupy a much more subordinate position than those in either Poland or Bulgaria. The comments of the PSD secretary-general offer an insight into the relationship between business and political parties in post-socialist Romania. The dominance of post-NSF elites created a rather surprising dynamic. Although Romanian politics was marked by a series of splits and party divisions among the group of elites that formed the initial National Salvation Front, these can be seen as conflicts within a narrow clique struggling for executive power. In this context, the left–right split is quite blurred, and parties that opposed each other in one election often became allies in a coalition government only a few years later. For example, between 2005 and 2008 the PSD was an opposition party after losing an election to a coalition comprised of the Democratic Party and the National Liberal Party (PNL). After various factional conflicts, the PD changed its name to the Democratic Liberal Party (PD-L). In 2008 the PD-L formed a coalition government with its former opponents, the PSD.

Strong expectations of dominance on the part of the post-NSF groupings conditioned business to seek ties primarily with politicians from these parties, but failed to create the conditions for lasting alliances as the dominance of a

When uncertainty increases cooperation 139

single party made firms vulnerable to extraction. The long success of the PSD gave it an advantage in this search for financing. A business leader noted, "The PSD has the most of them, contributors, because there are many people who are benefiting from favors from them. It is not possible for a big businessperson to prosper without political connections." The relationship between parties and firms was different from the partnership that had developed in Poland: business leaders had much more of a sense that parties had the upper hand in the relationship. Another top business owner observed, "We are providing a significant portion of the state revenues and they have to understand that they have to consult my business. But they don't. They are the rulers and they expect the subjects to contribute."

As a way around this dilemma, some powerful businesspeople tried to become major figures associated with a particular, personal, party. The oil magnate Dinu Patriciu has, for example, long been involved with the Liberal Party. In fact, he was one of the founders of the party, and worked to develop a political career at the same time as he was developing his fortune. Others established what could best be called vanity parties, such as the Humanist Party of Dan Voiculsecu. This was essentially a personal vehicle through which to lend support to the PSD while also obtaining some security.

The remaining companies try to follow a "swinging" pattern when political opportunity presents itself, jockeying for favor from a member of the dominant coalition, which has thus far meant figures from the various centrist groupings of post-NSF elites. Hence, the difficulty that the opposition faced in gaining seats was related to the fact that it also had a difficult time raising funds. It searched for economic allies among firms that were unable to attract the protection of the PSD, often at an exorbitant cost.

This pattern was documented in a White Paper issued in May 2001, in which the government of Adrian Năstase charged the opposition CDR for allowing arrears to grow rapidly and using concessions to favor particular interests. According to the White Paper, debts to the Finance Ministry stood at an overall lei 7,393 billion at the end of 1996, before the CDR took power. Concessions accounted for only 10.6 percent of this debt. In contrast, the value of debts at the end of the CDR mandate, in 2000, was estimated at around lei 60,000 billion, with concessions related to 60 percent. Debts to the Work and Social Security Ministry at the end of 1996 were worth lei 3,671 billion, and by the end of 2000 they had surged to lei 45,000 billion, of which concessions accounted for 15 percent (Government of Romania 2001). This dynamic, according to the White Paper, was the result of the restrictive economic policies followed between 1997 and 2000, which had led to the "rapid de-capitalization of economic agents coupled with a surge in their indebtedness to creditors" that was tolerated by the CDR.

The White Paper was highly criticized by the opposition as a political smear campaign that attempted to place blame on the CDR for difficulties facing Năstase's new government. Yet, if the data are reliable, they suggest where the

CDR's support lay within the economy: firms dependent on concessions that had not been able to obtain them under previous governments, and firms awarded concessions in an attempt to secure their future support and lure them away from the PSD.

Outstanding payments in the state sector diminished to the equivalent of 26.8 percent of GDP in the first half of 2000 from a high of 39.6 percent of GDP in 1996, during the CDR government. As the CDR's support did not come from this sector, it was able to call in the debts of large state-owned enterprises. In contrast, in the mixed-property sector, debt grew to 33.3 percent from 20.4 during the same period (Government of Romania 2001), reflecting the need of the CDR to offer more slack to such firms. A similar explanation could be offered for the rise in concessions. Combined with this first observation, the steep rise in concessions between 1997 and 2000 at the Finance Ministry and Ministry of Work and Social Security was a sign of the importance that giving out this form of preferences to private business held for the CDR. As the NSF and PSDR drew their support and finances largely from the state sector, they did not need to offer concessions to private firms.

Unsurprisingly, the PSD was able to leverage its political dominance into greater access to gains from illicit financing. Extracting money from the state sector was a key means of obtaining support. One method, for example, was for firms to place advertisements in newspapers. The firms would pay newspapers for "advertising," and the latter would funnel money to political parties. A telltale sign of this dynamic was when advertisements promoted unusual sectors. For example, a business leader pointed out in an interview that the control tower at Bucharest's Otopeni airport ran an advertisement despite the fact that it had no competition and there was no choice in the use of its services.

Over time, the dominant party was also able to attract well-known politicians. In the period leading up to and right after the 2000 electoral defeat of the CDR coalition, a series of senators and deputies migrated (*Stiri Politice* 2000). This mostly meant a move to post-NSF splinter groups such as the PDSR/PSD. Thus, Adrian Severin, Adrian Vilău, and Octavian Stireanu left the PD for the PDSR, the last giving up his seat in the senate for a deputies' seat. Similarly, George Pruteanu left the Christian Democratic PNTCD for the PDSR. Valentin Iliescu left the PUNR for the PDSR. Adrian Paunescu left the PSM for the PDSR. Trița Fanița was the leader of the PD and switched in 2000 to the PSD.

The lower degree of uncertainty in Romanian politics as a result of the dominance of the Social Democrats created a situation in which firms were unable to count on political alliances. The dominance of the Social Democrats also created a spiral of increasing support, as confirmed in the extent of party switching. As a result, there were none of the alliances between parties and firms that were such a central part of the Polish landscape.

When uncertainty increases cooperation

Bulgaria: firms against the state

The case of Bulgaria displays high uncertainty and narrow networks, resulting in an inability to coordinate and in the prevalence of preying and violence against the state. Bulgarian politics since 1989 has been marked by instability and contention over basic reform issues. The Bulgarian Socialist Party (formerly the Bulgarian Communist Party) won the first post-communist parliamentary elections in 1990, with 48 percent of the vote and 52 percent of seats. The BSP's support was drawn from pensioners, peasants fearful of land restitution, and the technical intelligentsia. However, the BSP's policies were largely driven by the old *nomenklatura*. Its official platform consisted of support for reform, but at a gradual pace.

After a series of failed attempts to form a coalition, the "go it alone" government of the BSP leader, Andre Lukanov, lasted only until late 1990, when it fell as a result of a general strike. A transitional coalition government comprised of members of the BSP, the Union of Democratic Forces, and the Bulgarian Agrarian National Union (BANU) – a party built on the platform of agricultural property restitution – replaced it.

The country's first fully democratic parliamentary election, in November 1991, resulted in a near-majority for the anti-communist and pro-reform UDF. A coalition government led by the UDF in partnership with an ethnic party, the Turkish Movement for Rights and Freedoms (MRF), was formed. Despite the passage of a privatization law and a foreign investment law, this coalition collapsed in late 1992 under a vote of no confidence and pressure from the Bulgarian president, Zhelyu Zhelev, also of the UDF. A compromise produced a government of experts put forward by the MRF and supported by the BSP and a breakaway faction of the UDF. This government became increasingly unpopular, culminating with the crash of the Bulgarian currency, the lev, in 1994, which forced the resignation of the prime minister.

The BSP won an absolute majority in the pre-term election in December 1994, with the support of the Bulgarian Business Block (BBB), a new force in Bulgarian politics that proposed to fight for the interests of small business, offering a nationalistic message. The BBB's leader, Georges Ganchev, became a popular candidate during the 1996 presidential election. The BSP was heavily allied with newly emergent "nomenklatura"-based economic interests, with links that often ran directly to senior party officials. Despite a public commitment to macro-reform, these behind-the-scenes conflicts of interest led to reform inertia. Ganchev remained in office until February 1997, when a populace alienated by the BSP's failed and corrupt government demanded its resignation and called for a new general election.

The crisis caused tensions among factions within the BSP. At the 1998 party congress, a faction known as "the generals," a reformist grouping of post-communist businessmen and former security officials determined to re-establish the party, cleared the top party ranks and installed Georgi Purvanov as leader

(BTA 1998c; *East European Constitutional Review* 1998). Little was heard of "the generals'" movement after the financial crisis wiped out many of their businesses, but Purvanov's presidential victory in 2001 strengthened the position of the BSP. "The generals" themselves moved to take over a number of companies making light firearms and armaments, one of Bulgaria's strong export product categories.

Once again, a caretaker Cabinet emerged, appointed by the president. Stefan Sofianski, Sofia's UDF mayor, became prime minister. By stabilizing the lev, proceeding with privatization, fighting corruption, driving down inflation, and vigorously purging the bureaucracy, Sofianski's government gained popularity, serving until a pre-term parliamentary election in April 1997.

In the general election that year, a pro-reform coalition, the United Democratic Forces (UtdDF), led by the Union of Democratic Forces, won 137 out of 240 seats – a landslide victory. (Other members of the UtdDF included the Bulgarian Agrarian People's Union, the Democratic Party, and the Bulgarian Social Democratic Party.) In contrast, the Bulgarian Socialist Party dropped from its 1994 majority of 125 seats to fifty-eight. Along with the Ecoglasnost Movement and the Aleksandar Stamboliyski faction of the Bulgarian Agrarian People's Union, the BSP stood as a member of the Democratic Left electoral alliance. The UDF leader, Ivan Kostov, formed a government that pushed ahead with privatization, signed a three-year agreement with the IMF, and set up a currency board.

Mounting public concerns about corruption caused the UDF to lose popularity as the July 2001 parliamentary election approached, however. As one official put it, "In the previous [Kostov] government, deals were made against the interest of the state. There is no evidence of payments but either the person making these deals was stupid or there was a financial incentive." The Bulgarian political scene was again disturbed with the entrance of the National Movement Simeon II. This also upset already weak party–economy ties, according to an official who said, "The arrival of Simeon (*Sakskoburggotski*) has destroyed the clear ties along left–right lines and reconstructed them for his party." The SNM won the general election and formed a coalition with the MRF. This government again lasted only one term. In 2005 the Socialists attempted to form a coalition government with the MRF, but its proposed Cabinet failed to receive parliamentary approval. Ultimately, a grand coalition of the Socialists, the SNM, and the Turkish minority party emerged. The parliamentary election of 2009 led to even more changes in the party system. The most votes were obtained by a new party, Citizens for European Development of Bulgaria, led by the brash Boyko Borisov, whose career ranged from security policeman to interior minister and mayor of Sofia. The formerly ruling SNM did not even reach the 4 percent threshold and thus obtained no seats.

This shifting party system also had an impact on patterns of party finance. Despite a law on party financing delivered at the roundtable talks in 1990 and a replacement of this law with a new one on March 28, 2001, financing

When uncertainty increases cooperation 143

irregularities are the norm. Official sources include public subsidy, own means, and income from assets and donations. Officially, anonymous donations can be equal to up to 25 percent of the public subsidy, which is determined for each election. The use of anonymous donations was seen as a major problem; as one politician noted, "The problem with party finance is that the audit mechanism is not very strong and there are still [speaking in 2003] anonymous donations."

Balances of official party financing are available to the public, but BBSS Gallup International estimates that more than 80 percent of party finances are "non-transparent" and illegal according to the reporting standards of the law (Alexandrova 2002). According to the World Bank, 42 percent of Bulgarian companies have paid money to political parties in return for favors. This situation is allowed to persist because no effective means for the supervision of party finances exists, and officials are effectively unable to do more than rubber-stamp party financial statements (Ikstens, Smilov, and Walecki 2001). According to one official, "The real problem is that the available money is dirty money, which is controlled by people in the business community involved in the black, grey and even the regular economy." As a consequence, another official concluded, "Many parties were using practices that ranged from the grey economy to plainly illegal practices to fund their campaigns."

The prevalence of illegal party finance in Bulgaria reflects a larger dilemma: the fact that a group of strong societal interests faced an unstable party system. In this context, political actors were more dependent on a small group of firms than the firms on parties. Describing how parties are impacted by the business elite, a party leader said, "Most parties are infected by big businesspeople. The parties need to reform themselves and stop taking money from the grey economy." Echoing these sentiments and pointing out that they have deep consequences for institutional development, an analyst noted, "The individuals who control the shadow business world persist in their activities undisturbed. Really this is a chain of corruption, which permeates all parties. Unfortunately, the Democrats are as corrupted as the Socialists, perhaps even more." Moreover, narrow networks meant that economic actors beyond these small groups had a difficult time mobilizing coalitions. Monitoring through networks was weak, as well. High levels of uncertainty and narrow networks made it difficult for parties to make credible commitments to firms and for firms to monitor the fulfillment of electoral bargains.

FIRMS AND PARTIES IN POLAND, ROMANIA, AND BULGARIA

In each country, the incentives for firms to be loyal to a particular party were shaped by the extent to which firms could estimate the future political success of a potential political partner and the likelihood that favors would be delivered once in office. In both Poland and Bulgaria, the political climate created uncertainty for firms, yet, in the Polish case, broad networks allowed reputation mechanisms to operate. As a consequence, firms eagerly gave to their favorite political side, because the latter could credibly commit to delivering favors. These were initially destined for a small circle of large backers. Over time the high level of political uncertainty and electoral competition caused an increasing number of firms to align themselves. As a result, parties distributed not only selective handouts but increasingly also broadly distributive regulation. By contrast, in Bulgaria, uncertainty combined with narrow networks undermined the ability of parties to enter into credible agreements with firms. The result was a lack of cooperation and firms engaging in open preying on and violence against the state. Finally, in Romania, the dominance of a coalition meant that firms were at the mercy of political elites who controlled the state.

5

Tracing elite career networks

This chapter builds on the political backgrounds and varying contexts of uncertainty presented in Chapter 4. Through a macro-level analysis of the career networks of elite state officials, it provides an empirically grounded theory of the interplay of uncertainty and networks in institutional development.

Scholars have examined the impact of different forms of embeddedness in accounts of the state's ability to govern the economy (Wade 1990; Evans 1995; Kang 2002). This chapter, however, offers one of few studies that use data to understand the role of networks between state officials and the private sector. As the coming pages show, these cleverly forged relations are only partly shaped by the individual ambitions of bureaucrats. Political parties also view the deployment of party members to other sectors as a way of creating relational assets that are important in securing political finance for parties and creating lasting bonds with firms. These maneuvers, in combination with the level of political uncertainty, generate different elite networks. As in the case of ownership networks, over time Poland developed the broadest elite network, whereas Bulgaria's and Romania's networks were both much more narrowly connected.

HOW ELITE NETWORKS FUNCTION

Across the post-socialist landscape, poorly paid bureaucratic positions are seen as a stepping stone for talented individuals on their way to the private sector. For example, the former head of the Bulgarian Parliamentary Energy Committee, Nikita Shervashidze, was influential in the signing of a controversial contract between the state gas monopoly Bulgargas and two companies owned by Multigroup, the company that has been described as a "state within the state" for its ability to evade official control (Ganev 2001). As a result of this contract, Multigroup's companies performed financial services that involved

145

transferring Bulgargas's receivables from two other large state companies, Chimco and Kremikovtsi, to itself. Shevarshidze subsequently left his government post and founded the National Gas Company, affiliated with Multigroup, and initiated the establishment of the Energia Invest privatization fund, which has acquired assets in a number of companies from the power industry through mass privatization.

Some authors have suggested that the post-communist left was better placed and more skillful at creating such networks (Staniszkis 2000). This is not substantiated by the historical record, however: the Bulgarian Socialist Party's conservative rival, the Union of Democratic Forces, also created a network through which it could control economic resources. Once the UDF gained control of the government in 1997, it began to introduce management–worker partnerships in a large number of Bulgarian state-owned companies as part of its privatization strategy. As part of this policy, the UDF managed to change the directorates of several companies and installed directors who were party allies or top members of the party. This move, according to the standard argument, was necessary to prevent the mismanagement of state-owned firms by former socialist managers. The main goal, however, was to remove firms from the political control of the Socialist party. Interviews with politicians of various parties reveal that this did not mean that the firms became depoliticized property; rather, in short order, firms were sold to the RMDs and became sources of UDF donations. The pressure to compete for economic resources with other parties meant that having politically connected managers in place was key to the activities of all political parties. Commenting on the view that these networks were a resource for parties even after the individuals left formally political postions, a politician observed, "The UDF elite is still here. And the BSP elite is still here. For example, after the UDF government a lot of the UDF people went into the high court, the constitutional court, the high police agencies. Some of them became businesspeople. So they didn't disappear."

Whereas Bulgarian parties struggled to retain control of economic assets, Polish firms established stable ties with political parties that included the exchange of elites. These ties were instrumental for both sides. For example, the former deputy minister of trade and industry, Kazimierz Adamczyk, became the president of EuRoPolgaz, a company that is a critical mediator and beneficiary of trade between Russia's Gazprom and the Polish natural gas monopoly. Adamczyk also sat on the supervisory board of the Cigna STU insurance company. One of Adamczyk's former colleagues made a career in the gas business: Roman Czerwinski, the president of PolGaz Telekom, a dependent company of Gazprom, used to be deputy minister of industry. When he was in government, Czerwinski was responsible for the power sector. As minister, he negotiated the contract of the Yamal gas pipeline with Gazprom, while PolGaz Telekom signed contracts on the construction and use of a fiber optic cable, which runs along the pipeline (Polish News Bulletin 2000).

Tracing elite career networks

Andrzej Śmietanko, a Polish Peasant Party activist, became minister of agriculture for the PSL government of Waldemar Pawlak and later an advisor to President Kwasniewski. On leaving government, he became the president of Brasco Inc., a company involved in natural gas and part of Gudzowaty's empire. Śmietanko was a good investment for Gudzowaty because he was a strong opponent of Poland's largest company and top fuels group, PKN Orlen, when it tried to prevent the passage of a law that would mandate the sale of biofuels in the Polish market. Gudzowaty, on the other hand, had already invested in several biofuel companies and needed Śmietanko's contacts to push the law through parliament. The latter remains an important figure in the PSL.

These examples suggest that the politicization of property did not end with privatization but instead spread to the emerging private sector. In other words, private property could also be politicized property. All political parties sought to control property in search of advantages during the intense political struggles after 1989. The more intense party competition became, the more deeply this logic took hold.

Whereas the development of a network of loyal party supporters across the state, private, and non-profit sectors took place in every country, these networks took different forms across cases. I explore the mobility of individuals, what sectors they moved between, and, most importantly, the structure of the network of elites that developed as a result of these individual moves.

Poland had an abundance of figures with one foot in the state and one foot beyond, on either the left or the right side of the political spectrum. Elite state officials also experienced a high degree of job mobility during their careers. This supports the argument, made throughout this book, that Poland represents a key variety of post-socialist capitalism that is structured around dense ties in the partisan division of the economy.

Romania instead was a dominant-party regime for much of the first decade, and was dominated by state elites who emerged from a single national unity coalition after the violent and still murky revolution. Overall, Romania has been marked by very low mobility, much of it occasioned by the entrance of the first opposition government in 1996 and its exit in 2000, when many bureaucrats who had served from 1990 to 1996 returned to their state positions. This low mobility was concentrated within the state and was also apparent in the movement of some state officials to the parliament.

Bulgaria experienced the highest degree of mobility, with a high frequency of placements. The range of movement was limited, however, as it was concentrated in moves between private business and the key state ministries that regulate finance and the economy, industrial policy, internal security, and matters related to defense, including highly profitable firms producing arms for export. Such trajectories reflect the ability of business to dominate the state, but, because Bulgarian elites were concentrated in firms and these ministries, the range of career paths was limited and the overall effect was that the Bulgarian network was much less broad than the Polish network.

NETWORKS OF INDIVIDUALS

What is the role of persons and personnel networks in the exercise of state power? Do dense networks linking the state to the public sphere enhance state power or impede the exercise of government? By developing the concept of "state embeddedness," Evans and others have argued that such networks can, under certain circumstances, enhance the state's ability to make and implement policy by improving information flows and coordination (Gerlach 1992; Evans 1995; Kang 2002). On the other hand, some have argued that networks constrain the state's ability to build institutions and develop autonomy from powerful interests (Jowitt 1983; Ledeneva 1998; Ganev 2007), although these arguments do not explicitly discuss the structure of networks.

As sets of ties that link two or more organizations in a structure that is not just hierarchical, networks connect actors in public administration to other actors in the same ministry or agency, other levels of government, other ministries, and outside the state to private and non-profit actors. Networks can be used to mobilize actors, acquire and share information, generate support, and move a set of actors toward an objective or goal (O'Toole 2010: 8). Networks related to public administration link actors through three basic kinds of ties – authority, common interest, and exchange (O'Toole and Montjoy 1984, cited by O'Toole 2010: 8) – and act as both capacity enhancers and constraints on action by raising the number of potential veto points (Simon 1964, cited by O'Toole 2010: 8). Thus, it is important to distinguish between different types of network structures in order to determine what a particular network can do best. Above all, narrow networks perform different functions from the ones that broad networks do (Scholz, Berardo, and Kile 2008). The former assist in the generation of credible commitments that support cooperation among a small set of actors, while the latter reduce search costs when these pose the greatest obstacle to collaboration. Thus, broad networks between public administration and non-state actors can assist with the conduct of policy by allowing affected groups to communicate concerns to policy makers, receive information about upcoming policy shifts, and generate coalitions of support or opposition by bringing together distant actors around credible commitments to collective action. Narrow networks do not perform these functions (O'Toole and Montjoy 1984; O'Toole 1997; Lazer and Friedman 2007; Feiock and Scholz 2009).

This view is in line with the argument made in this book, with the difference that I consider cases in which the institutional context is incomplete. In the absence of strong institutional constraints, networks matter even more in shaping and determining the types of policies that are chosen. Broad networks reduce search costs, spread information, and mobilize cooperation. The constraint-raising quality identified by Simon (1964) is what leads broad networks to support collective action, as large sets of actors are able to veto narrowly distributive outcomes. This is the dynamic at work in Poland. Narrow networks can support cooperation among small sets of actors and favor narrowly distributive outcomes; this describes the situation in both Bulgaria and

Romania. Building on previous chapters, however, the argument developed in the coming pages is that the presence of broader networks is not *of itself* sufficient to determine whether powerful societal interests collaborate to support the process of institutional development or to subvert it. Instead, network features must be examined together with uncertainty in order to determine how the path of institutional development unfolds.

This chapter considers the uncertainty of career paths that derive from political dynamics, and therefore it focuses on the extent to which job changes coincide with elections. The meaning of a job change is very different if one changes jobs for a better position by choice or if that change is involuntary, prompted by a political dismissal after an election. Frequent election-related job changes suggest the broad politicization of key jobs in a society but also imply that politics serves as an effective check against the prolonged use of powers connected to a particular position by a single individual. The less individuals change jobs over time, the more they are likely to become entrenched power holders. If mass changes occur in the year of or following an election, political ousters likely motivate these changes.

The extent to which an individual moves among jobs affects the density of networks of social ties. If a job holder moves among multiple spheres, he or she will accumulate more ties than someone who moves back and forth between two jobs. I consider historical links to be stored in an individual's biography as professional capital. Thus, an individual who once worked in a firm and transitioned to a ministry can call on acquaintances made in both positions. Upon moving to a third position, the individual's built-up professional capital includes networks from both prior contacts. These links are not lost simply because he or she moves on to a new job. Quite to the contrary, such ties can be utilized to build coalitions, and his or her ability to span and connect to individuals in other organizations may be part of what makes him or her attractive as a new hire. Thus, if he or she moves between jobs in different sectors, he or she accumulates historical links to a variety of spheres.

As the data discussed below show, countries vary significantly. Stories about the movement of individuals between the public and private sphere are hardly particular to the post-socialist situation, but they raise interesting questions about the relationship between individual spheres of power and the dynamics of institution building, thus allowing the study of variation in *levels* and *types* of systemic influence construction. The pathways of bureaucrats once they leave a particular office are important because they reinforce the popular notion in post-socialist countries that bureaucratic interactions with those who lobby them are part of a longer-term plan to convert political power into other types of power, primarily economic power.[1] As noted above, in most eastern

---

[1] Such activity is not restricted to the post-socialist area. The conversion of public into private power is known as the *amakudari* system in Japan or the often referred-to "golden parachute," which is in the toolbox of bureaucrats from Peru to Norway. The *amakudari* system and others

European countries the practice of appointing state personnel to firms was a strategy pursued by political organizations to extend political control.[2] A great deal has been written in the press about the process and purpose of these exchanges, but little more than anecdotal evidence has been offered to support macro-conclusions about its impact. One often hears, for example, of a bureaucrat being appointed to the board of a firm or an executive being appointed to some governing body in a process that is intended to extend or convert one kind of authority into another (Kublik 2008).

This practice is, of course, advantageous not only to political parties. It is also an attractive strategy to bureaucrats, because it generates "emergency exits" for those who face an uncertain future at each round of elections. For example, in Poland the members of the supervisory boards of the most important firms are also replaced after elections (Grzeszak *et al.* 1999; Staniszkis 2000). This applies to both public and private firms and is supported by journalistic accounts of individual cases. Similarly, ministerial positions, including lower-level positions, are reshuffled after each election. For example, on June 25, 1994, the leading Polish daily *Gazeta Wyborcza* commented in connection with the then prime minister, "The ease with which Pawlak's team disposes of the best professionals at every level of the government and ministerial administration prompts amazement and dismay" (Vinton 1994).

These practices are in line with a minimal conception of the state in postsocialist countries that has emerged in the literature. The post-socialist state was initially considered to be an autonomous and strong actor that needed to be dismantled, because it was assumed that the socialist state had been a strong state. More recent studies, in particular Grzymała-Busse and Jones-Luong's (2002) direct treatment of the question, have urged a reconsideration of these states as particularly weak, requiring rebuilding to meet new administrative challenges.

Yet rebuilding was unlikely to take place in the conventional fashion: by erecting new institutional structures that were legitimized and that bound actors in rule-following behavior. Even if the situation on the ground could have made this possible, pressure coming from international policy advisors tied the hands of the state and limited the extent to which state structures could take an active role in the construction of markets. As a consequence, alternative structures developed to link political and economic actors. For example, during this period state economic activities were largely controlled or bounded by clientelistic relationships with powerful actors who had the money or means

---

like it in east Asia developed in order to create channels of control, however, and the implementation of industrial policy through official as well as personal pathways.

[2] An impressive body of press articles exists on individual episodes. References to a "system" of politics that underpins it were first made in an interview with a prominent political commentator in Warsaw in May 2000.

to threaten the state. Political parties with access to decision-making authority were similarly drawn into this web of relations.

Thus, one promising avenue for a reconception of the state focuses on elites (Levi 1998; Waldner 1999; Migdal 2001; Grzymała-Busse and Jones-Luong 2002), implicitly exploring the notion that the extension of state control and prestige is largely connected to the paths, networks, and initiatives of individuals. This reconception requires a shift toward considering the state as a non-unitary actor – one that operates through disjointed areas of influence that are in the process of consolidation while under pressure from social forces.

In this conception, pathways and relations are strategically deployed so as to maximize the career prospects of the individual and the organization vis-à-vis the state. Such strategic behavior aims to increase individual holdings in one or more of the key currencies in circulation: money, policy influence, and information. These paths form a macro-structural pattern of behavior, which all elites attempt to read and estimate in order to plan their next move. And, with each new move, the value of all members' network capital grows.

Behind this conception is a particular assumption about the state and the individuals who constitute it. In the weak states considered here, politics penetrates all areas of the state, and individuals are part of this political structure more than they are part of the state agency in which they work. This dynamic can also be attributed to attitudes stemming from before 1989, when all positions were obtained through the ruling communist party. Rather than shedding this trend after transition, there is ample evidence that new political parties, such as the Polish SLD and AWS or the Bulgarian UDF and BSP, adopted it. Hence, it is useful to view the state as constituted by individuals in diffuse political organizations, in the sense that the individuals are not located in one particular place but have fanned out across a variety of social arenas, moving along mutually self-serving paths.

It follows that much can be learned by observing the macro-structural patterns of elite movement. When summed together, different patterns of movement will give rise to very different configurations of networks. In turn, this should lead to different types of states, as a greater or lesser number of individuals control or have access to a network that fulfills functions such as the transmission of information, the facilitation of coalition building, the creation of policy cliques, and an awareness of the interests in different policy arenas. Succinctly, networks facilitate or impede the group mobilization of resources.

By following the development of the networks below, I observe how the state comes to occupy a particular position of relational power. These ties are the "embeddedness" of which Evans and others have written, and which enables the state to make informed policy decisions that have the support of societal actors by taking advantage of the feedback that flows through these ties. The following pages analyze how state power and state consolidation were supported or constrained by the informal organization of networked individuals.

Anticipating the findings, the analysis indicates the importance of two dimensions. First, it highlights the role of elite mobility. I find a striking difference between the breadth of embeddedness in the three cases. The Polish network is much wider than the Bulgarian network, although elites are more mobile in the latter. In Poland, networks spread further and linked social spheres and power brokers more broadly over time. In Romania, network breadth is much lower and elites are much less mobile as a whole. The presence of broad relational contacts between the public and private sectors in Poland challenges the notion that network ties between elites generated many of the pathologies of post-socialist government. The lack of such ties in Romania and Bulgaria – countries known for their poor governance – provides negative cases.

Second, this analysis reveals very different patterns of movement between the state and sectors of the private economy. The closeness of certain areas of the private sector to the state go hand in hand with particular paths of institutional development. The frequent movement of individuals from the private sector into the state in Bulgaria is a central part of the story of state capture that has been told qualitatively elsewhere in the literature (Ganev 2001; Ganev 2007). This pattern is in stark contrast to the dominant movement in Poland: of party functionaries from the parliament to key ministries and sometimes private business. Romania represents a third variant, in which elites circulate from high positions within the state outward, although with far less frequency and more limited breadth.

HOW ELITE NETWORKS DIFFER ACROSS COUNTRIES

The argument in this chapter is based on a relational approach to the state. In political science, states generally continue to be conceptualized as black boxes. In some empirical studies, scholars explore the actual interactions of state bureaucrats with societal actors (Evans, Rueschemeyer, and Skocpol 1985; Evans 1995). Even in studies of the post-socialist countries, however, in which much of the political science literature has been focused on how ties between state bureaucrats and societal actors are responsible for corruption, there is a tendency to discuss what states "do" (Ledeneva 1998). Rarely, as a result, is the link made between the role that individual actors play and the enabling or constraining effects of individual relational ties.

One aim of this study is to develop a less unitary vision of the state and contribute with empirical substance to the conception of the state as an arena (Mann 1984). The analysis thus uncovers how the networks of individual state bureaucrats contribute to the development of state power. To this end, it traces the development of these networks, which are difficult to observe, from a perspective that is available to researchers. As in the example of the Baron Rothschild discussed in Chapter 1, when we move to a temporal conception of networks, network approaches are able to capture both structure and agency.

Tracing elite career networks

TABLE 5.1 *Comparison of cases*

Country	Impact of elections	Career heterogeneity
Bulgaria	High	Low
Poland	High	High
Romania	Low	Low

Thus, by observing the same network over time, we can observe the effect that structure has on individual choice within a network.

Summarizing the data presented below, Table 5.1 shows the sharp differences in personnel network development across countries. In the Polish case, networks were conditioned by high uncertainty in the form of frequent changes of the party in power, which led to the regular reshuffling of network ties because individuals were removed from their jobs by an external political shock (this is labeled in the table as the "Impact of elections"). Individuals also tended to move between sectors with a wider range than in the other two countries. As a result, the average individual occupied more positions, and the resulting career network linked many more individuals (this is labeled in the table as "Career heterogeneity").

In Bulgaria, ties were much more homogeneous but slightly more conditioned by political change over time than in Poland. Occupants of elite bureaucratic positions were significantly affected by electoral shocks and forced to switch jobs in post-election years. They also were highly mobile in non-election years. These moves tended to be within the same sector, however. Many simply returned to their pre-election positions once their own political party returned to power. As a result, Bulgarian personnel networks did not develop the same type of breadth as in Poland, and individual careers did not develop to link diverse organizations and sectors.

As a result of these network structures, Bulgaria became the victim of strong societal interests that had close ties to entrenched bureaucrats in key ministries, which is, in fact, a feature often identified to explain the laggardly performance of Bulgaria in building functional market institutions (Ganev 2007). The reasoning that is commonly implied – that networks link the early winners of reform, who colonize the state – is incorrect, however (Hellman 1998; Ganev 2001; Hellman, Jones, and Kaufmann 2003). As previous chapters have shown in other contexts, what differentiates Poland from Bulgaria is not the presence of networks but their structure.

In all three countries, career networks were affected by elections. Electoral turnover is high in Poland and Bulgaria and weak in Romania, however. Thus, if a single quality marks the careers of Romanian state personnel, it is stability. Individuals in Romania change jobs less frequently, and these changes are not affected by electoral outcomes nearly to the extent that is true in the other cases.

Data

The data used here were collected in Bulgaria, Poland, and Romania. I first collected a list of ministers, deputies, secretaries, and undersecretaries in the Ministries of Finance, Economy, Industry and Trade, Interior, and Defense for all governments during the period 1993 to 2003. Subsequently, a database that included the career paths and declared political affiliations of these individuals for the entire period was compiled. For each person, his or her primary or full-time occupation was coded. The Polish data set covers the complete careers of 105 persons from 1993 to 2003, the Bulgarian dataset covers 106 individuals from 1992 to 2003, and the Romanian dataset covers 149 people from 1990 to 2005. Each cell was recoded into one of eighteen possible job categories culled from the whole range of jobs occupied by members of the data set. These categories are: "Ministry of Finance," "Ministry of Economy," "Ministry of

TABLE 5.2 *Coding of data*[3]

Original job category	Data coding
Academic/journalist	Academic/journalist
Business organizations	Business organization
International organization/EU	INGO
Labor unions	Labor union
Ministry of Finance	Ministries
Ministry of Economy	Ministries
Ministry of Industry and Trade	Ministries
Ministry of Interior	Ministries
Ministry of Defense	Ministries
Ministry of Foreign Trade	Ministries
Non-governmental organizations	NGO
Parliament	Parliament
Political party	Party
Private firms	Private business
Other top government positions (Executive Office, staff member at Council of Ministers)	Other state
Diplomatic corps	Other state
Senior military and police officials	Other state
State firms	State business

---

[3] The category "Other state" was distinguished from the four core ministries in order to study specifically the career and recruitment patterns of individuals who served in the ministries that deal with regulation of the economy as well as strategic economic sectors.

Industry and Trade," "Ministry of Interior," "Ministry of Defense," "Ministry of Foreign Trade," "Other top government positions," "Business organizations," "International organization/EU," "Labor unions," "State firms," "Private firms," "NGOs" (non-governmental organizations), "Diplomatic corps," "Senior military and police officials," "Parliament," "Political party," and "Academic/ journalist." These were then recoded according to Table 5.2 into a reduced schema that captures the various sectors of society represented in the data set.

This database details joint membership in groups, parallels and divergences in the paths of individuals, and the potential "reach" that develops as the network becomes more connected. The codes represent the transformations undertaken by the governing elite as they moved between the state bureaucracy, the business sector (state and private), pressure groups in the NGO sector, international organizations, and the media.

COMPARATIVE NETWORK DEVELOPMENT

What macro-patterns can be identified in the data over time, and what differences emerge from a comparison of these three cases? The exploration of the data set described above highlights two dimensions in the configuration of elite career paths: (1) the impact of elections (which captures uncertainty by looking at the degree of mobility – i.e. the frequency of change in jobs); and (2) the range of career destinations (which captures network breadth). Pulling together the degree of mobility and destination range, career paths are a way to materially capture the different relationships between state and economy generated by the interaction of political uncertainty and network breadth.

The impact of elections

The stability of the network over time captures the extent to which individuals sit in their appointed positions. It expresses the amount of mobility or "turbulence" in the macro-social system as people shift across positions – the extent to which the broad system is disrupted. Some countries are generally more turbulent than others because their social systems – in this case the system of professional appointments – are subject to more frequent shifts. There are also some events that are turbulence-inducing. Elections are particularly significant events of this type. In all three cases in this book, elections bring about broad changes in the staffing of high-status jobs, indicating that high-level positions are political. The degree of such shifts varies, however. The job of an individual at any given time can be considered a state, and a career as a sequence of states. Figure 5.1 captures the average number of transitions across states in non-election years and post-election years.

The Romanian career network experiences the lowest number of state transitions per year in the year following an election. Individuals there are also highly unlikely to change jobs in any given year, although their chances of

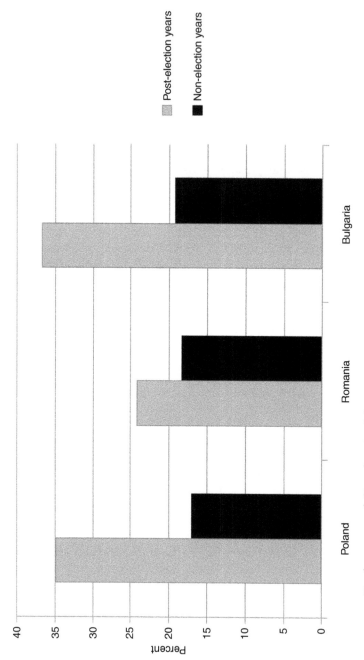

FIGURE 5.1 Yearly average of elites changing jobs
Note: Average percentage of job turnovers per year.

doing so rise in post-election years – as they do in other countries. This result is driven by the changes that took place after the 1996 victory of a broad coalition of parties that first interrupted the Social Democrats' hold on power after 1989. In other periods, the Romanian network experienced much less change. In any given non-election year an average of only 15 percent of individuals in this data set shifted career state.

By contrast, the Bulgarian network was highly turbulent; in any given year nearly a quarter of all individuals shifted jobs. In post-election years more than 35 percent were affected by job changes. Poland is much like Bulgaria: a highly fluid and deeply politicized society in which elite positions in both the public and the private sector are awarded according to political affiliation.

Considering the distribution of different levels of state transition in a population also reveals sharp differences between the cases. One useful measure is sequence entropy.[4] If each individual career is considered a sequence of states, then sequence entropy can be interpreted as the "uncertainty" of predicting the states in a given sequence. Sequence entropy is measured on a normalized scale of 0 to 1. If all states in the sequence are the same over time, the entropy is equal to 0. If every state is different, the value is 1. Values reported here are normalized and comparable across country data sets. The distribution of sequence entropies is shown in Figure 5.2, which presents frequency distributions for levels of sequence entropy in each country.

The variance is striking. Romania has a stable and static social system and is different from the other two cases, which experience a much higher degree of individual mobility. Poland and Bulgaria also differ in the extent to which individuals move, however. In Poland, the general population of elites shifts jobs regularly, with about 60 percent of the sample being highly mobile and transitioning through many jobs over the course of a career. By contrast, Bulgaria's elite tends not to transition through quite as many jobs, and a concentrated group of individuals is much more mobile than the rest of the population, as can be seen in the more bell-shaped distribution of frequencies.

The frequency of shifts reflects the extent to which individuals become entrenched office holders. Whereas, in Poland, no one can afford to be too comfortable in a given post, and this is true across the population in the public and private sectors alike, in Bulgaria only a subset of individuals is affected by the political forces that lead to frequent state transitions. The vast majority in Romania, instead, experience very few state changes. The distribution does indicate that some of those in a political office shift position, but they move on to a new job in which they are likely to become entrenched power holders. The great majority have quite stable careers.

---

[4] Sequence entropy was calculated using TraMineR in R. For more information about sequence entropy, see Gabadinho et al. (2011).

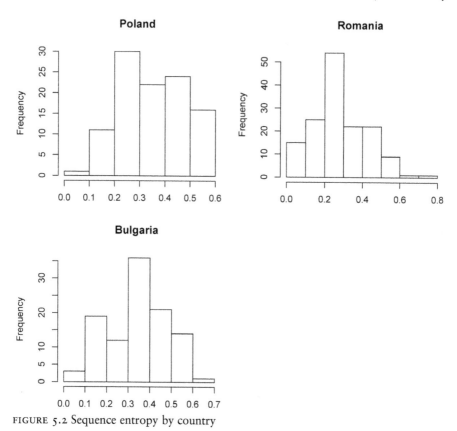
FIGURE 5.2 Sequence entropy by country

The effect of network breadth

The previous dimension captures the extent to which political shocks determine mobility. The analysis confirms that Romania is a country with little mobility, in response to a static political environment, while the elite in Poland is subject to frequent moves. Bulgaria is similar to Poland, although the elite is slightly less mobile.

Another important component for the argument is the extent to which accumulated contacts in any given country give an individual access to a heterogeneous network. In other words, the breadth of networks linking the state and the economy determines the range of opportunities for career shifts. One can imagine that, at every transition, individuals either fan out across the economy to take up positions in other sectors or perhaps return to an organization in which they previously held a job. The first is a more open system, in which individuals enjoy broad access to different types of organization. This produces individuals with diverse contacts, and organizationally benefits an elite that is jointly seeking to solve search and coordination problems. The second is much less open. Individuals move less, and, when they do move, they are less likely to change organizations

Tracing elite career networks

159

or sectors. Instead, they seek or are placed into entrenched positions of power. As an elite system, this second variant is well suited to small groups seeking to address problems of collaboration – behavior that may even be called collusion.

Thus, the analysis now turns to the ties that were formed by individuals changing jobs. A single tie between two organizations means that an individual worked in both and thus provides a human link between them. For example, if a single Romanian bureaucrat worked in the Ministry of Finance and then moved to work in the private business sector, he or she provides a single human pathway between two organizations and two spheres of the social world: the state and the private economy.

The graphics in Figures 5.3 to 5.5 were obtained by comparing the same eleven-year period for each country (1993–2003). The networks are presented in Figures 5.3 for Bulgaria, 5.4 for Poland, and 5.5 for Romania. These images represent the connectedness of the network at the end of the whole period under study. Although the networks pictured here actually represent a three-dimensional web that includes time, the two-dimensional image shows the state of the network at the end of 2003 and includes all of the relations that were formed from the first year of observation, 1993.

Thicker lines mean that more ties are present between two organizational nodes. Hence, the graphs give a cumulative historical impression of the network ties for all individuals in the data set in each country. These images convey information on both network breadth and the degree of mobility (discussed in the previous section). The latter is rendered by the thickness of the lines. Thus, the network graphs depict the relative interconnectedness of different social spheres throughout the period.

Previous analysis showed that, as a consequence of the high degree of political uncertainty, Polish and Bulgarian elites display high mobility, while Romanian elites are more stable. Figure 5.3 shows that, although Bulgaria is a country in which elites shift frequently among jobs, these shifts are limited to a few sectors. The densest ties are among ministries and other top state positions, and between ministries and the private business sector. Parliamentarians, for example, do not often seek or are not often recruited to jobs in the private sector. Business organizations are of little interest as a career destination at all, except for a few individuals, who go no further. The same can be said of labor unions. In all, these three organizational spheres are poorly networked to other social sectors. By contrast, private business is a core origin and destination in the network. In fact, Table 5.3 shows that individuals move most from private business to ministerial positions and, to a lesser extent, from ministerial positions in the core ministries back to other state positions.

In comparison, the Polish network shown in Figure 5.4 is much more broadly connected. This high mobility is spread out but especially focused between state bureaucratic positions, private business, state business, and parliament. This fits with the analysis presented in Chapter 3, which indicated mechanisms of control through personnel appointments in a variety of areas.

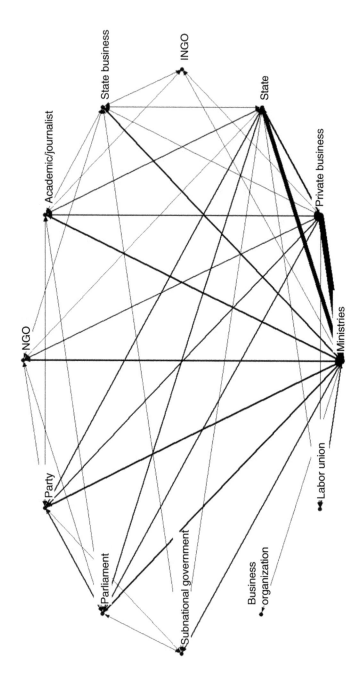

FIGURE 5.3 Bulgarian network of ties between social sectors, 1993–2003
Notes: Thickness of lines indicates density of ties. "Other state" is labeled "State" in order to minimize clutter.

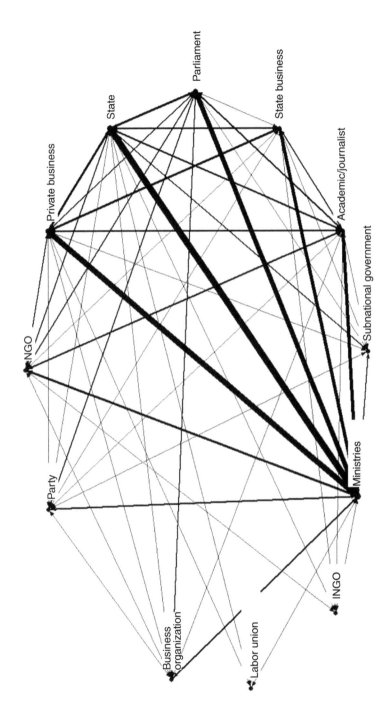

FIGURE 5.4 Polish network of ties between social sectors, 1993–2003.
Notes: Thickness of lines indicates density of ties. "Other state" is labeled "State" in order to minimize clutter.

161

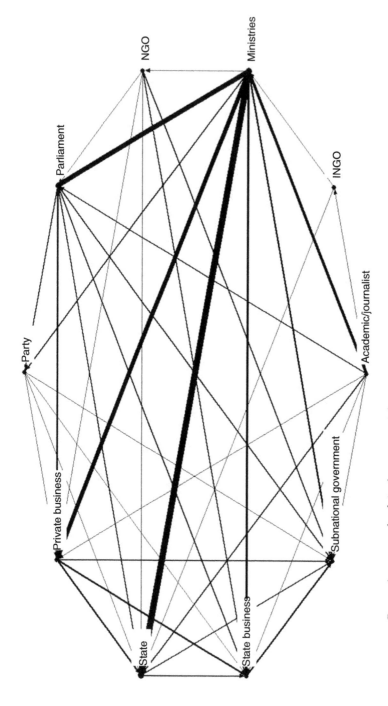

FIGURE 5.5 Romanian network of ties between social sectors, 1993–2003.
Notes: Thickness of lines indicates density of ties. "Other state" is labeled "State" in order to minimize clutter.

Tracing elite career networks

TABLE 5.3 *Most common career transitions*

	Bulgaria (N = 106)	Poland (N = 105)	Romania (N = 149)
1	Private business → ministries (42)	Parliament → ministries (33)	State → ministries (36)
2	Ministries → private business (36)	Ministries → state (21)	Ministries → state (28)
3	Ministries → state (34)	State → ministries (19)	Ministries → parliament (17)
4	State → ministries (18)	Ministries → private business (15)	Parliament → ministries (15)
5	Parliament → ministries (6)	Ministries → parliament (11)	Ministries → private business (11)

Notes: Descending order of frequency. Count in parentheses.

Romania has developed yet a different configuration, as shown in Figure 5.5. State and private business are both far less popular linkages. Further, because the system has a dominant party, the sphere of influence is parliament and bureaucracy rather than the market. This is the fundamental difference between Romania and Bulgaria. Business organizations are peripheral in Bulgaria, somewhat better connected in Poland, and do not appear at all in the Romanian network, meaning that no one who held a ministerial job also held a position in a business organization. This indicates strongly that the institutionalized representation of business is of marginal consequence. The same can be said of labor unions.

In reading these network graphs, it is important to keep in mind that the lack of movement to a sector does not mean that institutions in that social sphere do not play an important role in society. Instead, it indicates that those organizations are not sites that are being contested between elite groupings. For example, NGOs in Bulgaria are probably not an important destination, because many are already politically loyal to a single party and most do not have much influence on policy in Bulgaria. Some NGOs are known to be intermediaries of illegal party finance to political parties, however, and are established by the parties for this purpose. For example, when the UDF gained control of the government in 1997, it began to privatize companies that were performing well to investors allied with their party. These privatizations were allegedly reserved for investors who made donations to party-allied foundations. One such foundation, the Future of Bulgaria, was headed by Elena Kostova, the wife of the then prime minister (*Standart* 2001). Thus, NGOs can be important to elite groupings, but their political nature removes them from the struggle that is captured in these network graphs.

The sequence analysis shown in Table 5.3 confirms and expands on the differences shown in the network graphs by listing the most common transitions. In Bulgaria, the most common transition is between private business and core ministries. This shows the unique relation between private business and the state in Bulgaria. The dominant movement is from the private sector inward to state functions. Whereas Bulgaria is a state colonized by business, Poland is a state penetrated by political parties via parliament. Here, the dominant move is for party functionaries to take on elite state roles. The post-communist transition in Poland could be said to have been a move from a "party state" to a "parties' state." Romania, on the other hand, is an ossified social system in which a set of state elites dominates and has spread to other spheres. While in Bulgaria societal actors move inward to the state, Romanian state elites cycle between bureaucracy and government. The lack of early coherent political competition set up entrenched areas of influence that continue to slow reform progress. Beyond this, the state and the economy are clearly separate spheres, with little sharing of accumulated human capital.

CONCLUSION

The dynamics discussed above coincide with the characterizations of state types – the patronage state (Romania), the captured state (Bulgaria), and the concertation state (Poland) – set out at the beginning of this book. The analyses operationalize and reveal variation in embeddedness, a dimension of state–society relations that frequently figures in arguments about institutional development. The breadth or narrowness of networks – the extent to which distant individuals are connected to each other and have developed ties by working in the same places – structures their ability to engage in collective action.

While Romania is marred by career stability that stems from party dominance, Bulgaria and Poland display a high frequency of job changes, reflecting their turbulent political environments. Poland developed more autonomous institutions with less entrenched interests, however, while Bulgaria became the victim of strong societal interests that had close ties to entrenched bureaucrats in key ministries.

The implication is that we must adjust our understanding of network ties and consider uncertainties such as the role of elections in shaping and disturbing networks and the extent of individual mobility or entrenchment when theorizing about the role that societal actors play in the development of state power. The key lesson of this qualitative and quantitative comparison is that under high uncertainty, when networks are conditioned by political alternation, individuals circulate more often. The emergence of collective action depends on the combination of mobility and the range of career destinations, however. The greater the number of sectors in the public or private spheres, the broader the network of accumulated human capital and the larger the resources to bridge collective action among elites.

PART IV

BRINGING IT TOGETHER

6

Institutional development in new democracies

Network structure and uncertainty shape the incentives of political and economic elites to act collectively in the process of creating new institutions. The two previous chapters each explored the impact of uncertainty. Chapter 4 showed how political uncertainty structures ties between parties and firms. Chapter 5 demonstrated how political uncertainty interacts with network breadth to structure human ties, in the form of career networks, between the state and the economy.

In order to understand the link between networked societies and institutional development, this chapter identifies different forms of state–society relations that have emerged among eleven countries in post-socialist Europe through data that capture the two features identified as critical variables in this study: the breadth of social networks and the level of uncertainty in the political and economic field.

In describing the trajectories toward institutional development taken by the countries in question, I identify the following four types. First, there are the post-communist countries that have developed broad networks among firms and between the economic and political elite and have relatively high levels of uncertainty. These *concertation states* have made the most progress in the development of broadly distributive institutions. Second, countries with narrow networks and low levels of uncertainty have developed *patronage states*. These states have made moderate progress on the development of broad institutions. Third, countries with narrow networks and high levels of uncertainty have developed *captured states*. These countries have made the least progress in the development of broadly distributive institutions. Finally, the fourth category consists of *embedded corporatist states*, which comprise broad networks and low uncertainty. I do not expect to find countries with competitive elections that fit in this category. Rather, the combination of low uncertainty and broad networks describes Asian developmental states (for example, South Korea, as described by Evans 1995).

This chapter confirms the finding that in countries in which dramatic reform and institutional development are taking place simultaneously – as in many

167

emerging market countries and all the post-socialist nations – one tends to observe the emergence of broadly distributive institutions when uncertainty is higher and social networks are broader. This is counterintuitive, and in striking contrast to arguments in economics and political science that strong social networks hamper institutional autonomy, which is instead reinforced by predictable, fast, and early reform (Lipton and Sachs 1990a; Lipton and Sachs 1990b; Sachs 1994; Shleifer and Vishny 1998). Rather, the argument presented here draws on a long tradition in sociology focusing on the advantages of broad networks of weak ties for generating diverse resources (Granovetter 1973), as well as a literature in comparative politics that points to the role of historical struggles, social dislocations, relational ties, and negotiated institutions as the source of autonomous state power (Moore 1967; Mann 1984; Evans 1995; Waldner 1999).

MARKETS AND NETWORKS: EMPIRICAL PUZZLES

This chapter is motivated by an empirical puzzle about networks and uncertainty that undermines traditional explanations and suggests that the alternative spelled out above might have more leverage in explaining the emergence of institutional development. Take the comparison of two countries – the Czech Republic and Albania – at opposite extremes of the European post-socialist experience. The former is one of the success stories of transition, ranked as a regional leader in terms of government effectiveness – defined by the World Bank's "Worldwide governance indicators" as "the quality of public services, the quality of the civil service and the degree of its independence from political pressures, the quality of policy formulation and implementation, and the credibility of the government's commitment to such policies" (Kaufmann, Kraay, and Mastruzzi 2009). Albania, by contrast, has been the basket case of Europe. In both countries, however, firms express the same level of confidence (high) in their ability to find recourse without resorting to illegal payments in a case when an official acts against the rules (EBRD 2005b).

This surprising result raises more questions than it answers and suggests that there are two different dynamics generating the certainty of recourse, which likely does not have the same significance in both countries. As survey data show in the coming pages, two different orders frame and support market activity and the development of market institutions in these two countries, and we do not have a satisfying account of this process.

Albania and Poland provide another interesting contrast. Poland also ranked among the top regional countries for government effectivness in the late 1990s and 2000s.[1] Yet, in Albania, firms find interpretations of the law more

---

[1] Poland's ranking for governance effectiveness declined somewhat with the entrance of a new set of political parties that governed in a chaotic fashion.

Institutional development in new democracies 169

consistent and predictable. In fact, on average, they express the highest level of confidence in the sample. Most firms in Poland find them inconsistent and unpredictable (EBRD 2005b). This comparison suggests that the level of institutional performance varies significantly across the region and is not directly linked to the traditional indicators of quality of governance, such as levels of corruption.

In a further example, one of the basic components of a market economy – lending – shows an unexpected difference and dynamic in the last pair of countries. Albanian banks carry half as many non-performing loans on their balance sheets as (often partly party-owned) Polish banks, despite lending approximately the same percentage of GDP. This may be because Polish banks undertake more risky lending based on network ties. In fact, Polish firms use network sources of finance as a key source of investment capital, according to BEEPs (EBRD 2005b).

These cases could not be more different in most dimensions, and thus they make clear that there is good reason to revisit assumptions about the mechanisms that link networks and network-based practices, uncertainty, and institutional development in order to understand the divergence we now see across the region.

All the comparisons above highlight the different foundations on which interactions between firms and the state are structured. As discussed in the Introduction, the early literature on institutional reform in post-socialist states identified a core set of desirable features in this relationship. One key feature was an emphasis on the sociological dimensions of the Washington Consensus: disruption of network ties and state autonomy. These were critical components of the move toward privatization, liberalization, deregulation, fiscal discipline, and the withdrawal of subsidy spending associated with planned or coordinated market economies. Scholarship on corruption also broadly supported convergence on a set of institutions associated with market liberalism.[2] Deviations from these goals, it was argued, generated pathologies of reform (Hellman 1998; Hellman, Jones, and Kaufmann 2003). Arguments in these literatures became heavily politicized and came to reflect dominant positions in the debate on the Washington Consensus package of reforms.[3] Along the way, much of the complexity of models of economic development emerging in the post-socialist region was lost.

This chapter shows that a variety of novel solutions to the fundamental problem of economic transition have emerged in each of the eleven countries surveyed. In some countries firms and politicians turned to networks, while in others they individually turned to the state. For example, medium and large

---

[2] The literature here is vast. Some prominent exponents of this view are Rose-Ackerman (1999), Shleifer and Vishny (2002), and Holmes (2006).

[3] Authors have noted this in other regions of the world as well. See, for example, Serra and Stiglitz (2008).

firms use network ties to existing customers as the leading source of new business in Poland, while the government primarily performs this function in Hungary (EBRD 2005b). Although horizontal network ties support business in the former, vertical ties do so in the latter.

I have identified two key features in previous chapters that broadly distinguish countries: network breadth and uncertainty. I categorize state types by the combination of these two dimensions. Each possible pairing shapes the payoffs of making long-term investments in building institutions. As a result, each combination generates a different state type. The next section empirically explores this typology, and the final section shows that each state type has an impact on the institutional development that takes place.

DATA AND METHODS

The analysis of state types is based on two factors: (1) the extent to which networks that link the state and the market are narrow or broad; and (2) the extent to which the future is uncertain for economic and political actors. These are latent qualities, however, that can be accessed only by using data that function as manifestations of broader characteristics in each national system (Shawn and Simon 2008). To capture these latent qualities, one must construct country-level measures based on more concrete manifestations. Two key methods, factor analysis and cluster analysis, are available to build measures that capture the latent qualities of countries on the basis of sets of more directly measureable variables. Factor analysis is useful in generating latent measures out of similar variables, assembling them into a single new variable. Cluster analysis is deployed here because it captures latent similarity among cases. In other words, it accomplishes exactly what is called for by assembling similar groups of cases based on a set of variables that describe them. These cases share a latent characteristic that emerges from the mosaic of values on the underlying variables (Aldenderfer and Blashfield 1984; Kaufman and Rousseeuw 1990). Cluster analysis thus permits the identification of groups of cases based on the values that together express the level of uncertainty and the breadth of social networks in each case.

The breadth of networks and uncertainty are explored in this chapter by the use of data from the survey conducted by the EBRD in 2005 (EBRD 2005b). Numerous data sources provide insight into the nature of state–business interaction and reflect the level of cooperation, accountability, stability, and predictability of this relationship. Such indicators are not without flaws, however. For example, surveys whose purpose is to study state capture more easily detect administrative corruption, because respondents have much more contact with low-level corruption than high-level capture and tend to infer the presence of the latter from the former (Knack 2006). Despite such drawbacks, firms are a leading source of information on government political and bureaucratic conduct, and the survey responses they provide offer hard evidence about the

Institutional development in new democracies

nature of interaction with the state. The indicators used also report on the ability of firms to resist and cooperate with both low-level decision makers and high-level political actors on an everyday basis.

Using cluster analysis on social linkage indicators and on levels of uncertainty, state types can be created to group countries that are most similar. There are many variants of clustering methods, which use different procedures to join cases into groups. The two most commonly applied methods, hierarchical and k-means cluster analysis, generate similar results for the data used here. Three robust groups of countries emerge. One of the countries, Albania, is an outlier on many measures. The analysis was conducted both with and without Albania to confirm that the pull of its extreme values did not affecting the clustering solutions.

Cluster analysis requires the scholar to make a decision about the clustering method and the distance measurement used to assess similarity between cases. The scaling of variables has been thought to influence clustering outcomes by giving more weight to variables with larger scales, while some have found that standardization does not affect results in most cases (Aldenderfer and Blashfield 1984). All analyses were performed with variables standardized to z-scores to neutralize any effect that different scales may have and compared to results on unstandardized variables. Cluster assignments remained robust.

VARIABLES

In the pages that follow, results are reported from clustering cases using questions that measure network breadth and uncertainty. The analysis was conducted with questions from the 2005 BEEPS data (EBRD 2005b) that reveal the importance of networks to firm interactions with political actors. Although the questions ask about individual firm perceptions and behavior, aggregated they reveal the role that networks play in firm interactions in a given country. The following variables were created.

- SUPP, a variable that captures the stability of firm–firm networks. The question asks if firms would continue to use a supplier despite a significant price rise. I interpret persistent customer–supplier ties despite a price increase to mean that economic relationships between firms exist in the context of other types of ties that bind firms to each other. The extent to which firms choose not to switch suppliers in spite of economic motivations (rising cost) reveals the degree to which firm–firm networks underpin economic activity. Higher values indicate that firm–firm networks are broader.
- NETFIN, a variable that expresses the extent to which firms obtain working capital from network sources (informal sources, friends, state-owned banks, credit from customers, and credit from suppliers) as opposed to market sources (foreign banks, private banks, and equity markets). Higher values indicate broader networks.

- BUSORG, a variable that captures the extent to which business organizations are valuable in lobbying business. High values indicate that more firms use collective bodies for interest expression. In other words, networks between firms are broader.

A second set of indicators was developed to assess the uncertainty that firms and parties face. For this analysis, the following variables were used.

- COMPET, a variable that expresses the number of competitors firms face in the national market. Higher values indicate high levels of competition, and thus uncertainty in the market.
- TAXINS, a variable that captures the frequency of annual inspections by the tax authority and thus another element of uncertainty that firms face. Higher levels indicate frequent inspections.
- IDTURN, a variable that captures the extent to which ideological turnovers, as opposed to simply leadership turnover, of the party in power are a source of institutional uncertainty for firms (Horowitz, Hoff, and Milanovic 2009). Ideological turnovers are turnovers across the ideological divide. Higher values indicate more frequent turnover. The choice of ideological turnover is discussed in Chapter 1. Briefly, ideological turnover captures the number of political events that disrupt the networks linking firms to power holders.

Three groupings of countries emerge when these variables are clustered together.[4] Cluster centers are reported in Table 6.1. These are interpreted as the mean score of a value for a cluster on a given variable. Traditional significance tests are not available or appropriate for cluster analysis, as the analysis itself is designed to find the most significant cluster possible (Aldenderfer and Blashfield 1984; Everitt, Landau, and Leese 2011).

Cluster analysis differentiates the way that networks and uncertainty are present to create three groupings. Cluster 1, the grouping of concertation states, is marked by broad networks and high levels of uncertainty. In these countries, firm–firm networks are very stable. This is shown by the above-average use of business organizations and the persistence of customer–supplier networks independent of price levels. On both these variables, cluster 1 has the highest relative values. Firms also make frequent use of network sources of finance. When disaggregated, the data show that firms in cluster 1 make frequent use of informal sources of finance, supplier credit, and state-owned banks. While networks between

---

[4] Multiple cluster solutions were explored. The explanatory power of a three-cluster solution was confirmed by referring to pseudo-F values, which capture the increase or decrease in fit of 1 to n-cluster solutions.

Institutional development in new democracies

TABLE 6.1 *Networks and uncertainty in the Baltics, east central Europe, and the Balkans*

	Cluster		
	1. Concertation states (Hungary, Lithuania, Poland)	2. Patronage states (Czech Republic, Estonia, Latvia, Romania, Slovak Republic, Slovenia)	3. Captured states (Albania, Bulgaria)
SUPP	0.96	−0.25	0.02
NETFIN	0.12	0.09	1.14
BUSORG	0.90	−0.21	−1.51
COMPET	0.96	−0.22	0.27
TAXINS	0.10	−0.48	2.62
IDTURN	0.79	−0.60	1.10

Note: Final cluster center scores.
Source: BEEPS (EBRD 2005b).

firms as well as ties to the state typify these economies, business exists in an environment of uncertainty, with high competition between firms and frequent political alternation.

In cluster 2, patronage states, firms have narrow networks and face low levels of uncertainty. They do not use collective organizations, and horizontal ties between them are unstable. Customer–supplier relations are sensitive to price. Network sources of finance are still used by firms, but not as frequently as in cluster 1. Political alternation is also relatively low, and the level of competition between firms is the lowest of the three clusters.

Firms in cluster 3, captured states, have narrow networks and face high levels of uncertainty. The use of collective organizations by firms is low relative to the other clusters, and customer–supplier ties are more sensitive to price than in cluster 1. The exception to this is that network sources of finance are quite commonly used. Disaggregating reveals that firms, particularly in Bulgaria, rely on "family and friends" as sources of capital. Since I consider only medium- and large-sized firms, I interpret this as meaning allied firms and their executives. Supplier credit is also common. These narrow networks coincide with high levels of uncertainty. High political turnover and frequent tax inspections suggest a state that is weak, chaotic, and predatory. In contrast to cluster 1, this uncertainty does not extend to inter-firm competition, which is significantly lower.

The two dimensions in the cluster analysis can be reformatted into the typology proposed in Table 1.1. The resulting classification is shown in Table 6.2.

174 *Bringing It Together*

TABLE 6.2 *Networks, uncertainty, and state types*

		Uncertainty	
		Low	High
Network structure	Narrow	*Patronage states* Czech Republic, Estonia, Latvia, Slovak Republic, Slovenia, Romania	*Captured states* Albania, Bulgaria
	Broad	*Embedded corporatist*	*Concertation states* Hungary, Lithuania, Poland

The analysis groups cases together on political uncertainty that are not normally considered similar, but this follows from the data used here. Uncertainty is composed of three individual components: the level of competition from other firms, the level of intrusion from the state, and the unpredictability of politics. The latter was captured using data on ideological turnovers for each country. Lithuania is thus classified as a case with high uncertainty because it had four ideological turnovers between 1990 and 2005, according to Horowitz, Hoff, and Milanovic (2009). This is the highest number for the region, achieved only by two other countries: Bulgaria and Hungary. Poland trailed slightly, with three ideological turnovers. By contrast, Latvia had only one ideological turnover, although it had three government turnovers (recompositions of the governing coalition). These were episodes when the majority coalition changed but did not shift across the ideological divide. While Latvia is an example of a country known for government instability, these changes did not take place across the ideological divide. As regards ideological turnover, Latvia has instead been very stable despite frequent recompositions of government. The distinction is important, because we expect changes in government to have a different and arguably less disruptive effect than ideological shifts of power (Horowitz, Hoff, and Milanovic 2009: 121).

IMPACTS ON GOVERNANCE

This section shows how different combinations of network breadth and uncertainty pair with patterns of institution building. Thus, it becomes possible to determine whether, for example, societies in which firms are linked by broad networks but also face higher levels of uncertainty tend to progress to broader institutional development than those in which networks are narrow and uncertainty is high.

Institutional development in new democracies　　　　　　　　175

External factors have driven some countries in the post-communist region to move ahead on institutional reform in specific areas. Given the external pressure for reform and liberalization related to European Union accession, according to the EBRD, trade and foreign exchange liberalization are at high levels across the region. Nevertheless, there are significant differences between the clusters. Averages across six policy areas – enterprise restructuring, price liberalization, trade and foreign exchange policy, competition policy, banking reform and interest rate liberalization, and securities market and non-bank financial institution reform – show that the three clusters have performed as expected.

The following graphs of outcome variables show only small numerical differences between clusters. The differences between whole numbers in the EBRD scoring scheme represent big outcome differences, however. The EBRD's scoring system rates countries on different policy areas on a scale ranging from 1 to 4+. With minor differences between the policy areas, a 1 indicates little progress from a planned economy or an absence of policy in a given area. A 2 indicates the existence of some institutions, while a 3 indicates "some progress" in the development of a regulatory framework. A 4 means that the policy framework approaches Western standards, while a 4+ indicates a framework on the level of advanced industrial countries. The difference between a 2 and a 4 is therefore enormous. Figure 6.1 shows that captured states have made the least progress. Patron states are also in the same general category of reform, although they have made slightly more progress. Concertation states are in the highest category. The large difference between the concertation and captured cluster, for example, indicates a sizeable gap between the quality and implementation of policy frameworks in countries belonging to the two clusters.

The clusters vary especially when compared on areas of policy that are largely determined by factions. For example, institutional reforms that regulate the internal market framework and are more easily subject to pressure from interest groups display more variance, and countries from the same wave of EU integration, such as Poland, Hungary, and the Czech Republic, or Romania and Bulgaria, score differently from each other. This is consistent with the literature on the impact of EU expansion discussed in Chapter 1.

Competition policy

One major indicator that can be used to judge the impact of firms on the state is the progress that a country has made on competition policy. Competition policy and the structures that enforce it by definition harm the interests of insiders, so the development of a competent body that monitors and

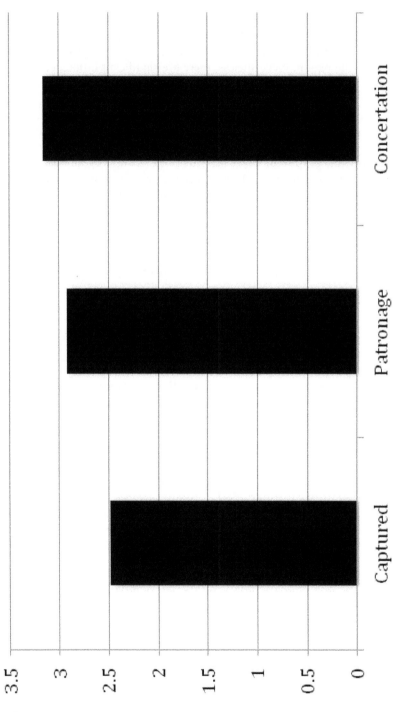

FIGURE 6.1 Progress on six major policy areas, 1990–2005
Source: EBRD "Transition indicators."

Institutional development in new democracies

enforces such policies requires the support of a broad coalition of firms. The EBRD "Transition indicators" provide a comparative measure of progress on competition policy. There is a range of outcomes across the typology presented in Figure 6.2. As predicted above, where networks are strong and uncertainty is highest – the concertation states – progress on competition policy is greatest. Differences across full integers represent large differences in outcome.[5]

Recapitulating the mechanisms at work here, the enforcement of competition policy is taken as a result of the struggles of diverse groups to create an institution that "levels the playing field." Thus, competition policy is also a good indicator of the distribution of the power of groups. Where progress is made, competing factions have brokered a structure to make sure that all parties stick to the rules of the market and abide by whatever joint conception of fair competitive practices obtain in a given context. Where such structures are lacking, one group of insiders is likely to dominate and block the development of competition enforcement. These results are in line with the argument that concertation states, with broad networks and high levels of uncertainty stemming from a rapid development of institutions and frequent political turnovers, have competing factions of business elites who gradually recognize the benefits of an enforcement authority that reduces selective benefits. By contrast, in patronage states, there are much weaker incentives to build such leveling institutions. Captured states have the weakest incentives for collective action. In Bulgaria, when the business community attempted to coordinate and create an institutional infrastructure that would provide stability for repeated interactions, the attempts repeatedly broke down as calculations about future political counterparts became difficult to make and dominant firms were unable to look beyond their very short time horizons.

---

[5] Competition policy reform is scored by the EBRD as follows.

1	No competition legislation and institutions.
2	Competition policy legislation and institutions set up; some reduction of entry restrictions or enforcement action on dominant firms.
3	Some enforcement actions to reduce abuse of market power and to promote a competitive environment, including break-ups of dominant conglomerates; substantial reduction of entry restrictions.
4	Significant enforcement actions to reduce abuse of market power and to promote a competitive environment.
4+	Standards and performance typical of advanced industrial economies: effective enforcement of competition policy; unrestricted entry to most markets.

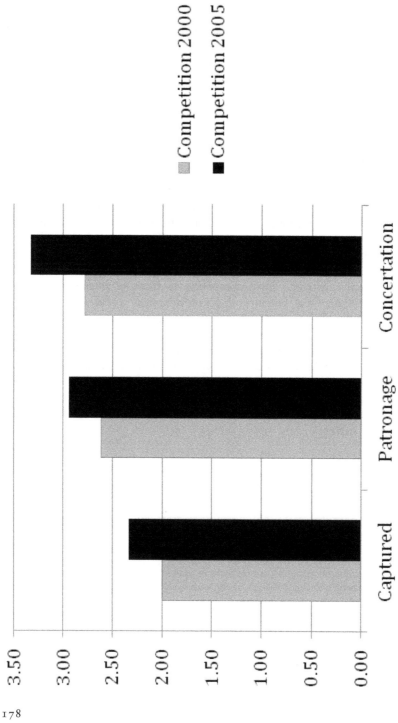

FIGURE 6.2 Competition policy, 2000–2005
Source: EBRD "Transition indicators."

Institutional development in new democracies   179

Financial institutions and secured transactions policy

As seen in Figure 6.3, securities market and non-bank financial institution reform shows similar divergence in the amount of reform undertaken.[6] The ability to regulate securities transactions and safeguard the rights of minority shareholders is a critical component of sophisticated markets, giving firms the ability to raise capital and reassuring shareholders that their interests will be protected. Thus, this is another variable that measures the extent to which the framework benefits the interests of broad versus narrow coalitions. Although standards in the region fall below the level of advanced industrialized countries, in the case of concertation states we see a development of institutions that protect minority shareholder rights, settlement procedures, and a regulatory framework.

Banking

Differences are also to be found in banking law, although they are narrower than in the two prior areas, as shown in Figure 6.4.[7] Again, concertation states lead in the area of banking reform.

---

[6] Securities market and non-bank financial institution reform is scored by the EBRD as follows.

1	Little progress.
2	Formation of securities exchanges, market-makers and brokers; some trading in government paper and/or securities; rudimentary legal and regulatory framework for the issuance and trading of securities.
3	Substantial issuance of securities by private enterprises; establishment of independent share registries, secure clearance and settlement procedures, and some protection of minority shareholders; emergence of non-bank financial institutions (for example, investment funds, private insurance and pension funds, leasing companies) and associated regulatory framework.
4	Securities laws and regulations approaching IOSCO [International Organization of Securities Commissions] standards; substantial market liquidity and capitalisation; well-functioning non-bank financial institutions and effective regulation.
4+	Standards and performance norms of advanced industrial economies: full convergence of securities laws and regulations with IOSCO standards; fully developed non-bank intermediation.

---

[7] Banking regulation reform is scored by the EBRD as follows.

1	Little progress beyond establishment of a two-tier system.
2	Significant liberalisation of interest rates and credit allocation; limited use of directed credit or interest rate ceilings.
3	Substantial progress in establishment of bank solvency and of a framework for prudential supervision and regulation; full interest rate liberalisation with little preferential access to cheap refinancing; significant lending to private enterprises and significant presence of private banks.
4	Significant movement of banking laws and regulations towards BIS [Bank for International Settlements] standards; well-functioning banking competition and effective prudential supervision; significant term lending to private enterprises; substantial financial deepening.
4+	Standards and performance norms of advanced industrial economies: full convergence of banking laws and regulations with BIS standards; provision of full set of competitive banking services.

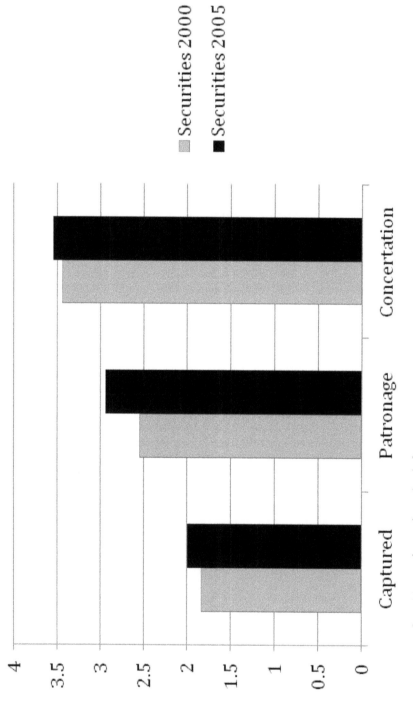

FIGURE 6.3 Securities market and non-bank financial institution reform, 2000–2005
Source: EBRD "Transition indicators."

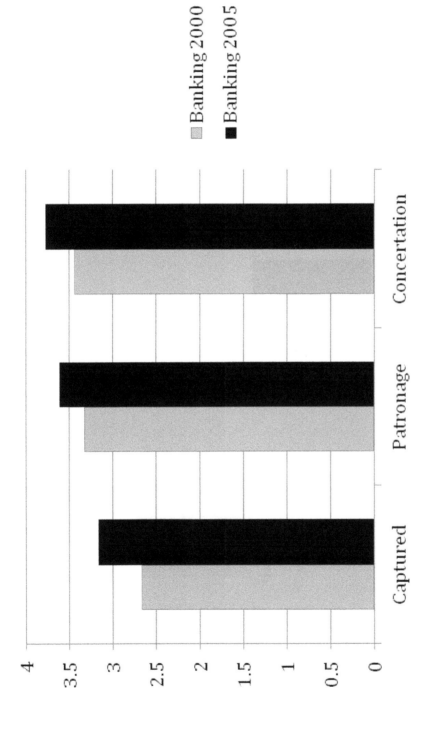

FIGURE 6.4 Banking regulation reform, 2000–2005
Source: EBRD "Transition indicators."

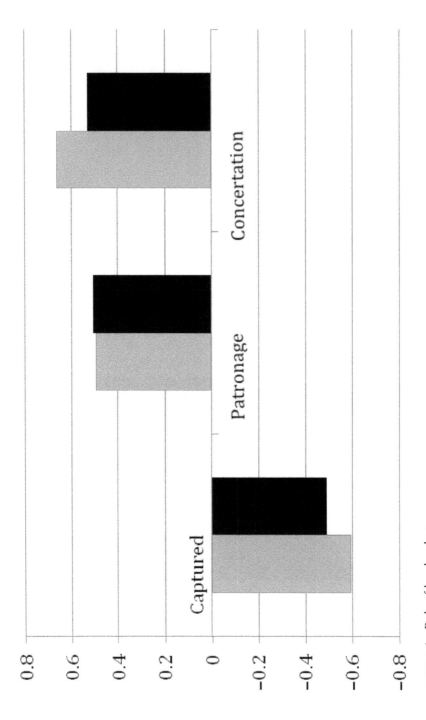

FIGURE 6.5 Rule of law by cluster
Source: World Bank "Worldwide governance indicators."

Institutional development in new democracies

Rule of law

A final broad measure that sustains the findings of this chapter is drawn from the World Bank "Worldwide governance indicators" of the rule of law, as shown in Figure 6.5. This indicator expresses the extent to which the rule of law is applied equally to all affected parties, ranging from −2.5 to 2.5. It captures the extent to which "agents have confidence in and abide by the rules of society, and in particular the quality of contract enforcement, property rights, the police, and the courts, as well as the likelihood of crime and violence" (Kaufmann, Kraay, and Mastruzzi 2009). This is a composite measure that also includes factors such as trust in the police that are not relevant here. Nevertheless, quite a few of the components of the rule of law indicator give a sense of the selective or broad nature of institutions emerging in each cluster.

Concertation states were significantly more advanced on this measure after a decade of reform but had lost ground by 2005. Poland and Hungary both received weaker scores in the latter year, driving down the result for the whole cluster. As a result, the difference between the concertation states cluster and the patronage states cluster is not likely to be significant by the end of the period. This raises an interesting question about why patronage states have done surprisingly well on the development of the rule of law. One possible explanation is that patronage states may have reasons to develop the rule of law despite the disproportionate power of political actors because the political elite still depend on firms to generate revenue and thus have some incentives to provide an institutional framework that can support market activity. I discuss this further in the conclusion. Captured states trail dramatically on this indicator.

CONCLUSION

This chapter grouped together post-communist countries on the basis of two characteristics: (1) the extent to which networks are narrow insider networks or broad heterogeneous networks; and (2) the predictability of the environment in which firms operate. Four groups were posited and countries then placed into a typology that expressed variation along these dimensions. Once clusters were identified, it was demonstrated that membership in a cluster has significant and, in the case of several clusters, unexpected impacts.

Three principal findings emerge from the large-n analysis. First, unsurprisingly, captured states have performed poorly in the development of institutions that serve the broad interest. Narrow societal networks and high levels of uncertainty have given narrow groupings the ability to influence the course of institutional development.

With regard to patronage states, one might expect them to perform as poorly as captured states. The second finding of the large-n analysis is that patronage states fall between captured and concertation states on measures of institutional development. On some dimensions, such as the development of the rule of law, they perform as well as concertation states by the end of the period under observation. They also fall between captured and concertation states in the development of competition policy and securities market regulation, however. How can we interpret this result? In patronage states, political elites are able to dominate economic elites because of narrow networks and low levels of uncertainty. Nevertheless, political elites in patronage states have an interest in institutional development because they rely on funds extracted from business. Patrons are both grantors of benefits and extractors of resources. To this end, institutional development is useful for promoting business performance. As outlined by Greif, Milgrom, and Weingast (1994), rulers must tie their own hands with institutionalized procedures to be able to extract resources effectively. Patronage states have undertaken some institutional development in order to facilitate economic development because they rely on business for resources. This impetus for institutional performance is not as great as in the concertation states, however, because of the lower level of party competition and the narrowness of business networks. The third finding, which supports the argument made in earlier chapters, is that the combination of high uncertainty and broad networks correlates strongly with countries that have the highest levels of institutional development of the three clusters identified in the analysis.

7

Conclusion: political varieties of capitalism in emerging markets

What was hailed as a transition to democracy and markets over twenty years ago has turned out to be a long and arduous struggle on the path to develop effective institutions that can support economic development. This book began by observing that, after two decades of reform and two waves of European integration, a surprising diversity of relationships between economic and political actors is still evident in the post-communist world. Notably, countries such as Poland, which have been among the leaders of institutional development and economic growth, also display dense ties between the economy and the polity, while countries such as Romania and Bulgaria do not. The early literature on post-socialist reform viewed such ties between the polity and the economy as the source of poor progress on institutional development because powerful insiders hijacked reform agendas. I have observed a number of cases, however, in which the opposite seemed to be true. Armed with this puzzle, I set out to understand the conditions under which networks could support institutional development. At the core of this analysis is a desire to understand the conditions under which political and economic elites are able to use networks to act collectively.

A literature on the economic growth miracle that took place in east Asia in the 1990s offered tools to explore the role that networks play in structuring the choices that elites make. Scholarship on the developmental state in east Asia focused precisely on the powerful role that embeddedness played in helping political elites cooperate with business leaders, resulting in rapid growth. The case studies were mostly non-democratic countries, however, and the outcomes seemed heavily dependent on a special set of cultural circumstances and international political economy pressures. With few exceptions (Kang 2002), the east Asian "tigers" were seen as having internal cultural characteristics and external security pressures that made embedded elites work together and limited the abuse of embedded ties. These limiting factors were not present in post-socialism.

186   *Bringing It Together*

In contrast, one powerful limiting factor present in the transition countries was the extent of political uncertainty related to democratic elections. All the cases investigated here had regular electoral contests but different levels of competition. As culture and the international pressures of the post-war international system were the exogenous factor that limited pernicious collaboration in east Asia, so political uncertainty served as the factor that conditioned how networks were used in post-socialism.

I thus explored how the structure of network ties between the polity and the economy, together with the level of uncertainty, affect the ability of elites to engage in collective action. Different combinations of these two variables shape the incentives of political and economic elites to cooperate, resulting in different and specific patterns of institutional development. The pages that follow review the findings and discuss the implications of this argument for countries undergoing large-scale economic transformations.

THE IMPACT OF NETWORKS AND UNCERTAINTY

I argue that the different combinations of the structure of networks and the level of uncertainty determine the path of collective action that political and economic elites take. This shapes the trajectory of institutional development. Where narrow networks are combined with high levels of uncertainty, economic actors have the upper hand against political elites. Because economic elites have few incentives to forge long-term bargains with political elites, these countries have made very poor progress on institutional development. I label these *captured states*.

In *patronage states*, narrow networks and low levels of uncertainty allow political elites to dominate atomized economic actors. Similarly, few incentives exist for institutional development, as economic actors are poorly coordinated, and political actors do not need to be responsive to their demands.

Finally, in *concertation states*, broad networks link economic and political actors and lead them to take a long view in economic exchange. As a result, they create rules of the game that are broadly distributive.

FINDINGS

Key finding I: different network structures emerged across post-socialism

Through a survey of firm network structure and a comparison of firm networks in Bulgaria, Romania, and Poland, I have shown that different network structures emerged across the post-socialist world. Taking just the comparison of Poland, Romania, and Bulgaria, different owner types emerged as the organizing poles in each economy, as a result of the varying approaches to transformation outlined in Chapter 3. The Polish network of firms was

Political varieties of capitalism in emerging markets

structured by the key role of banks, which came to own large numbers of firms through debt-to-equity swaps that were common during the early phase of transition. This resulted in a broad network with many ties between firms. The largest firms in both Romania and Bulgaria were, instead, organized around industrial firms and individual investors, creating much narrower networks.

Elite networks also took on different structures. In Poland, individuals shifted jobs often and between more sectors than did individuals in Romania. Although Bulgarians also shifted jobs often, they tended to have less diverse careers. As a result, the latter two cases had much narrower career networks.

Key finding II: broad networks raise the likelihood of collective action

Broader networks that include more heterogeneous agents also raise the incidence of collective action among firms. Instead of lobbying for themselves using insider channels, firms in countries in which networks broadly linked them were more likely to use business associations for political ends. In turn, in most cases they were also less likely to use private channels to parties or bureaucrats.

Key finding III: broad networks combined with high uncertainty improve institutional development

Where networks were broad and uncertainty was high, greater progress was made in institutional development. More progress was made in the reform of banking law. The development of competition policy and an authority that could monitor it also progressed much further. Finally, measures of the rule of law showed higher levels of performance. The development of institutions for the oversight of party finance – another particularly sensitive area of regulatory development – also developed further. On this last measure, none of the three, Poland, Romania, or Bulgaria, approaches an ideal level of oversight that would render it free of illicit activity. Poland made greater advances than the other two countries, however. Institutions of oversight were created when all three faced tremendous external pressure from the European Union to reduce levels of corruption. Yet Poland developed the most functional system. The empirical findings are summarized in Table 7.1.

The differing role of institutions of collective action described in Chapter 2, the varying role of inter-firm ties discussed in Chapter 3, the different combinations of uncertainty and network structure discussed in Chapter 4, and the stark differences in career patterns across countries described in Chapter 5 are all features of three distinct trajectories of institutional development that have emerged out of the rapidly developing market economies of post-socialist Europe. These three forms are the captured, patronage, and concertation states. Each of these orders is supported by a series of complementary institutions that emerged as solutions to the problem of uncertainty that business elites and politicians faced over the period of the transformation.

188   *Bringing It Together*

TABLE 7.1 *Summary of findings*

Chapter	Findings
Chapter 2	Ownership networks that are broad and include heterogeneous agents increase the incidence of business collective action.
Chapter 3	Ownership networks have developed around different types of firms, and inter-firm ties create networks of sharply varying breadth.

		Bulgaria	Poland	Romania
	Network breadth	Narrow inter-firm networks	Broad inter-firm networks	Narrow inter-firm networks
	Dominant owner	Industrial firms	Financial firms	Industrial firms

Chapter	Findings
Chapter 4	Party finance: stable firm–party alliances emerge when parties can make credible commitments to electoral bargains. Broad networks and high uncertainty make political parties accountable to electoral deals through monitoring and electoral competition. Narrow networks and low uncertainty weaken monitoring and the electoral mechanism. Narrow networks and high uncertainty make the future uncalculable, lowering the likelihood of credible commitments.

	Bulgaria	Poland	Romania
	Weak party–firm alliances	Strong party–firm alliances	Weak party–firm alliances

Chapter	Findings
Chapter 5	Elite career networks: political uncertainty promotes mobility as elites are replaced after alternation in government. Network breadth determines the range of placements. The combination of these two factors determines the type of elite career paths and explains variance in the emergence of elite cooperation.

	Bulgaria	Poland	Romania
Career mobility	High	High	Low
Career heterogeneity	Low	High	Low

Chapter	Findings
Chapter 6	Country clusters perform differently on measures of institutional development. Concertation states have made the most progress on institutional reform. Captured states have made the least progress. Patronage states exhibit moderate progress.

BROADER IMPLICATIONS

What insights and broader conclusions can be derived from the findings of this book? One goal of the book has been to shed light on the process of post-communist development and the critical role of both networks and democratic competition in it. One of the key lessons of the post-communist transformation is that networks provide a vital resource to economic and political actors during periods of rapid change. These networks can be utilized in a variety of ways depending on their structure and the constraints placed on them, however. As scholars such as Kang (2002) have pointed out in the context of non-democratic east Asian states, how ties between political and economic elites are put to use depends on the limitations facing these elites. If the arguments made in the preceding pages are convincing, then the central policy implications are to promote orderly political competition and support the development of networks both within the economy and between the state and business actors. The cases examined here illustrate the consequences of weak competition and sparse networks that took hold in some countries. Consequently, one wonders about the future for both the desirable and less desirable paths. Of particular concern is the question of the stability of the three paths – concertation, patronage, and captured states – identified here after the period 1990–2005 that is covered in this book. For the paths that generate poor outcomes of institutional development – captured and patronage – it is particularly important to ascertain if states eventually emerge from them, even if they do so slowly. It would also be useful, however, to ascertain if the networks that link parties and business in concertation states eventually give way to stable and "hardened" institutions. Is it the case that this arrangement, while important during the early phase of development and high levels of uncertainty, is displaced by more formal structures? Or do networks continue to play a role even when functioning institutions have emerged?

These questions can be considered in two different ways. First, we can examine changes that have taken place in the case studies after 2005, the end point of both the data and the case study research conducted for this book. Second, we can examine cases in other regions that might shed light on possible future developments.

Regional changes

Changes in the party system are one way that shifts out of a particular party–business alignment might come about. It is also possible that party system development will bring about a breakdown altogether of the network-based dynamic. Of particular concern are the concertation states, in which, I have argued, stable party–economy ties have supported post-communist development. It is worth considering how Poland has been affected by changes in the party system that began in 2005. At that time the dominant social division in post-socialist Poland began to shift from an anti-communist/post-communist cleavage to a new division between those who have benefited from reform and those left behind. This shift brought the end of the left SLD and post-Solidarity coalition AWS and their seeming replacement" with two new main center-right parties and a host of smaller partners.

It would be reasonable to expect that such a shift in the party system would have unsettled the dynamic that existed until 2005. This unsettling could result from the scrambling of existing networks linking politicians to business leaders, or from the nature of political competition having shifted. Both seemed likely with the emergence of the Law and Justice party (PiS), which formed a minority coalition government that lasted until 2007, and vocally attacked the business elite, called for an end to the Polish oligarchy's influence, and pledged to move the country into a "Fourth Republic" free of the corruption and cronyism of the post-communist period (Markowski 2008: 1056). Early elections in 2007 brought yet another new party, Civic Action (PO), to power. PO instead presented itself as an economically liberal party with conservative positions on social issues, and governed in coalition with the Polish Peasant Party. At the time of this writing, the PO–PSL coalition is still in power, having been returned to power in 2011.

Based on the election of 2007, Gwiazda (2009) argues that we may finally be seeing the settling of the party system. This remains a minority view, however, and others continue to view the system as unsettled. Szczerbiak (2012), for example, sees the first re-election of an incumbent government, in 2011, as a potential sign of stabilization, but points to the strong performance of a new anti-clerical liberal party, Palikot's Movement, as a sign of continued instability. Most scholars continue to classify Poland as a weakly institutionalized party system with high levels of volatility, poor party discipline, and high fractionalization (Lewis 2006; Markowski 2008). There is, consequently, no reason to believe that the level of political uncertainty has declined. On the other hand, Shabad and Slomczynski (2002) argue that Poland is in the process of developing career politicians, which would reinforce networks despite the emergence of new political parties.

There is little recent research on the connection of Polish political parties with the economy in the period after 2005. Despite the changes in the party system, available sources suggest that the ties between the state and the economy continue. Gwiazda (2008) finds that, following the emergence of new party organizations, party patronage is as extensive after the shift as it was before 2005. Specifically, she finds that PiS, elected on a strong anti-corruption platform, "was relentlessly involved in the central government and economy, [and,] in addition, it extracted resources from quangos. Moreover, the new Civil Service Law increased state politicization" (Gwiazda 2008: 821).

The dynamic underpinning the concertation state is also reinforced by the attitudes of business leaders. In a survey conducted in 2009 and 2010 in Poland, Hungary, and Germany, Bluhm, Martens, and Trappmann (2011: 1024–5) find that Polish managers in top firms have a preference for an "active role of state" and "alienation towards capitalistic principles of competition" combined with a disposition toward "collective regulation of social partners." Poland is exceptional

Political varieties of capitalism in emerging markets 191

in that feelings of alienation from capitalist principles of competition are particularly strong among business leaders in large firms. These attitudes suggest that managers view the benefits of collectively binding rules as outweighing their costs and risks while also being skeptical of market rules. This is particularly striking because business leaders in Poland are mostly drawn from a new, young managerial elite that has replaced the older generation of managers. It is also worth noting that all the large entrepreneurs of the pre-2005 period survived the party system change unscathed. Together, these findings suggest that the Polish economy will continue to develop toward some hybrid form of market. This will likely be based on networks and collective organization continuing to play an important role despite the emergence of functioning institutions. And, given the generational replacement of managers that has already taken place, it will likely develop with support from managers who are skeptical of liberal capitalism and welcome the active intervention of the state and political parties. The adoption of earlier practices of patronage by PiS, a party that came to power with a pledge to wipe away the pathologies of post-communism, indicates that even a disruption as large as a party system shift has not moved Poland toward a less network-dependent and more institutionalized arrangement.

Bulgaria, a captured state, has similarly not shifted path radically. New political parties have continued to emerge as Bulgarians shift their votes from one party to the next. In particular, dissatisfaction with the government of Simeon II gave rise to the Citizens for the European Development of Bulgaria party (GERB) led by a former chief secretary in the Interior Ministry and mayor of Sofia, Boyko Borisov. GERB won the election in 2009 and Borisov formed a "no coalition" minority government, which nevertheless often relied on the support of potential coalition partners. Borisov enjoyed broad support because of a shift toward programmatic politics and, in particular, a hardline approach to corruption, spearheaded by Borisov's interior minister, Tsvetan Tsvetanov (Kolev 2012: 41). To some, this signaled a potential shift in Bulgarian politics (Kolev 2012). GERB governed only until Borisov's resignation in February 2013, however, over popular opposition to rising energy prices (Ehl 2013). Subsequent elections in March 2013 gave the most votes to GERB but failed to generate a clear outcome. The election also had the lowest turnout since 1989 – widely taken as an indication of voter resignation and disillusion even with GERB. A government formed out of this election is likely to be unstable.

It thus seems reasonable that Bulgaria will continue to operate in an environment of high uncertainty. In the economy, many of the leaders of the business community who emerged in the first wave of private property creation have been displaced by new figures. Nevertheless, Bulgaria is widely seen as a mafia state in which policy is determined by organized crime and the shadow economy. Unfortunately for Bulgaria, large legitimate business is also controlled by these actors. Further, Bulgaria continues to be plagued by a weak institutional environment and corrupt management practices in firms (Center for the Study of Democracy 2013). In fact, it seems likely that captured states have a very hard time emerging from the circumstances that have placed them there in the first place. The state capacity to make such a shift is simply lacking in the long run. As a government official in Bulgaria argued, "There is not a vicious circle of corruption. The real problem is administrative capacity." Without the development of state capacity, it is difficult to emerge from the cycle imposed by narrow networks and high uncertainty. Bulgaria, therefore, has been unable to move from being a captured state to some other form despite even GERB's quite aggressive attempt to tackle corruption head-on.

Romania is perhaps the case that experienced the most change from the period before 2005. Between 2004 and 2008 Romania was governed by a coalition that emerged in opposition to the Social Democratic Party, which had through various mutations dominated Romanian politics for much of the last two decades. An electoral alliance called the Justice and Truth Alliance (DA), composed of the Democratic Party and the National Liberal Party, emerged in 2003. The priorities of this alliance were in line with the center-right ideology of its members and focused on attracting investment to Romania and empowering private initiatives, fighting corruption, creating a more fiscally responsible social policy, and depoliticizing the judiciary. In 2004 Traian Basescu was elected president and appointed Calin Popescu-Tariceanu, head of the PNL, to form a government, which resulted in a weak coalition of the PNL, the PD, the Democratic Union of Hungarians in Romania (UDMR) and the Conservative Party (PC). The DA split in 2007 when Tariceanu excluded the PD from the governing coalition. As a result, the 2008 legislative election gave birth to a new coalition government composed of the PSD and Democratic Liberal Party, the latter a union of the PD and the Liberal Democratic Party. The first designated prime minister of this coalition government, Theodor Stolojan, resigned after four days, and President Basescu then appointed Emil Boc, who would govern Romania during the economic crisis. Boc's government collapsed in December 2009 when the PSD left the coalition. Romania's government collapsed for a second time in February 2012, after protests that had erupted in January in opposition to austerity measures. This brought down Boc's second government. The collapse took place against the background of heightened political struggle between Boc's PD-L and the opposition PNL and PSD. A no-confidence vote sponsored by the opposition Social-Liberal Union (USL), seizing upon popular opposition to austerity cuts, caused the most recent governmental collapse: that of Mihai Razvan Ungureanu, in April 2012. The USL, a coalition formed by the PSD, the PNL, and the PC, won the general election in December 2012.

Although new alliances have emerged, the Romanian political leadership remains remarkably closed. Chiru and Gherghina (2012: 511) show that for more than two decades major Romanian parties (they examine the PSD, the PD-L, the PNL, the UDMR, and the Greater Romania Party – PRM) have displayed an "uninterrupted oligarchic inertia" in which parties have highly centralized leadership selection and removal procedures with low party membership and little member involvement. Coman (2012) also argues that a

Political varieties of capitalism in emerging markets 193

reform that introduced single-member districts in 2008 had minimal impact on the power of party leaders. Moreover, despite the reformist and anti-corruption campaign that brought Basescu to power in 2004, much of the political elite colluded to reverse the reforms (Spendzharova and Vachudova 2012: 41). All three observations suggest that the political elite is insulated from societal actors and in a position to use patronage-based exchanges with business. This reinforces the view that Romania is still set in a form of patronage state, although this order may be more fragile than it was before 2004.

Lessons beyond the region

The western European experience also sheds light on the future development of at least two of the state types: concertation and patronage. There are no readily available examples of a captured state in the region.

Italy offers a western European case of patronage state. Governed by a dominant Christian Democratic (DC) party from the formation of the republic in 1948 until the Tangentopoli scandal in the early 1990s, it fits the definition of a low-uncertainty environment. Firms were also organized hierarchically through the Confindustria, which managed and structured relationships between different factions. The Confindustria served as the representative of the business community to the dominant DC (Martinelli 1979). This resembled closely the patronage state type identified in this book, with high ownership concentration in pyramidal groups (Barca and Trento 1997; Aganin and Volpin 2005). The Tangentopoli scandal that swept away the Christian Democrats reshaped the party system, however, and brought this order to an end. Certainly, patronage states that depend on the dominance of a party or coalition are vulnerable to these types of shifts.

After Tangentopoli, it becomes more difficult to classify Italy. Firms are politicized. For example, Sapienza (2004) shows that Italian state-owned banks, key suppliers of finance to firms, charge lower interest rates than privately owned banks (by forty-four basis points on average). She also finds, however, that the political affiliation of the state-owned bank drives its lending behavior. The stronger the bank's affiliated political party is in an area, the lower the interest rates that bank charges (Sapienza 2004: 359).

Political competition is intense, however, between the disorganized and frequently reorganized leftist parties and a right dominated by Silvio Berlusconi since the early 1990s. The elite on the left is closed but internally deeply split between a center-left and parties further left of center. At the same time, reforms in the financial system since the 1990s should have brought significant changes to the Italian ownership structure. The evidence suggests that such a change has not taken place, however (Bianchi and Bianco 2006). Overall, it would seem that Italy has devolved from a patronage state but not yet moved to a new type.

More examples are available of countries resembling concertation states in western Europe. According to Hall and Soskice (2001), firms in coordinated market economies (CMEs) in continental Europe coordinate economic activity using nonmarket methods. This is accomplished by relying on informal networks or corporatist arrangements between firms. Germany is the central example of a CME for Hall and Soskice, and a country in which networks serve the purpose of facilitating economic activity and have played a key role in the country's post-war success. In addition to allowing firms to share information, engage in "network reputational monitoring," set collective standards, develop collaborative systems of vocational training and engage in relational contracting, these networks have also helped German firms coordinate in response to the increasing competition associated with globalization (Hall and Soskice 2001: 23; Kogut and Walker 2001). These networks persist and play a key role in supporting market activity despite the highly institutionalized environment in which German firms operate.

This is consistent with the broadly held view that markets rely on networks to function (White 1981; Fligstein 2001; White 2004). We can conclude from this that the emergence of well-formed institutions does not necessarily mean that networks will be displaced, as they are an essential part of certain forms of capitalism, such as the CME. It is likely also the case that, as in the CMEs, institutionalization will transform the nature of networks so that they can be incorporated into more institutionalized but pluralistic processes of economic management. This is not yet the case in any of the post-communist countries. There is evidence, however, that similar processes have been under way as a result of democratic deepening in other regions where networks play a key role in the economy. East Asian states that were identified as developmental states have seen the evolution of networks and their incorporation into collaborative relationships with the state and political actors as a result of democratic deepening (Kim 1999; Wong 2004). As with the CMEs of western Europe, this suggests that networks persist even at the advanced stage of institutional development.

NETWORKS AND POLITICS

Throughout this book, I have argued for the importance of social networks in political processes, and one key aim of this work has been to give them a central role in explanations of post-socialist development. North (2010) has argued that rationalist approaches to institutional change miss a key feature of institution building: historical forces and social structures that bind and limit the choices available to rational actors, as well as the inability of those actors to know ex ante which institutions will reduce transaction costs.

Social network analysis addresses these shortcomings, as has been shown by studies in economics and political science (Carpenter, Esterling, and Lazer 1998; Lazer and Friedman 2007). Often, however, in such work "networks" constitute a variable added to the analysis to capture the effect of social relations on outcomes (Putnam 1994), with little consideration of the impact that the structure of ties might have. As I can testify, data on networks are

Political varieties of capitalism in emerging markets   195

notoriously difficult to obtain, and even more so for multiple countries. Yet the benefits of such endeavors are significant, as they grant empirical foundation to the key notion of embeddedness, bringing testable hypotheses and theory building to a new level.

MULTIPLE LEVELS OF ANALYSIS

The question of when elites cooperate to build institutions is a central question of development. The main lesson that I have drawn from this exploration is that broad networks under conditions of uncertainty create the conditions and incentives for elites to cooperate toward institution building. I have tried to address questions about the dynamics of institutional development in post-socialism by appealing to multiple levels of analysis. Behind this research design is a belief that generating insight into large-scale dynamics requires both the global view of quantitative social science and a thick understanding of dynamics on the ground. An exciting trend in recent political science is the tendency to conduct "mixed-methods" research (Lieberman 2005; Collier, Brady, and Seawright 2010), which most commonly combines quantitative analysis, allowing researchers to make sense of many cases, with deep analysis of a few cases, in order to understand the mechanisms that generate outcomes. I have followed in the footsteps of this scholarship. The ambition of this study has been to confirm the theory by utilizing data at three different levels: cross-national large-n data; within-country large-n data; and deep qualitative analysis. To this end, the study employed survey data that allow for cross-national comparisons, as well as two original data sets – of ownership and of careers – that allow for the quantitative exploration of within-country dynamics in three countries. Finally, extensive field research was conducted in each of these three countries to understand the forces driving what I observe in the data, and to supplement these understandings with the point of view of the individuals themselves through elite interviews.

At times, working at these three levels has seemed akin to the Sufi poet Rumi's tale of "The elephant in the dark," in which three men are led to feel an elephant in a dark room and come away with dramatically different impressions of its shape. The dynamic under study here is difficult to observe and understand. The preceding chapters represent a vigorous attempt to creatively investigate it. The challenge and the value of this study both lie in the fact that it seeks to identify the complex story of post-socialist development, told and cross-validated by what sometimes seemed like different glimpses of an elephant in the dark. Actors in this period of tumultuous change are agents within a social structure that they only partly perceive, yet they respond to it and also shape it. The dynamic is huge and its movements impressive, and yet it is hard to grasp its shape completely. The story of the elephant has endured because, while the men fight over who has correctly described it, we know that they each have a partial view. If only all three knew that each component is part of the larger whole. It is precisely this larger, cumulative impression of the beast that I have sought to deliver.

List of interviews

All individuals listed below consented to interviews about the sensitive topic of state–business relations. Given the nature of the topic, I withhold names when citing interviews in the text and refer instead to the position (official, business leader, politician, party leader, etc.) of the individual being quoted. In a few instances I have attributed comments to individuals with their permission.

Dimitar Abadjiev, MP, vice-chairman, Committee on Foreign Policy, Defense and Security, Sofia, June 2003.

Mieczyslaw Bak, Institute for the Study of Democracy and Private Enterprise, National Chamber of Commerce, Warsaw, June 2011.

Ryszard Bankowicz, general director, Polish Business Roundtable, Warsaw, July 2001.

Cristine Barbu, Tax Advisory Program assistant, Ministry of Finance, Bucharest, June 2003.

Gigi Becali, entrepreneur, owner of FC Steaua, and chairman of the New Generation Party, Bucharest, June 2004.

Maxim Behar, chairman, Bulgarian Business Leaders Forum, Sofia, June 2003.

Alicja Beras, head specialist, Polish Ministry of Treasury, Warsaw, February 2001.

Andrzej Bratkowski, Centrum Analiz Społeczno-Ekonomicznych (Center for Social and Economic Research), Warsaw, June 2000.

Guy Burrow, general manager, CEC Government Relations, Bucharest, May 2003.

Cristian Butuman, manager, industrial policy, delegation of the European Commission in Romania, Bucharest, June 2003.

Gabriel Calinescu, general secretary, New Generation Party – Christian Democratic, Bucharest, June 2004.

Marian Chichosz, director, Polish National Audit Office, May 2001.

Eugenia Liliana Constantinescu, vice-president, New Generation Party, Bucharest, July 2004.

List of interviews　　　197

Kazimirz Cwalina, head of Department of Economic Strategy, Ministry of Economy, Warsaw, July 2001.

Dariusz Czerniak, director, Greenbriar Poland, Warsaw, August 2001.

Bozena Czyzkkowska-Majak, advisor to the minister, Ministry of Treasury, Warsaw, June 2001.

Marek Dabrowski, Centrum Analiz Społeczno-Ekonomicznych, Warsaw, May 2000.

Alexander Dimitrov, economic analyst, Bulgarian Chamber of Commerce and Industry, Sofia, June 2003.

Tatiana Doncheva, MP, Bulgarian Socialist Party, Sofia, June 2003.

Stelian Dorobantu, general manager, General Confederation of Industrial Employers UGIR-1903, Bucharest, June 2003.

Bozena Dyjak, head of oversight, Ministry of Treasury, Warsaw, February 2001.

Mike Farnworth, director, National Democratic Institute, Sofia, June 2003.

Michal Fedorowicz, Institute of Philosophy and Sociology, Polish Academy of Sciences, Warsaw, June 2000.

William Furman, CEO, Greenbriar Inc., New York, September 2001.

Zofia Gaber, president of the Supervisory Board, Agros Holding, Warsaw, May 2001.

Juliusz Gardawski, Sociology Department, Warsaw School of Economics, Warsaw, June 2000.

Borislav Georgiev, Bulgarian Industrial Association, Sofia, June 2001.

Dariusz Grabowski, Coalicja dla Polski, Warsaw, May 2001.

Aleksander Gudzowaty, president, Bartimex, Warsaw, May 2001.

Adriana Halpert, editor, *Capital Weekly* magazine, Bucharest, June 2004.

Robert Hofnar, advisor, Ministry of Finance, Bucharest, June 2003.

Alina Hussein, advisor to the president, National Audit Office, Warsaw, February 2001.

Sorin Ionita, Romanian Academic Society, Bucharest, June 2003.

Tudor Irimescu, deputy general director of industrial policy, Ministry of Industry and Resources, Bucharest, May 2003.

Beata Jarosz, press secretary, Ministry of Treasury, Warsaw, February 2001.

Krszysztof Jasiecki, Institute of Political Studies, Polish Academy of Sciences, Warsaw, 2000–2001.

Grazyna Jaskula-Pereta, vice-president and general director, Business Centre Club, Warsaw, July 2001.

Ivailo Kalfin, economic advisor to the president, Sofia, June 2004.

Antoni Kaminski, Transparency International, Warsaw, October 2000.

Nikolai Kamov, MP and chairman, Social Democratic Movement, Sofia, June 2003.

Joanna Karman, director, Oversight of PKO BP, Ministry of Treasury, Warsaw, February 2001.

Urzula Karpinska, deputy director, Polish Confederation of Private Employers, Warsaw, July 2001.

198 *List of interviews*

Aleksander Kashukeev, chairman, Metalsnab Holding, Sofia, June 2003.

Krszysztof Kelian, former telecommunications minister (1992–1993), Warsaw, May 2000.

Jacek Kolaskinski, director, International Affairs Division, National Audit Office, Warsaw, July 2001.

Grażyna Kopińska, director, Anti-Corruption Program, Batory Foundation, Warsaw, December 2000.

Emil Koshlukov, chairman of the Committee on Civil Society Affairs and MP, National Movement of Simeon II, Sofia, September 2003.

Ivan Kostov, former prime minister, Sofia, June 2003.

Iwona Kubik, Department of Economic Development, Government Center for Strategic Studies, Warsaw, July 2001.

Warren Kuhler, resident tax advisor, Sofia, June 2003.

Jan Kulczyk, president, Kulczyk Holding, Warsaw, August 2001.

Younal Loutfi, deputy chairman, Movement for Rights and Freedoms, and MP, National Assembly of Bulgaria, Sofia, June 2004.

Elzbieta Lutow, tax specialist, Polish Craft Association, Warsaw, June 2000.

Scott McLeod, resident tax advisor, Ministry of Finance, Bucharest, June 2003.

Ligia Medrea, director general, Natural Gas Regulatory Authority, Bucharest, June 2003.

Dan Mihalache, executive secretary, Social Democratic Party of Romania, Bucharest, July 2004.

Georgi Milkov, 24 *Chasa* (24 *Hours*) newspaper, Sofia, June 2004.

Plamen Minchev, president, BBB Group, Sofia, June 2003.

Nikolay Minkov, Bulgarian International Business Association, Sofia, June 2003.

Jeremi Mordasiewicz, Business Center Club, Warsaw, May 2000.

Florin Negrutiu, senior reporter, Banii Nostri, Bucharest, June 2004.

Vera Nicheva, legal counsel, Bulgarian Chamber of Commerce and Industry, Sofia, June 2003.

Ioan Niculae, president, InterAgro, Bucharest, June 2004.

Kazimierz Nowak, director, Investment Division, Polish Oil and Gas Company, Warsaw, July 2001.

Konstantin Palikarsky, legal advisor to the prime minister, Sofia, June 2003.

Dinu Patriciu, CEO, Rompetrol Group, Bucharest, June 2004.

Enrico Perini, director, Romstal, Bucharest, June 2004.

Ion Pop, director, Research and Strategy Department, Chamber of Commerce and Industry, Bucharest, May 2003.

Marian Popa, president, Transparency International Romania, and founding member of the Businessmen's Association of Romania, Bucharest, May 2003.

Boyko Radaev, MP, Social Democratic Movement, Sofia, June 2003.

Marin Roumenov, expert, JSC Gazprom and JSC Topenergy, Sofia, June 2003.

Andrzej Sadowski, Adam Smith Center, Warsaw, February 2001.

Joseph Seroussi, CEO, J&R Enterprises, Bucharest, June 2004.

List of interviews

Ognian Shentov, chairman, Center for the Study of Democracy, Sofia, June 2003.

Tsvetan Simeonov, vice-president and CEO, Bulgarian Chamber of Commerce and Industry, Sofia, June 2003.

Margarit Slevoaca, councillor, Ministry of Industry and Resources, Bucharest, June 2003.

Anna Smołka, Confederation of Polish Employers, Warsaw, June 2000.

Pawel Soroka, Polish industrial lobby, Warsaw, September 2000.

Mikolaj Stasiak, deputy director, Office for Competition and Consumer Protection, Warsaw, July 2001.

Jan Stefanowicz, attorney, Warsaw, November 2000.

Krystyna Szajdakowska, director, Department of Administration and European Integration, Warsaw, July 2001.

Anna Szczesniak, Institute for the Study of Democracy and Entrepreneurship, Warsaw, February 2001.

Kiril Tekeliev, head of cigarette manufacturing, Bulgartabac Holding Group, Sofia, June 2003.

Petar Terziyski, economic analyst, Bulgarian Chamber of Commerce and Industry, Sofia, June 2003.

Emil Tsenkov, Center for the Study of Democracy, Sofia, June 2003.

Stefan Varfalvi, General Union of Romanian Industrialists, Bucharest, May 2003.

Valeriu Velciu, president, Unicapital Holding, Bucharest, June 2003.

Valentin Vidolov, deputy general tax director, Ministry of Finance, Sofia, June 2003.

Sevdalina Voynova, deputy director, National Democratic Institute, Sofia, June 2003.

Jan Waga, chairman of the board, Kulczyk Holding, Warsaw, August 2001.

Wlodzimierz Wesolowski, Institute of Philosophy and Sociology, Polish Academy of Sciences, Warsaw, June 2000.

Sylwia Wilkos, assistant to Henry Wujec, MP (Unia Wolnosci), Warsaw, May 2001.

Pawel Witkowski, director of chemical industry oversight, Ministry of the Treasury, Warsaw, February 2001.

Edmund Wnuk-Lipinski, Institute of Political Studies, Polish Academy of Sciences, Warsaw, June 2000.

Rick Woodward, Centrum Analiz Społeczno-Ekonomicznych, Warsaw, May 2000.

Damian Zaczek, editor-in-chief, *Decydent & Decision Maker*, lobbying trade magazine, Warsaw, September 2000.

Marek Ziolkowski, Institute of Philosophy and Sociology, Polish Academy of Sciences, Warsaw, June 2000.

Elzbieta Znosko-Lapczynska, director general, Polish Craft Association, Warsaw, June 2000.

References

Emerging European Markets (1998). "A real turn-around." *Emerging European Markets*, June 1.

Acemoglu, D., S. Johnson, and J. A. Robinson (2005). "Institutions as a fundamental cause of long-run growth," in P. Aghion and S. N. Durlauf, eds., *Handbook of Economic Growth*, vol. IA. Amsterdam, Elsevier: 385–472.

Aganin, A., and P. Volpin (2005). "The history of corporate ownership in Italy," in R. K. Morck, ed., *A History of Corporate Governance around the World: Family Business Groups to Professional Managers*. University of Chicago Press: 325–61.

Aghion, P., and O. J. Blanchard (1994). "On the speed of transition in central Europe," in S. Fischer and J. J. Rotemberg, eds., *NBER Macroeconomics Annual 1994*. Cambridge, MA, MIT Press: 283–330.

———— (1998). "On privatization methods in eastern Europe and their implications." *Economics of Transition* 6(1): 87–99.

Ahrend, R., and J. Oliveira Martins (2003). "Creative destruction or destructive perpetuation: the role of large state-owned enterprises and SMEs in Romania during transition." *Post-Communist Economies* 15(3): 331–56.

Aidt, T. S. (2009). "Corruption, institutions, and economic development." *Oxford Review of Economic Policy* 25(2): 271–91.

Aldenderfer, M. S., and R. K. Blashfield (1984). *Cluster Analysis*. Beverly Hills, CA, Sage.

Alexandrova, G. (1998). "Heads rolling in the state sector." *Capital Weekly*, July 15.

Alexandrova, P. (2002). "Under-the-table funding." Transitions Online, September 27, www.tol.org/client/article/7414-under-the-table-funding.html?print.

Almeida, H. V., and D. Wolfenzon (2006). "A theory of pyramidal ownership and family business groups." *Journal of Finance* 61(6): 2637–80.

Alt, J. E., and R. C. Lowry (1994). "Divided government, fiscal institutions, and budget deficits: evidence from the states." *American Political Science Review* 88(4): 811–28.

Andreev, S. A. (2009). "The unbearable lightness of membership: Bulgaria and Romania after the 2007 EU accession." *Communist and Post-Communist Studies* 42(3): 375–93.

Andreff, W. (2005). "Corporate governance structures in postsocialist economies: toward a central eastern European model of corporate control," working paper. University of Paris I, Panthéon–Sorbonne.

References

Åslund, A. (1995). *How Russia Became a Market Economy*. Washington, DC, Brookings Institution Press.

Axelrod, R. M., and M. D. Cohen (1999). *Harnessing Complexity: Organizational Implications of a Scientific Frontier*. New York, Free Press.

Balcerowicz, E., and A. Bratkowski (2001). "Restructuring and development of the banking sector in Poland: lessons to be learnt by less advanced transition countries," Case Report no. 44. Warsaw, Centrum Analiz Społeczno-Ekonomicznych.

Banker Daily (1997). "The privatization of Bulgartabac is close at hand." *Banker Daily*, December 4.

Barca, F., and S. Trento (1997). "State ownership and the evolution of Italian corporate governance." *Industrial and Corporate Change* 6(3): 533–59.

Bartolini, S., and P. Mair (2001). "Challenges to contemporary political parties," in L. Diamond and R. Gunther, eds., *Political Parties and Democracy*. Baltimore, Johns Hopkins University Press: 327–43.

Bates, R. H. (1981). *Markets and States in Tropical Africa: The Political Basis of Agricultural Policies*. Berkeley, University of California Press.

Beckert, J. (2007a). "The great transformation of embeddedness: Karl Polanyi and the new economic sociology," Discussion Paper no. 07/1. Cologne, Max-Planck-Institut für Gesellschaftsforschung.

——— (2007b). "The social order of markets," Discussion Paper no. 07/15. Cologne, Max-Planck-Institut für Gesellschaftsforschung.

Belka, M., and A. Krajewska (1997). "The Polish bank and enterprise restructuring programme: debt/equity swaps: survey results," Discussion Paper no. 97/14. Edinburgh, Centre for Economic Reform and Transformation, School of Management, Heriot-Watt University.

Berglof, E., and E. Perotti (1994). "The governance structure of the Japanese financial keiretsu." *Journal of Financial Economics* 36(2): 259–84.

Berle, A. A., and G. C. Means (1991). *The Modern Corporation and Private Property*. New Brunswick, NJ, Transaction Publishers.

Bianchi, M., and M. Bianco (2006). "Italian corporate governance in the last 15 years: from pyramids to coalitions?" Finance Working Paper no. 144/2006. Brussels, European Corporate Governance Institute.

Bielasiak, J. (2002). "The institutionalization of electoral and party systems in post-communist states." *Comparative Politics* 34(2): 189–210.

——— (2005). "Party competition in emerging democracies: representation and effectiveness in post-communism and beyond." *Democratization* 12(3): 331–56.

Birch, S. (2003). *Electoral Systems and Political Transformation in Post-Communist Europe*. London, Palgrave Macmillan.

Black, B. S. (1992). "Agents watching agents: the promise of institutional investor voice." *UCLA Law Review* 39(4): 811–93.

Black, B. S., R. Kraakman, and A. Tarassova (2000). "Russian privatization and corporate governance: what went wrong?" *Stanford Law Review* 52(6): 1731–808.

Błaszczyk, B., I. Hashi, A. Radygin, and R. Woodward (2003). "Corporate governance and ownership structure in the transition: the current state of knowledge and where to go from here," Network Study and Analysis no. 264. Warsaw, Centrum Analiz Społeczno-Ekonomicznych.

Bluhm, K., B. Martens, and V. Trappmann (2011). "Business elites and the role of companies in society: a comparative study of Poland, Hungary and Germany." *Europe–Asia Studies* **63**(6): 1011–32.

Bohle, D., and B. Greskovits (2007). "Neoliberalism, embedded neoliberalism, and neocorporatism: paths towards transnational capitalism in central-eastern Europe." *West European Politics* **30**(3): 443–66.

Bonin, J., and P. Wachtel (1999). "Lessons from bank privatization in central Europe," Working Paper no. 245. Ann Arbor, William Davidson Institute, Stephen M. Ross School of Business, University of Michigan.

Boycko, M., A. Shleifer, and R. W. Vishny (1995). *Privatizing Russia*. Cambridge, MA, MIT Press.

Brada, J. C. (1996). "Privatization is transition – or is it?" *Journal of Economic Perspectives* **10**(2): 67–86.

Brown, J. D., J. S. Earle, and S. Gehlbach (2009). "Helping hand or grabbing hand? State bureaucracy and privatization effectiveness." *American Political Science Review* **103**(2): 264–83.

BTA (1997). "Bulgartabac Holding increases capital to 7.122 mln leva." BTA, December 6.

——— (1998a). "Minister expects privatization to end by 2000." BTA, May 3.

——— (1998b). "Cabinet approves list of companies to be privatized." BTA, May 18.

——— (1998c). "Privatization chief outlines strategy for 1999." BTA, October 28.

Campos, N. F., and F. Giovannoni (2008). "Lobbying, corruption and other banes," Working Paper no. 930. Ann Arbor, William Davidson Institute, University of Michigan School of Business.

Capital Weekly (1998a). "Redistribution of the cigarette market begins." *Capital Weekly*. February 20.

——— (1998b). "Bulgartabac shares to be traded on international stock market." *Capital Weekly*, May 1.

Carpenter, D. P., K. M. Esterling, and D. M. J. Lazer (1998). "The strength of weak ties in lobbying networks." *Journal of Theoretical Politics* **10**(4): 417–44.

Carruthers, B. G. (1996). *City of Capital: Politics and Markets in the English Financial Revolution*. Princeton University Press.

Center for the Study of Democracy (2013). "The hidden economy in Bulgaria: 2011–2012," Policy Brief no. 37. Sofia, Center for the Study of Democracy.

Chibber, V. (2003). *Locked in Place: State-Building and Late Industrialization in India*. Princeton University Press.

Chiru, M., and S. Gherghina (2012). "Keeping the doors closed: leadership selection in post-communist Romania." *East European Politics and Societies* **26**(3): 510–37.

Chrisman, J. J., L. P. Steier, and J. H. Chua (2006). "Personalism, particularism, and the competitive behaviors and advantages of family firms: an introduction." *Entrepreneurship Theory and Practice* **30**(6): 719–29.

Cialdini, R. B. (1989). "Indirect tactics of image management: beyond basking," in R. A. Giacalone and P. Rosenfeld, eds., *Impression Management in the Organization*. Hillsdale, NJ, Erlbaum Associates: 45–56.

Collier, D., H. E. Brady, and J. Seawright (2010). "Outdated views of qualitative methods: time to move on." *Political Analysis* **18**(4): 506–13.

Coman, E. E. (2012). "Legislative behavior in Romania: the effect of the 2008 Romanian electoral reform." *Legislative Studies Quarterly* **37**(2): 199–224.

References

Crawford, B., and A. Lijphart (1995). "Explaining political and economic change in post-communist eastern Europe: old legacies, new institutions, hegemonic norms, and international pressures." *Comparative Political Studies* 28(2): 171–99.

Crouch, C., and W. A. Brown (1993). *Industrial Relations and European State Traditions*. Oxford, Clarendon Press.

Crowley, S. (2004). "Explaining labor weakness in post-communist Europe: historical legacies and comparative perspective." *East European Politics and Societies* 18(3): 394–429.

Dalton, R. J. (2008). *Citizen Politics: Public Opinion and Political Parties in Advanced Industrial Democracies*. Washington, DC, CQ Press.

Dalton, R. J., and P. M. Wattenberg (2000). *Parties without Partisans: Political Change in Advanced Industrial Democracies*. Oxford University Press.

Davis, G. F., and M. S. Mizruchi (1999). "The money center cannot hold: commercial banks in the US system of corporate governance." *Administrative Science Quarterly* 44(2): 215–39.

Detterbeck, K. (2005). "Cartel parties in western Europe?" *Party Politics* 11(2): 173–91.

Dewatripont, M., and G. Roland (1992a). "The virtues of gradualism and legitimacy in the transition to a market economy." *Economic Journal* 102: 291–300.

——— (1992b). "Economic reform and dynamic political constraints." *Review of Economic Studies* 59(4): 703–30.

——— (1995). "The design of reform packages under uncertainty." *American Economic Review* 85(5): 1207–23.

Dimitrova Grajzl, V. (2007). "The Great Divide revisited: Ottoman and Habsburg legacies on transition." *Kyklos* 60(4): 539–58.

Doner, R. F. (2009). *The Politics of Uneven Development: Thailand's Economic Growth in Comparative Perspective*. Cambridge University Press

Doner, R. F., B. K. Ritchie, and D. Slater (2005). "Systemic vulnerability and the origins of developmental states: northeast and southeast Asia in comparative perspective." *International Organization* 59(2): 327–61.

Dzierwa, J. (1999). "Foreigners bank on Poland." *Warsaw Voice*, April 11.

Dzierzanowski, M., and P. Tamowicz (2003). "Setting standards of corporate governance: the Polish experience of drafting governance codes." *European Business Organization Law Review* 4(2): 273–99.

Earle, J., and A. Telegdy (1998a). *Istoria Zbuciumata a Programului de Privatizare in Masa: Rezultate si Evaluare*. Bucharest, Centrul Pentru Reforma Institutionala.

——— (1998b). "The results of 'mass privatization' in Romania: a first empirical study." *Economics of Transition* 6(2): 313–32.

——— (2002). "Privatization methods and productivity effects in Romanian industrial enterprises." *Journal of Comparative Economics* 30(4): 657–82.

East European Constitutional Review (1998). "Constitution watch: Bulgaria." *East European Constitutional Review* 7(3); available at www1.law.nyu.edu/eecr/vol7num3/constitutionwatch/Bulgaria.html.

EBRD (2005a). *Transition Report 2005: Business in Transition*. London, EBRD.

——— (2005b). "Business environment and enterprise performance survey," EBRD; available at www.ebrd.com/pages/research/economics/data/beeps/beeps05.shtml.

Edgardo Campos, J., D. Lien, and S. Pradhan (1999). "The impact of corruption on investment: predictability matters." *World Development* 27(6): 1059–67.

Ehl, M. (2013). "A state of depression." Transitions Online, May 14, www.tol.org/client/article/23769-a-state-of-depression.html?print.

EIU (2001). *Country Report: Romania.* London, EIU.

Ekiert, G. (1999). "Do legacies matter? Patterns of postcommunist transitions in eastern Europe," Occasional Paper no. 53. Washington, DC, Woodrow Wilson International Center for Scholars.

Ekiert, G., J. Kubik, and M. A. Vachudova (2007). "Democracy in the post-communist world: an unending quest?" *East European Politics and Societies* 21(1): 7–30.

Epperly, B. (2011). "Institutions and legacies: electoral volatility in the postcommunist world." *Comparative Political Studies* 44(7): 829–53.

Evans, P. B. (1995). *Embedded Autonomy: States and Industrial Transformation.* Princeton University Press.

Evans, P. B., D. Rueschemeyer, and T. Skocpol (1985). *Bringing the State Back In.* Cambridge University Press.

Everitt, B. S., S. Landau, and M. Leese (2011). *Cluster Analysis,* 5th edn. Hoboken, NJ, John Wiley.

Faccio, M. (2006). "Politically connected firms." *American Economic Review* 96(1): 369–86.

Feiock, R. C., and J. T. Scholz (2009). *Self-Organizing Federalism: Collaborative Mechanisms to Mitigate Institutional Collective Action Dilemmas.* New York: Cambridge University Press.

Feldmann, M. (2006). "Emerging varieties of capitalism in transition countries: industrial relations and wage bargaining in Estonia and Slovenia." *Comparative Political Studies* 39(7): 829–54.

Fesnic, F., and O. Armeanu (2010). "Party system change in Romania: institutional versus structural explanations." Paper presented at annual meeting of American Political Science Association.

Finance East Europe (1994). "Conflict within entrepreneurs lobby." *Finance East Europe.*

Fischer, S., and A. Gelb (1991). "The process of socialist economic transformation." *Journal of Economic Perspectives* 5(4): 91–105.

Fligstein, N. (2001). *The Architecture of Markets: An Economic Sociology of Twenty-First-Century Capitalist Societies.* Princeton University Press.

Fogel, K. (2006). "Oligarchic family control, social economic outcomes, and the quality of government." *Journal of International Business Studies* 37(5): 603–22.

Frieden, J. (1988). "Sectoral conflict and foreign economic policy, 1914–1940." *International Organization* 42(1): 59–90.

Frydman, R., and A. Rapaczynski (1994). *Privatization in Eastern Europe: Is the State Withering Away?* Budapest, Central European University Press.

Frye, T. (2010). *Building States and Markets after Communism: The Perils of Polarized Democracy.* Cambridge University Press.

Gabadinho, A., G. Ritschard, M. Studer, and N. S. Müller (2011). *Mining Sequence Data in R with the TraMineR Package: A User's Guide.* University of Geneva.

Gabryel, P., and M. Zieleniewski (1998). *Piata Wladza: Czyli kto Naprawde Rzadzi Polska.* Warsaw, Wydawnictwo Naukowe PWN.

Ganev, V. I. (2001). "The Dorian Gray effect: winners as state breakers in postcommunism." *Communist and Post-Communist Studies* 34(1): 1–25.

——— (2007). *Preying on the State: The Transformation of Bulgaria after 1989.* Ithaca, NY, Cornell University Press.

References

Gerlach, M. L. (1992). *Alliance Capitalism: The Social Organization of Japanese Business*. Berkeley, University of California Press.

Ghatak, M., and R. Kali (2001). "Financially interlinked business groups." *Journal of Economics and Management Strategy* 10(4): 591–619.

Gherghina, S., M. Chiru, and F. Casal Bértoa (2011). "State resources and pocket money: shortcuts for party funding in Romania," Legal Regulation of Political Parties Working Paper no. 8. Leiden University.

Gilson, R. J., and M. J. Roe (1993). "Understanding the Japanese keiretsu: overlaps between corporate governance and industrial organization." *Yale Law Journal* 102(4): 871–906.

Gourevitch, P. A., and J. Shinn (2005). *Political Power and Corporate Control: The New Global Politics of Corporate Governance*. Princeton University Press.

Government of Romania (2001). *Carta Alba a Preluarii Guvernarii in Luna Decembrie*. Bucharest, Monitorul Oficial.

Grahovac, B. (2004). *East and West European Public–Private Partnerships: Public Companies in Restructuring and Privatization*. Hauppauge, NY, Nova Publishers.

Granovetter, M. S. (1973). "The strength of weak ties." *American Journal of Sociology* 78(6): 1360–80.

———— (1983). "The strength of weak ties: a network theory revisited." *Sociological Theory* 1(1): 201–33.

———— (1985). "Economic action and social structure: the problem of embeddedness." *American Journal of Sociology* 91(3): 481–510.

———— (1995). *Getting a Job: A Study of Contacts and Careers*. University of Chicago Press.

Greif, A., P. Milgrom, and B. R. Weingast (1994). "Coordination, commitment, and enforcement: the case of the merchant guild." *Journal of Political Economy* 102(4): 745–76.

Gross, J. (1989). "Social consequences of war: preliminaries to the study of imposition of communist regimes in east central Europe." *East European Politics and Societies* 3(2): 198–214.

Grzeszak, A., W. Markiewicz, J. Dziadul, J. Wilczak, M. Urbanek, J. Mojkowski, and M. Pokojska (1999). "Kraj rad (nadzorczych)." *Polityka*, February 27: 3–8.

Grzymała-Busse, A. (2007). *Rebuilding Leviathan: Party Competition and State Exploitation in Post-Communist Democracies*. Cambridge University Press.

Grzymała-Busse, A., and P. Jones-Luong (2002). "Re-conceptualizing the state: lessons from post-communism." *Politics and Society* 30(4): 529–54.

Gustafson, T. (1999). *Capitalism Russian-Style*, Cambridge University Press.

Gwiazda, A. (2008). "Party patronage in Poland." *East European Politics and Societies* 22(4): 802–27.

———— (2009). "Poland's quasi-institutionalized party system: the importance of elites and institutions." *Perspectives on European Politics and Society* 10(3): 350–76.

Hall, P. A., and D. W. Soskice (2001). *Varieties of Capitalism: The Institutional Foundations of Comparative Advantage*. Oxford University Press.

Hamilton, G. G., and N. W. Biggart (1988). "Market, culture, and authority: a comparative analysis of management and organization in the Far East." *American Journal of Sociology* 94(S1): 52–94.

Hanson, S. E. (1995). "The Leninist legacy and institutional change." *Comparative Political Studies* 28(2): 306–14.

Hawley, J., and A. Williams (1997). "The emergence of fiduciary capitalism." *Corporate Governance* 5(4): 206–13.

Hellman, J. S. (1998). "Winners take all: the politics of partial reform in postcommunist transitions." *World Politics* 50(2): 203–34.

Hellman, J. S., G. Jones, and D. Kaufmann (2003). "Seize the state, seize the day: state capture and influence in transition economies." *Journal of Comparative Economics* 31(4): 751–73.

Hoff, K., and J. E. Stiglitz (2002). "After the Big Bang? Obstacles to the emergence of the rule of law in post-communist societies," Working Paper no. 9282. Cambridge, MA, National Bureau of Economic Research.

Holmes, L. (2006). *Rotten States? Corruption, Post-Communism, and Neoliberalism.* Durham, NC, Duke University Press.

Höpner, M., and A. Schäfer (2010). "A new phase of European integration: organised capitalisms in post-Ricardian Europe." *West European Politics* 33(2): 344–68.

Horowitz, S., K. Hoff, and B. Milanovic (2009). "Government turnover: concepts, measures and applications." *European Journal of Political Research* 48(1): 107–29.

Ikstens, J., D. Smilov, and M. Walecki (2001). "Party and campaign funding in eastern Europe: a study of 18 member countries of the ACEEEO." Washington, DC, International Foundation for Electoral Systems.

Ilieva, G. (1998). "New replacement of Bulgartabac chiefs." *Capital Weekly*, August 3.

Innes, A. (2002). "Party competition in postcommunist Europe: the great electoral lottery." *Comparative Politics* 35(1): 85–104.

Jacoby, W. (1999). "Priest and penitent: the European Union as a force in the domestic politics of eastern Europe." *East European Constitutional Review* 8(1/2): 62–7.

——— (2006). "Inspiration, coalition, and substitution: external influences on post-communist transformations." *World Politics* 58(4): 623–51.

Janos, A. C. (1993). "Continuity and change in eastern Europe: strategies of post-communist politics." *East European Politics and Societies* 8(1): 1–31.

Jarosz, M., ed. (2001). *Manowce Polskiej Prywatyzacji.* Warsaw, Naukowe PWN.

Jensen, M. C., and W. H. Meckling (1976). "Theory of the firm: managerial behavior, agency costs and ownership structure." *Journal of Financial Economics* 3(4): 305–60.

Johnson, S., and G. Loveman (1995). *Starting Over in Eastern Europe: Entrepreneurship and Economic Renewal.* Cambridge, MA, Harvard Business School Press.

Jowitt, K. (1983). "Soviet neotraditionalism: the political corruption of a Leninist regime." *Europe–Asia Studies* 35(3): 275–97.

——— (1992). *New World Disorder: The Leninist Legacy,* Berkeley, University of California Press.

——— (1996). "Undemocratic past, unnamed present, undecided future." *Demokratizatsiya* 4(3): 409–19.

Kang, D. C. (2002). *Crony Capitalism: Corruption and Development in South Korea and the Philippines.* Cambridge University Press.

Katz, R. S., and P. Mair (1995). "Changing models of party organization and party democracy." *Party Politics* 1(1): 5–28.

Katz, R. S., P. Mair, L. Bardi, L. Bille, K. Deschouwer, D. Farrell, R. Koole, L. Morlino, W. Müller, J. Pierre, T. Poguntke, J. Sundberg, L. Svasand, H. van de Velde,

References

P. Webb, and A. Widfeldt (1992). "The membership of political parties in European democracies, 1960–1990." *European Journal of Political Research* **22**(3): 329–45.

Kaufman, L., and P. J. Rousseeuw (1990). *Finding Groups in Data: An Introduction to Cluster Analysis*. Hoboken, NJ, John Wiley.

Kaufmann, D., A. Kraay, and M. Mastruzzi (2009). "Governance matters VIII: aggregate and individual governance indicators, 1996–2008," Policy Research Working Paper no. 4978. Washington, DC, World Bank.

Kawalec, S. (1994). "Polska droga restrukturyzacji złych kredytów" ("Polish method of bad debt restructuring"), in "Polska droga restrukturyzacji złych kredytów," Notebook no. 12. Warsaw, Centrum Analiz Społeczno-Ekonomicznych and Polski Bank Rozwoju: 7–9.

Khanna, T. (2000). "Business groups and social welfare in emerging markets: existing evidence and unanswered questions." *European Economic Review* **44**(4/6): 748–61.

Khanna, T., and K. Palepu (1997). "Why focused strategies may be wrong for emerging markets." *Harvard Business Review* **75**(4): 41–51.

——— (1999). "Emerging market business groups, foreign investors and corporate governance," Working Paper no. 6955. Cambridge, MA, National Bureau of Economic Research.

Kilduff, M., and D. Krackhardt (1994). "Bringing the individual back in: a structural analysis of the internal market for reputation in organizations." *Academy of Management Review* **37**(1): 87–108.

Kim, S. J. (2004). "Bailout and conglomeration." *Journal of Financial Economics* **71**(2): 315–47.

Kim, Y. T. (1999). "Neoliberalism and the decline of the developmental state." *Journal of Contemporary Asia* **29**(4): 441–61.

Kitschelt, H. (1992). "The formation of party systems in east central Europe." *Politics and Society* **20**(1): 7–50.

——— (1999). "Accounting for outcomes of post-communist regime change: causal depth or shallowness in rival explanations?" Paper presented at annual meeting of American Political Science Association.

——— (2000). "Linkages between citizens and politicians in democratic polities." *Comparative Political Studies* **33**(6/7): 845–79.

——— (2003). "Accounting for postcommunist regime diversity: what counts as a good cause?" in G. Ekiert and S. E. Hanson, eds., *Capitalism and Democracy in Central and Eastern Europe: Assessing the Legacy of Communist Rule*. Cambridge University Press: 49–86.

Knack, S. F. (2006). "Measuring corruption in eastern Europe and central Asia: a critique of the cross-country indicators," Policy Research Working Paper no. 3968. Washington, DC, World Bank.

Kochanowicz, J. (1997). "Incomplete demise: reflections on the welfare state in Poland after communism." *Social Research* **64**(4): 1445–69.

Kogut, B. (2012). "The small world of corporate governance: an introduction" in B. Kogut, ed., *The Small Worlds of Corporate Governance*. MIT Press: 2–51.

Kogut, B., and G. Walker (2001). "The small world of Germany and the durability of national networks." *American Sociological Review* **66**(3): 317–35.

Kolev, K. (2012). "Bulgaria: electoral volatility, polarization and financial deficits lead to reduction in clientelism," in H. Kitschelt and Y.-T. Wang, eds., *Research and Dialogue on Programmatic Parties and Party Systems: Case Study Reports.* Stockholm, International Institute for Democracy and Electoral Assistance: 35–54.

Kolodko, G. (1999). "Ten years of postsocialist transition: lessons for policy reforms," Policy Research Working Paper no. 2095. Washington, DC, World Bank.

Kolodko, G., and D. Nuti (1997). "The Polish alternative: old myths, hard facts and new strategies in the successful transformation of the Polish economy," Research for Action no. 33. Helsinki, World Institute for Development Economics Research, United Nations University.

Kopecky, P. (2006). "Political parties and the state in post-communist Europe: the nature of symbiosis." *Journal of Communist Studies and Transition Politics* 22(3): 251–73.

Kopstein, J. S., and D. A. Reilly (2000). "Geographic diffusion and the transformation of the postcommunist world." *World Politics* 53(1): 1–37.

Kornai, J. (1986). *Contradictions and Dilemmas: Studies on the Socialist Economy and Society.* Cambridge, MA, MIT Press.

——— (1990). *The Road to a Free Economy: Shifting from a Socialist System – the Example of Hungary.* New York, W. W. Norton.

——— (2000). "Ten years after *The Road to a Free Economy*: the author's self-evaluation," in B. Pleskovic and N. Stern, eds., *Annual World Bank Conference on Development Economics 2000.* Washington, DC, World Bank: 49–63.

Krueger, A. O. (1974). "The political economy of the rent-seeking society." *American Economic Review* 64(3): 291–303.

Kublik, A. (2008). "PSL wciska swoich działaczy do państwowych spółek." Gazeta Wyborcza, March 19, http://wyborcza.pl/1,75968,5036991.html.

Lachmann, R. (2000). *Capitalists in Spite of Themselves: Elite Conflict and Economic Transitions in Early Modern Europe.* New York, Oxford University Press.

Laporta, R., F. Lopez-de-Silanes, and A. Shleifer (1999). "Corporate ownership around the world." *Journal of Finance* 54(2): 471–517.

Lazer, D., and A. Friedman (2007). "The network structure of exploration and exploitation." *Administrative Science Quarterly* 52(4): 667–94.

Ledeneva, A. V. (1998). *Russia's Economy of Favours: Blat, Networking, and Informal Exchange.* Cambridge University Press.

Leff, N. H. (1978). "Industrial organization and entrepreneurship in the developing countries: the economic groups." *Economic Development and Cultural Change* 26(4): 661–75.

Levi, M. (1988). *Of Rule and Revenue.* Berkeley, University of California Press.

Lewis, P. G. (2002). *Political Parties in Post-Communist Eastern Europe.* London, Routledge.

——— (2006). "Party systems in post-communist central Europe: patterns of stability and consolidation." *Democratization* 13(4): 562–83.

Leys, C. (1965). "What is the problem about corruption?" *Journal of Modern African Studies* 3(2): 215–30.

Lieberman, E. S. (2005). "Nested analysis as a mixed-method strategy for comparative research." *American Political Science Review* 99(3): 435–52.

Lipton, D., and J. Sachs (1990a). "Creating a market economy in eastern Europe: the case of Poland." *Brookings Papers on Economic Activity* 1990(1): 75–147.

——— (1990b). "Privatization in eastern Europe: the case of Poland." *Brookings Papers on Economic Activity* 1990(2): 293–341.

References

Lui, F. T. (1985). "An equilibrium queuing model of bribery." *Journal of Political Economy* 93(4): 760–81.

Mair, P., and I. van Biezen (2001). "Party membership in twenty European democracies, 1980–2000." *Party Politics* 7(1): 5–21.

Mancheva, M. (1998). "The new government gives signs of upcoming changes in Bulgartabac." *Capital Weekly*, July 1.

Mann, M. (1984). "The autonomous power of the state: its origins, mechanisms and results." *European Journal of Sociology* 25(2): 185–213.

Mares, I. (2003). "The sources of business interest in social insurance: sectoral versus national differences." *World Politics* 55(2): 229–58.

Markowski, R. (2008). "The 2007 Polish parliamentary election: some structuring, still a lot of chaos." *West European Politics* 31(5): 1055–68.

Martinelli, A. (1979). "Organised business and Italian politics: Confindustria and the Christian Democrats in the postwar period." *West European Politics* 2(3): 67–87.

Matichescu, M. L., and O. Protsyk (2011). "Political recruitment in Romania: continuity and change", in R. F. King and P. Sum, eds., *Romania under Basescu: Aspirations, Achievements, and Frustrations during His First Presidential Term*. Lanham, MD, Lexington Books.

Maw, J. (2002). "Partial privatization in transition economies." *Economic Systems* 26(3): 271–82.

McDermott, G. A. (2002). *Embedded Politics: Industrial Networks and Institutional Change in Postcommunism*. Ann Arbor, University of Michigan Press.

——— (2007). "Politics, power and institution building: bank crises and supervision in east central Europe." *Review of International Political Economy* 14(2): 220–50.

McMenamin, I., and R. Schoenman (2007). "Together forever? Explaining exclusivity in party–firm relations." *Political Studies* 55(1): 153–73.

McMillan, J., and B. Naughton (1992). "How to reform a planned economy: lessons from China." *Oxford Review of Economic Policy* 8(1): 130–43.

Mendelski, M. (2008). "Institutional reforms in south-eastern Europe: a comparative analysis during different periods of transition," working paper. University of Trier.

Mèon, P.-G., and L. Weill (2010). "Is corruption an efficient grease?" *World Development* 38(3): 244–59.

Meyer-Sahling, J.-H. (2006). "The rise of the partisan state? Parties, patronage and the ministerial bureaucracy in Hungary." *Journal of Communist Studies and Transition Politics* 22(3): 274–97.

Migdal, J. S. (2001). *State in Society: Studying How States and Societies Transform and Constitute One Another*. Cambridge University Press.

Miller, J. H., and S. E. Page (2007). *Complex Adaptive Systems: An Introduction to Computational Models of Social Life*. Princeton University Press.

Milner, H. V. (1997). *Interests, Institutions, and Information: Domestic Politics and International Relations*. Princeton University Press.

Mintz, B., and M. Schwartz (1981). "Interlocking directorates and interest group formation." *American Sociological Review* 46(6): 851–69.

——— (1983). "Financial interest groups and interlocking directorates." *Social Science History* 7(2): 183–204.

——— (1985). *The Power Structure of American Business*. University Of Chicago Press.

Mizruchi, M. S. (1992). *The Structure of Corporate Political Action: Interfirm Relations and Their Consequences.* Cambridge, MA, Harvard University Press.

Mizruchi, M. S., and L. B. Stearns (2001). "Getting deals done: the use of social networks in bank decision-making." *American Sociological Review* 66(5): 647–71.

Montgomery, J. D. (1992). "Job search and network composition: implications of the strength-of-weak-ties hypothesis." *American Sociological Review* 57(5): 586–96.

Moore, B. (1967). *Social Origins of Dictatorship and Democracy: Lord and Peasant in the Making of the Modern World.* London, Penguin Books.

Moravcsik, A., and M. A. Vachudova (2003). "National interests, state power, and EU enlargement." *East European Politics and Societies* 17(1): 42–57.

Morck, R. K., D. Strangeland, and B. Yeung (2000). "Inherited wealth, corporate control, and economic growth: the Canadian disease?" in R. K. Morck, ed., *Concentrated Corporate Ownership.* University of Chicago Press: 319–69.

Morck, R. K., and B. Yeung (2003). "Agency problems in large family business groups." *Entrepreneurship Theory and Practice* 27(4): 367–82.

——— (2004). "Family control and the rent-seeking society." *Entrepreneurship Theory and Practice* 28(4): 391–409.

Nee, V. (1989). "A theory of market transition: from redistribution to markets in state socialism." *American Sociological Review* 54(5): 663–81.

Newsweek Polska (2009). "SLD dostała od Gudzowatego 3 mln zł. I oddała." *Newsweek Polska,* March 24.

Nölke, A., and A. Vliegenthart (2009). "Enlarging the varieties of capitalism: the emergence of dependent market economies in east central Europe." *World Politics* 61(4): 670–702.

North, D. C. (1990). *Institutions, Institutional Change and Economic Performance.* Cambridge University Press.

——— (2010). *Understanding the Process of Economic Change.* Princeton University Press.

O'Dwyer, C. (2006). *Runaway State-Building: Patronage Politics and Democratic Development.* Baltimore, Johns Hopkins University Press.

O'Toole, L. J. (1997). "Treating networks seriously: practical and research-based agendas in public administration." *Public Administration Review* 57(1): 45–52.

——— (2010). "The ties that bind? Networks, public administration, and political science." *PS: Political Science and Politics* 43(1): 7–14.

O'Toole, L. J., and R. S. Montjoy (1984). "Interorganizational policy implementation: a theoretical perspective." *Public Administration Review* 44(6): 491–503.

Olson, M. (1963). *The Economics of the Wartime Shortage: A History of British Food Supplies in the Napoleonic War and in World Wars I and II.* Durham, NC, Duke University Press.

——— (1982). *The Rise and Decline of Nations: Economic Growth, Stagflation, and Social Rigidities.* New Haven, CT, Yale University Press.

——— (2000). *Power and Prosperity: Outgrowing Communist and Capitalist Dictatorships.* New York, Basic Books.

Ost, D. (2000). "Illusory corporatism in eastern Europe: neoliberal tripartism and postcommunist class identities." *Politics and Society* 28(4): 503–30.

——— (2006). *The Defeat of Solidarity: Anger and Politics in Postcommunist Europe.* Ithaca, NY, Cornell University Press.

Ostrom, E. (1990). *Governing the Commons: The Evolution of Institutions for Collective Action.* Cambridge University Press.

References

Panther, S. (1997). "Cultural factors in the transition process: Latin center, Orthodox periphery," in J. G. Backhaus and G. Krause, eds., *Issues in Transformation Theory*. Marburg, Metropolis: 95–122.

Paradowska, J. (2001). "Ruch dwóch." *Polityka*, July 21: 20–3.

Pari Daily (1998). "In a nutshell." *Pari Daily*, February 2.

Pasti, V. (1997). *The Challenges of Transition: Romania in Transition*. New York, East European Monographs.

Perotti, E. C. (1995). "Credible privatization." *American Economic Review* 85(4): 847–59.

Perotti, E. C., and S. Gelfer (2001). "Red barons or robber barons? Governance and investment in Russian financial–industrial groups." *European Economic Review* 45(9): 1601–17.

Persson, T., and G. Tabellini (2000). *Political Economics: Explaining Public Policy*. Cambridge, MA, MIT Press.

Pistor, K., M. Raiser, and S. Gelfer (2000). "Law and finance in transition economies." *Economics of Transition* 8(2): 325–68.

Polanyi, K. (2001). *The Great Transformation: The Political and Economic Origins of Our Time*. Boston, Beacon Press.

Polish News Bulletin (2000). "Ministers and businessmen in one." Polish News Bulletin.

——— (2004). "Privatisation debate: treasury minister saves his job by abandoning controversial plans and proposing PKO BP-PZU merger." Polish News Bulletin, March 23, www.pnb.pl/clientarea/pnb-economic-review/139301-privatisation_debate_treasury_minister_saves.html.

Pollert, A. (1999). *Transformation at Work in the New Market Economies of Central Eastern Europe*. London, Sage.

Popov, V. (2000). "Shock therapy versus gradualism: the end of the debate (explaining the magnitude of transformational recession)." *Comparative Economic Studies* 42(1): 1–57.

——— (2007). "Shock therapy versus gradualism reconsidered: lessons from transition economies after 15 years of reforms – I." *Comparative Economic Studies* 49(1): 1–31.

Portes, R. (1990). "Introduction," in *European Economy March 1990: Economic Transformation in Hungary and Poland*. Brussels, Commission of the European Communities: 11–18.

Poterba, J. M. (1994). "State responses to fiscal crises: the effects of budgetary institutions and politics." *Journal of Political Economy* 102(4): 799–821.

Prohaska, M. (2002). *Privatisation Funds: The Bulgarian Model*. Sofia, Center for the Study of Democracy.

Prohaski, G. (1998). "A review of Bulgarian privatisation." Paris, Organisation for Economic Co-operation and Development.

Protsyk, O., and M. L. Matichescu (2011). "Clientelism and political recruitment in democratic transition: evidence from Romania." *Comparative Politics* 43(2): 207–24.

Przeworski, A. (1991). *Democracy and the Market: Political and Economic Reforms in Eastern Europe and Latin America*. Cambridge University Press.

Putnam, R. D. (1994). *Making Democracy Work: Civic Traditions in Modern Italy*. Princeton University Press.

Rajan, R. G., and L. Zingales (2003). "The great reversals: the politics of financial development in the twentieth century." *Journal of Financial Economics* 69(1): 5–50.

Rogowski, R. (1989). *Commerce and Coalitions: How Trade Affects Domestic Political Alignments*. Princeton University Press.

Roland, G. (1991). "Political economy of sequencing tactics in the transition period," in L. Csaba, ed., *Systemic Change and Stabilization in Eastern Europe*. Aldershot, Dartmouth Publishing: 47–64.

————— (1994). "The role of political constraints in transition strategies." *Economics of Transition* 2(1): 27–41.

————— (2002). "The political economy of transition." *Journal of Economic Perspectives* 16(1): 29–50.

Roper, S. D. (2000). *Romania: The Unfinished Revolution*. London, Routledge.

————— (2006). "The influence of party patronage and state finance on electoral outcomes: evidence from Romania." *Journal of Communist Studies and Transition Politics* 22(3): 362–82.

Roper, S. D., A. Moraru, and E. Iorga (2008). "Romania: the secondary influence of public finance on the party system," in S. D. Roper and J. Ikstens, eds., *Public Finance and Post-Communist Party Development*. Aldershot, Ashgate Publishing: 143–54.

Rose-Ackerman, S. (1999). *Corruption and Government: Causes, Consequences, and Reform*. Cambridge University Press.

Rumi, C. (2009). "Political alternation and the fiscal deficits." *Economics Letters* 102(2): 138–40.

Rutland, P. (1993). "Thatcherism, Czech style: transition to capitalism in the Czech Republic." *Telos* 94: 103–29.

Rzeczpospolita (2013). "Gudzowaty: człowiek z gazu." *Rzeczpospolita*, 15 February.

Sachs, J. (1994). *Poland's Jump to the Market Economy*. Cambridge, MA, MIT Press.

Sachs, J., and D. Lipton (1989). "Summary of the proposed economic program of Solidarity," report prepared for Solidarity leadership.

Sanders, G., and D. Bernstein, eds. (2002). *Law in Transition Autumn 2002: Ten Years of Legal Transition*. London, EBRD.

Sapienza, P. (2004). "The effects of government ownership on bank lending." *Journal of Financial Economics* 72(2): 357–84.

Scarrow, S. E. (1996). *Parties and Their Members: Organizing for Victory in Britain and Germany*. Oxford University Press.

Schoenman, R. (2005). "Captains or pirates? State–business relations in post-socialist Poland." *East European Politics and Societies* 19(1): 40–75.

Scholz, J. T., R. Berardo, and B. Kile (2008). "Do networks solve collective action problems? Credibility, search, and collaboration." *Journal of Politics* 70(2): 393–406.

Serra, N., and J. E. Stiglitz (2008). *The Washington Consensus Reconsidered: Towards a New Global Governance*. New York, Oxford University Press.

Shabad, G., and K. M. Slomczynski (2002). "The emergence of career politicians in post-communist democracies: Poland and the Czech Republic." *Legislative Studies Quarterly* 27(3): 333–59.

Shawn, T., and J. Simon (2008). "Democracy as a latent variable." *American Journal of Political Science* 52(1): 201–17.

Shleifer, A., and R. W. Vishny (1997). "A survey of corporate governance." *Journal of Finance* 52(2): 737–83.

————— (1998). *The Grabbing Hand: Government Pathologies and Their Cures*. Cambridge, MA, Harvard University Press.

Sikk, A. (2005). "How unstable? Volatility and the genuinely new parties in eastern Europe." *European Journal of Political Research* 44(3): 391–412.

References

Sikora, S. (1996). "Warianty przekształceń systemu bankowego w Polsce" ("Transformation variants of the banking system in Poland"), in "Jak dokończyć prywatyzację banków w Polsce" ("How to complete the bank privatization in Poland"), notebook. Warsaw, Centrum Analiz Społeczno-Ekonomicznych and Polski Bank Rozwoju: 18–23.

Simon, H. A. (1964). "On the concept of organizational goal." *Administrative Science Quarterly* 9(1): 1–22.

Solnick, S. L. (1998). *Stealing the State: Control and Collapse in Soviet Institutions.* Cambridge, MA, Harvard University Press.

Solska, J. (2012). "Kto chce pogrążyć Kulczyka: Wielkie wizje...i prowizje." *Polityka,* June 26: 1–3.

Spendzharova, A. B., and M. A. Vachudova (2012). "Catching up? Consolidating liberal democracy in Bulgaria and Romania after EU accession." *West European Politics* 35(1): 39–58.

Stan, L. (2003). "Fighting the demons of the recent past: prospects for Romanian reconstruction and development." Paper presented at "Southeastern Europe: moving forward" conference, Carleton University, Ottawa; available at www.carleton.ca/ces/papers/january03/stan03.pdf.

Stanchev, K. (1999). "Democrats go populist." Sofia, Institute for Market Economics.

Standart (2001). "Interior Ministry to investigate Elena Kostova." *Standart,* October 20.

Staniszkis, J. (2000). *Post-Communism: The Emerging Enigma.* Warsaw, IFiS PAN.

Stark, D. (1986). "Rethinking internal labor markets: new insights from a comparative perspective." *American Sociological Review* 51(4): 492–504.

———— (1996). "Recombinant property in east European capitalism." *American Journal of Sociology* 101(4): 993–1027.

Stark, D., and L. Bruszt (1998). *Postsocialist Pathways: Transforming Politics and Property in East Central Europe.* Cambridge University Press.

Stark, D., and B. Vedres (2006). "Social times of network spaces: network sequences and foreign investment in Hungary." *American Journal of Sociology* 111(5): 1367–411.

———— (2012). "Political holes in the economy: the business network of partisan firms in Hungary." *American Sociological Review* 77(5): 700–22.

Stearns, L. B., and M. S. Mizruchi (1993). "Board composition and corporate financing: the impact of financial institution representation on borrowing." *Academy of Management Journal* 36(3): 603–18.

Stigler, G. J. (1961). "The economics of information." *Journal of Political Economy* 69(3): 213–25.

Stiri Politice (2000). "Politicienii Romani migreaza din patru in patru ani." *Stiri Politice,* December 7.

Svejnar, J. (1989). "A framework for the economic transformation of Czechoslovakia." *Planecon Report* 5(52): 1–18.

———— (2002). "Transition economies: performance and challenges." *Journal of Economic Perspectives* 16(1): 3–28.

Synovitz, R. (1996). "Bulgaria: the death of the once-mighty nomenklatura business groups." Radio Free Europe/Radio Liberty, October 9; available at www.rferl.org/content/article/1081896.htm.

Szczerbiak, A. (1999). "Interests and values: Polish parties and their electorates." *Europe–Asia Studies* 51(8): 1401–32.

———— (2006). "State party funding and patronage in post-1989 Poland." *Journal of Communist Studies and Transition Politics* 22(3): 298–319.

———— (2012). "Poland (mainly) chooses stability and continuity: the October 2011 Polish parliamentary election," Working Paper no. 129. Brighton, Sussex European Institute, University of Sussex.

Szelenyi, I. (1988). *Socialist Entrepreneurs: Embourgeoisement in Rural Hungary.* Madison, University of Wisconsin Press.

Sztompka, P. (1992). "Dilemmas of the Great Transition." *Sisyphus* 2(8): 9–28.

———— (1993). "Civilizational incompetence: the trap of post-communist societies." *Zeitschrift für Soziologie* 22(2): 85–95.

Tavits, M. (2005). "The development of stable party support: electoral dynamics in post-communist Europe." *American Journal of Political Science* 49(2): 283–98.

———— (2008). "Party systems in the making: the emergence and success of new parties in new democracies." *British Journal of Political Science* 38(1): 113–33.

Thelen, K. A. (2004). *How Institutions Evolve: The Political Economy of Skills in Germany, Britain, the United States, and Japan.* Cambridge University Press.

Tilly, C. (2001). *Coercion, Capital, and European States, AD 990–1992.* Malden, MA, Blackwell Publishers.

Useem, M. (1984). *The Inner Circle: Large Corporations and the Rise of Business Political Activity in the US and UK.* New York, Oxford University Press.

Uzzi, B. (1999). "Embeddedness in the making of financial capital: how social relations and networks benefit firms seeking financing." *American Sociological Review* 64(4): 481–505.

Vachudova, M. A. (2005). *Europe Undivided: Democracy, Leverage, and Integration after Communism.* New York, Oxford University Press.

Van Biezen, I. (2003). *Political Parties in New Democracies.* London, Palgrave Macmillan.

———— (2004). "Political parties as public utilities." *Party Politics* 10(6): 701–22.

Van Biezen, I., and P. Kopecky (2007). "The state and the parties: public funding, public regulation and rent-seeking in contemporary democracies." *Party Politics* 13(2): 235–54.

Van Biezen, I., P. Mair, and T. Poguntke (2012). "Going, going, ...gone? The decline of party membership in contemporary Europe." *European Journal of Political Research* 51(1): 24–56.

Veblen, T. (1994 [1899]). *The Theory of the Leisure Class: An Economic Study of Institutions.* Mineola, NY, Dover Publications.

Viktorova, O. (1998). "General meetings of shareholders in Bulgartabac Holding postponed." *Pari Daily*, May 8.

Vinton, L. (1994). "Shake-up in Polish Finance Ministry." *Radio Free Europe/Radio Liberty*, June 27.

Volkov, V. (2002). *Violent Entrepreneurs: The Use of Force in the Making of Russian Capitalism.* Ithaca, NY, Cornell University Press.

Wade, R. (1990). *Governing the Market: Economic Theory and the Role of Government in East Asian Industrialization.* Princeton University Press.

Waldner, D. (1999). *State Building and Late Development.* Ithaca, NY, Cornell University Press.

Walecki, M. (2000). *Finansowanie Polityki: Wybory, Pienia Dze, Partie Polityczne.* Warsaw, Wydawnictwo Sejmowe.

References

———— (2005). *Money and Politics in Poland*. Warsaw, Institute of Public Affairs.

———— (2007). "Political finance in Poland," in D. Smilov and J. Toplak, eds., *Political Finance and Corruption in Eastern Europe: The Transition Period*. Aldershot, Ashgate Publishing: 123–42.

Weber, M. (1978 [1922]). *Economy and Society* (ed. G. Roth and C. Wittich, trans. E. Fischoff, H. Gerth, A. M. Henderson, F. Kolegar, C. Wright Mills, T. Parsons, M. Rheinstein, G. Roth, E. Shils, and C. Wittich). Berkeley, University of California Press.

Weimer, D. L. (1997). *The Political Economy of Property Rights: Institutional Change and Credibility in the Reform of Centrally Planned Economies*. Cambridge University Press.

White, H. C. (1981). "Where do markets come from?" *American Journal of Sociology* 87(3): 517–47.

———— (2004). *Markets from Networks: Socioeconomic Models of Production*. Princeton University Press.

Whiteley, P. F. (2011). "Is the party over? The decline of party activism and membership across the democratic world." *Party Politics* 17(1): 21–44.

Williamson, O. (1985). *The Economic Institutions of Capitalism: Firms, Markets, Relational Contracting*. New York, Free Press.

Windolf, P. (1998). "Elite networks in Germany and Britain." *Sociology* 32(2): 321–51.

Winiecki, J. (2004). "Determinants of catching up or falling behind: interaction of formal and informal institutions." *Post-Communist Economies* 16(2): 137–52.

Wong, J. (2004). "The adaptive developmental state in east Asia." *Journal of East Asian Studies* 4(3): 345–62.

Woodruff, D. (2009). "The economist's burden: David Woodruff on Anders Åslund, *How Capitalism Was Built*: a vocal advocate of shock therapy casts a blinkered eye over its results in the former Eastern Bloc." *New Left Review* 55, January/February: 143–52.

Żakowski, J. (2009). "Szkoda ludzi!" *Polityka*, April 4: 14–16.

Zinnes, C., Y. Eilat, and J. Sachs (2001). "The gains from privatization in transition economies: is 'change of ownership' enough?" *IMF Staff Papers* 48(S): 146–70.

Index

Adamczyk, Kazimierz 146–7
advanced industrial states 23
agency problems 57, 67, 69, 83
Albania
  networks and uncertainty 173
  uncertainty type 174
Allianz Capital 96–7
Allied Irish Bank 96–7
AOAR (Businessman's Association of
    Romania) 80–1
assets
  diversity 59, 67, 69–70, 72, 83
  effects on state 86
  specificity 58
AWS–UW government coalition (Poland) 96–8,
    133–4, 152, 189

Bakurdzhiev, Evgeni 109–10
Bank Gdansky (Poland) 94
Bank Handlowy (Poland) 96, 118
Bank Staropolski (Poland) 135
Bank Zachodni (Poland) 96–7
banks
  banking reform 179
  banking regulation 31
  Bulgaria 70, 102
  Japan (keiretsu) 63
  and ownership of firms 63, 90–1, 118
  Poland 2, 21, 70, 85, 90–8, 114–16, 118,
    168–9, 186–7
  post-communist countries 70
  Romania 70
  see also individual banks
BANU (Bulgarian Agrarian National Union) 141

Basescu, Traian 192–3
BBB (Bulgarian Business Block) 141
BDK (Poland) 96–7
Becali, Gigi 101
Beckert, J. 37–8
BEEPS 7, 56, 72, 170
Berle, A. A. 57
Berlusconi, Silvio 193
BGZ Cooperative Bank (Poland) 96–7
BIBA (Bulgarian Investors Business Association)
    81, 105
BIG (Poland) 94
Boc, Emil 192
book plan 24–5
Borisov, Boyko 142, 191–2
Bozhkov, Aleksandur 108
BPH (Bank Przemyslowo-Handlowy) (Poland)
    93–4
Brasco Inc. 146–7
broad business groups 64–5
broad distributive policies 132
broad networks see networks
broadly distributive institutions 3, 5–6, 10, 168
BSK (Bank Slaski) (Poland) 95
BSP (Bulgarian Socialist Party) 141–2, 145–6
  "the generals" faction 141–2
budget constraints 13
Bulgargas 107, 109, 145–6
Bulgaria
  administrative weakness 191–2
  assassinations 8–9, 104–5
  asset diversity 67, 70, 72
  banks 70, 102
  decentralization 102

216

Index

ineffectiveness of 102
broadly distributive institutions 10
business associations 72–6, 81–3
business collective action 70–6
business domination, of political parties/state
30, 52, 102–10, 123–7
business groups
and insiders 104–5
semi-criminal 104–5, 191–2
business leaders' influence 83
capital sources 173
as captured state 25, 84, 164, 173
collective action and self-interest 78
competition policy 9, 175–7
corruption 8, 52, 104–5, 142–3, 191–2
direct control struggles 107–10
elite career networks 188
elite mobility 152, 155–64
elite networks 145–7, 186–7
elite network ties 152
elites and elections 150, 153–7
embeddedness breadth 152
financial firms' role 60, 70
firms against the state 141–3
firms and political parties 102
G-13 ("Group of Thirteen") 82–3, 104–5
GDP in private sector 15–17
hierarchical ownership 127
horizontal ties 123–7
ideological turnover 174
and IMF 103, 142
imperial legacies 19–20
informal groups 82–3
law enforcement weakness 8–9, 191–2
lobbying 81–2
narrow networks 132, 141–3, 148–9, 152,
173, 191–2
national investment funds 105–7
network breadth, effects of 158–64
network ties 113–14
networks
limited access to 8–9
personnel 153–5
and uncertainty 173
organizations as irrelevant 69
owners by type 89
ownership concentration 59, 70, 72
ownership decentralization 91
ownership development 91, 102
ownership networks 102, 128, 188
ownership structures 123, 127
ownership types 186–7

path to privatization 102–10
political instability 45, 141–3, 191
political party finance 142–3, 188
post-transition 191–2
privatization 85, 102–10
opposition to 102–3
Privatization Act (1992) 102
privatization funds 106
RMDs (management–worker partnerships)
106–7, 145–6
and Russian financial crisis 105
shifting party system 141–3
socialist re-election 102–3
stakeholders 127
state ownership 91, 127
state/private mobility of individuals
152
tobacco industry 107–10
transaction law 9
uncertainty 174, 191–2
violent business methods 8–9, 104–5
see also institutions; networks
Bulgarian Agrarian People's Union 142
Bulgarian Industrial Association 81
Bulgarian Industrial Capital Association
81
Bulgarian miracle 108
Bulgarian Social Democratic Party 142
Bulgartabac 107–10, 123
bureaucratic institutions 23
bureaucrats' careers and influence 25
business associations
Bulgaria 72–6, 81–3
Poland 72–9
Romania 72–6, 79–81
Business Centre Club 79
business collective action 70–6
business political action 67
businesspeople and politicians 43
BUSORG analysis variable 172–3
Buzek, Jerzy 2
Bykowski, Piotr 135

capital markets development 86–7
capitalism
financial 58
forms of 38–9, 58
industrial 58
institutional 58
managerial 58
VoC (varieties of capitalism) 22, 32,
33–6

Index

captured states 25, 84, 164, 168, 173
  competition policy 175–7
  institutional development 183, 187
  networks and uncertainty 173, 186
  stability 189
  uncertainty type 174
  see also Bulgaria
career politicians, Poland 45–6
careers
  bureaucrats' careers and influence 25
  elite bureaucrats and influence 25
  elite career destinations 155, 158–64
  elite networks 145–64
  elites and elections 150, 153–7
  overlapping career paths 56
  strategic behaviour 151
Carruthers, B. G. 86–7
case study selection 22–3
CCIR (Romanian Chamber of Commerce) 81
CDR (Romanian Democratic Convention) 137, 139–40
Ceausescu, Nicolae 137
Chimco 145–6
CIGNA 97–8
Cigna STU 146–7
Cimoszewicz, Włodzimierz 135
Ciorbea, Victor 100
civil society role, in democracy 48–9
cluster analysis, and state types 170–5
CMEs (coordinated market economies) 33–5, 193–4
collaborative relationships 34, 83
collective action
  between firms and parties 131–44
  and broad networks 187
  and institutional factors 76–7
  and privatization 77
COMPET analysis variable 172–3
competition
  and corruption 46–7
  and political influence 56–7
  weak 189
competition law 31
competition levels 11
competition policy 175–7
competition problems 37–8
complementarities 32, 34
complex adaptive systems 41
concertation, as collective action 131–2
concertation states 25, 84, 164, 167–8
  banking reform 179
  cluster analysis 172–3

competition policy 175–7
institutional development 187
networks and uncertainty 173, 186
political party system changes 189–90
rule of law 183
stability 189
uncertainty type 174
western Europe 193–4
see also Poland
conditionality, and reform 11
Confederation of Bulgarian Industrialists 82–3, 104–5
Confindustria (Italy) 193
contractual governance 64
cooperation problems 37–8
coordination
  between firms 55
  non-market modes of 34
  problems 37–8
corporate governance
  of firms 24, 55, 57–8
  Poland 7, 93
corruption 49–50, 169, 46–7
  Bulgaria 8, 52, 104–5, 142–3, 191–2
  as inefficient 43–4
  and investment 39
  Poland 5–6, 190
  Romania 138
credible commitments 56
cross-ownership 64
cultural legacies 17–21
customer-supplier relations 173
Czech Republic
  effectiveness contrast with Albania 168
  networks and uncertainty 173
  uncertainty type 174
Czerwinski, Roman 146–7

DA (Justice and Truth Alliance) (Romania) 192
DC (Christian Democratic) party (Italy) 193
debt/equity swaps 92
decision making
  and geography 17–21
  and historical legacies 17–21
democracy, civil society role 48–9
Democratic Left alliance (Bulgaria) 142
democratic states, institutional development in 167–84
developmental states 23
  literature 24, 32–3
dispute resolution 7
dynamic of insubordination 108

Index

east Asian growth 185
EBRD (European Bank for Reconstruction and Development) 1–19, 36, 94, 175, 177
Ecoglasnost Movement (Bulgaria) 142
economic governance, and embeddedness 37
economic policy, and incorporation of networks 30–1
economic and political elites 24, 55–6
economic reform *see* reform
economic/political stakeholders, interaction patterns 84–5
elections
  and elite careers 150, 153–7
  and political uncertainty 186
electoral volatility 48
elites
  agencies' role in network structure 11
  balance of 87–8
  and banks 63
  bureaucrats' careers and influence 25
  career destinations 155, 158–64
  career networks 145–64, 188
  careers and elections 150, 153–7
  competition 39
  concentrated ownership 67–8
  conflict between 37
  cooperation between 86–7
  coordination of 39–40
  dispersed 68–9
  elections and personnel movement 150
  exchanges between 63
  functioning of networks 145–7
  incentives to act collectively 5, 30–1
  individuals' networks 148–52
  mobility of 152, 155–7
  political and economic 24, 55–6
  in state building 38–9
  state leaders' motivations 35
  and state reconception 151
  state/private mobility of individuals 152
  see also Bulgaria; Poland; Romania
embedded corporatist states 168
  uncertainty type 174
embeddedness 32–3
  breadth 152
  and economic governance 37
  multiple forms of 36–8
  of owners 123–7
  post-communist lack of 48
  state 148
  and state policy 151
emerging markets 38–9

employee buyouts 91
employer coordination 58
employer–worker relations 35, 58, 76–7
Energia Invest 145–6
"Enterprise and Bank Financial Restructuring Program" (Poland) 94
Estonia
  networks and uncertainty 173
  uncertainty type 174
European Union conditionality 21–2, 175
EuRoPolgaz 146–7
Evans, P. B. 31, 36–7, 148, 151
export sector size 58
external actors, influence of 21–2

factor analysis, and state types 170
Faniţa, Triţa 140
financial capitalism 58
financial firms' role 60, 70
financial institutions 45
  and secured transaction policy 179
financial transaction regulation 31
firm–firm networks 171
firms
  agency problems 57, 67, 69
  asset diversity 67, 69
  authority structures 58
  behavior of 24
  business collective action 70–6
  in central and eastern Europe 69–76
  coalition of 35
  collaboration 83
  collective action 67–9
    and institutional factors 76–7
  competition policy 175–7
  coordination 55
  coordinated political action 67
  corporate governance 24, 55, 57–8
  credible commitments 56
  director networks 24
  German 193–4
  hierarchically integrated 64–5
  influence on political actors 56–7, 131–44
  involvement with state 56–7
  and legal system 59
  networks 118, 123–7
  network structure types 186–7
  ownership *see* ownership
  and parties 56–7, 131–44
  and party finance 131–44
  and party network density 131–2
  and political relations 42–3, 131–44

Index

firms (cont.)
  in post-communist Europe 69–76
  sanitizing 93
  and the state *see* institutional development
  state capture 56–7
  top connected 115
  see also Bulgaria; Poland; Romania

G-13 ("Group of Thirteen") 82–3, 104–5
Ganchev, Georges 141
Gazprom
  and Gudzowaty 1–3
  and Poland 1–3, 146–7
GDP in private sector 15–17
geographic proximity to West 20
GERB (Citizens for European Development of
  Bulgaria) 142, 191–2
Germany, as concertation state 193–4
government turnover, and rule of law 46–7
"grabbing hand" approach 14
gradualism 11–17
Granovetter, M. S. 40–1
Grzymała-Busse, A. 46–7
Gudzowaty, Aleksander 1–3, 97–8, 135, 146–7
guilds tradition 58
Gwiazda, A. 190

Hall, P. A. 35
Hellman, J. S. 31–2
hierarchical cluster analysis 171
historical legacies, and reform 11, 17–22
Humanist Party (Romania) 9, 101, 139
Hungary
  ideological turnover 174
  legacies 20
  networks and uncertainty 173
  rule of law 183
  uncertainty type 174

ideological turnover 46–7, 172, 174
IDTURN analysis variable 172–3
Iliescu, Ion 100
Iliescu, Valentin 140
Iliev, Vasil 104
imperial legacy inconsistencies 19–20
industrial capitalism 58
inflation 12
informal coalitions 21–2
information sharing 37
ING (Poland) 95, 114–16
insider interests 13
insider networks 35

institution building 44, 84–5
  historical forces and social structures 194–5
institutional bargains 64
institutional capitalism 58
institutional choice 42–3
institutional design 42–3
institutional development 10–11
  captured states 183
  competition policy 175–7
  EBRD 1–19, 36, 94, 175
  effects on governance 174–83
  effects of networks 40–4
  effects of ownership structures 57
  in new democracies 167–84
  and uncertainty 38–40, 52
institutional factors, and collective action
  76–7
institutional investors 60–2, 65
institutions
  broadly distributive 3, 5–6, 10, 168
  complementarities 32, 34
  definition 3
  and economic reform 33
  employer–worker relations 35, 58, 76–7
  financial institutions 45
  formal 3
  and geography 17–21
  hardened 189
  and historical legacies 17–22
  incomplete 5
  market institutions and political struggle
    87–8
  and networks 3, 5–6, 17, 43–4
  redistributive consequences 3
  selective advantage 3
  and VoC (varieties of capitalism) research 32
  see also Bulgaria; networks; Poland;
    Romania
interaction patterns 84–5
interest groups, and external pressures 22
investment distortions 12
investors 60–2
Italy, as patronage state 193

Jacoby, W. 21–2

k-means cluster analysis 171
Kaczynski brothers 134
Kamela-Sowińska, Aldona 133–4
Kang, D. C. 37
key findings 186–9
Kitschelt, H. 21

Index

Kostov, Georgi 109
Kostov, Ivan 102–3, 106–9, 142
Kostova, Elena 106–7
Krackhardt, D. 42
Kremikovtsi 145–6
Kulczyk, Jan 3, 97–8, 135–6
Kwasniewski, Aleksander 94, 136, 146–7
Kyulev, Emil 104–5

labor contracts 35, 58
labor mobility 35
labor reallocation/layoffs 12
Latvia
  ideological turnover 174
  networks and uncertainty 173
  uncertainty type 174
law
  rule of 31, 183
    and concertation states 183
    and government turnover 46–7
Law on Campaign Finance (1997) (Poland)
  134
leadership coalitions 47
legal regime uncertainty 15
legal systems, inherited 23
Lewandowski, Janusz 136
Lipton, D. 12–13
literatures
  networks/uncertainty 32–3
  in political economy 24, 31
Lithuania
  ideological turnover 174
  networks and uncertainty 173
  uncertainty type 174
LMEs (liberal market economies) 33–5
lobbying 58, 72–6, 78, 81–2, 172
Lukanov, Andre 141

managerial capitalism 58
market institutions and political struggle 87–8
markets and networks 170
Matei Agathon, Dan 138
Means, G. C. 57
Meciar, Valdimir 20
Michailov, Dako 107
Minchev, Ognyan 103
Moore, B. 86
MRF (Turkish Movement for Rights and
  Freedoms) 141–2
Multigroup 8, 105, 108, 123, 145–6
Musetescu, Ovidiu 101
mutual hostages 37

mutual interests 51
mutual monitoring 37

narrow networks see networks
National Gas Company (Bulgaria) 145–6
NEC (National Electric Company) (Bulgaria)
  109–10
NETFIN analysis variable 171, 173
network advantages 30–1
network analysis 41–2, 195
network breadth, effects of 158–64
network capital sources 172
network coalitions 22, 39, 47
network reconfigurations 87
network reputational monitoring 194
network-sourced capital 41
networks
  acquaintance relationships 41
  actors 148–9
  broad/breadth of 30–1, 40–5, 50, 59, 92–8,
    131–2, 148–9, 155, 158–64, 170–1,
    186–7
  and broadly distributive institutions 6, 10
  businesspeople and politicians 43
  and corruption/violence 5, 8–9
  and diversity 41–2
  effect on institutional development 40–4
  elite career networks 145–64
  elite individuals 148–52
  and external stimuli 87
  firm–firm 171
  firm–party 13, 131–44
  and firms' behavior 24
  and firms' ownership/director networks 24
  functioning of elite networks 48–9
  and individials' ability 42
  of individuals 43, 133–4
  information sharing 37
  and institutions 3, 5–6, 17, 32, 34, 43–4
    see also institutions
  inter-firm 32–4
  joint memberships 56
  and key job movement 149–50
  long-term 6–7
  and markets 170
  mutual monitoring 37
  narrow 30–1, 50, 59, 132, 148–9, 170–1,
    186
  as obstacles to institutions 29
  and opportunity 50
  overlapping career paths 56
  ownership 44, 56

Index

networks (cont.)
party–society linkage 47–8
personal ties 133–4
personnel network development 153–5
and political competition 24, 40
public administration 148–9
reasons for emergence 5
reasons for variations in 5
relationships with institutions 3, 5–6
as resources 11
social network analysis 194–5
and social structures 43
state–economy ties 36–7
strong ties 40
structure and agency 42, 152–3
tight 40
types of 6
and uncertainty 5–6, 10, 22, 24–5, 30–3,
50–1, 173, 186
and violence 8–9
VoC (varieties of capitalism) research
literature 32–3
weak ties theory 40–1
see also Bulgaria; embeddedness; firms;
Poland; Romania
New Generation Party (Romania) 101
NFIs (national investment funds) (Poland)
94
Niculae, Ioan 101
nonmarket modes of coordination 34
North, D. 194–5
NSF (National Salvation Front) (Romania) 9,
138, 140

Oleksy, Josef 2–3
Orion group 105
outsider stakeholders 13
ownership
banks 63, 90–1, 118
broad business groups 64–5
business/industrial pyramids 60–2, 65–7
cross-holdings 6
cross-ownership 64–5
decreasing concentration 69
director networks 24
dispersed 68–9
diversified 65
and economic development 86–8
elite 67–8
external stakeholders 58–9
family group 60–2, 65–8
firms' ownership data 88–90, 115

hierarchical structure 60, 65–7
horizontal structure 60, 62–5, 67, 92
hybrid 85
institutional investors 60–2, 65
investors 60, 65
owners by type 89
and privatization 84
shareholders 57–9
see also Bulgaria; firms; Poland; Romania
ownership concentration 59, 67–8, 70, 72
ownership development 88–92
ownership networks 44, 56, 128
broad 59
findings summary 188
narrow 59, 98
and politics–business relations 86–8
ownership reconfigurations 87
ownership structure 24, 44–5, 56–62
and configuration of interests 87–8
hierarchical structure 60
horizontal structure 60, 62–5
ownership ties 55
ownership types 186–7

Palikot's Movement (Poland) 190
parties see political parties
Patriciu, Dinu 139
patronage states 25, 84, 164, 168
cluster analysis 173
competition policy 175–7, 183–4
institutional development 183–4, 187
Italy as western European example 193
networks and uncertainty 173, 186
political elites 183–4
rule of law 183–4
stability 189
uncertainty type 174
see also Romania
Paunescu, Adrian 140
Paunescu family (Romania) 80, 100–2
Pavlov, Ilya 7–9, 104–5
Pawlak, Waldemar 146–7, 150
PBG (Poland) 96–7
PBK (Poland) 96
PBKS (Poland) 96–7
PC (Centrum Alliance) (Poland) 134
PC (Conservative Party) (Romania) 192
PD (Democratic Party) (Romania) 100, 138, 192
PD-L (Democratic Liberal Party) (Romania)
138, 192
PDSR (Party of Social Democracy of Romania)
9

Index

PEKAO (Poland) 96–7
personal ties 133–4
personnel network development 153–5
PiS (Law and Justice Party) (Poland) 97–8, 190–1
PKN Orlen 146–7
PKO BP 96–7
planning structure collapse 13
PNL (National Liberal Party) (Romania) 138, 192
PO (Civic Action) (Poland) 190
PO–PSL coalition (Poland) 190
Poland
  asset diversity 67, 70, 72
  banks 70, 85, 90–8
    centrality 118
    foreign 114–16
    inefficiency 168–9
    key role of 186–7
    privatization 93–7
    restructuring 93, 95
    as shareholders 97, 118
  broad networks 92–8, 127, 131–2, 152
  broad organizations 78
  broadly devised institutions 7
  broadly distributive institutions 3, 5
  business associations 72–9
  business collective action 70–6
  business groups 97–8
  business and political left 135
  business and political right 135–6
  business–party alliances 132–7
  business–politics connections 97–8, 100–2
  and capitalist competition 190–1
  career politicians 45–6
  Civil Service Law 190
  collective action organizations 69
  common owners 78
  communist influence, post-transition 133
  as concertation state 25, 84, 131–2, 164
  corporate governance
    law 7
    structure 93
  corruption 5–6, 190
  cross-ownership networks 92
  debt/equity swaps 92
  decentralized structures 94
  dispute resolution 41
  economic reform 4
  effectiveness contrast with Albania 168–9
  elite career networks 188
  elite mobility 152, 155–64

elite network ties 152
elite networks 146–7, 186–7
elites and elections 150, 153–7
embeddedness breadth 152
financial firms' role 60, 70
financial institutions 118
financial law 7
firm networks 118
firms' collaboration 83
firms' management and active role of state 190–1
foreign banks 114–16
foreign investment/ownership 90–1, 93–5, 114–16
gas supply and Gazprom 1–3
gas supply and Gudzwaty 1–3
GDP in private sector 15–17
hybrid institutions 127, 190–1
ideological turnover 174
imperial legacies 19–20
industrial policy 133–4
leadership coalitions 47
lobbying 7
long-term networks 6–7
mutual interests 51
narrow networks 148–9
national investment funds 106
network breadth, effects of 158–64
network emergence 29–30
network formation 3–5
network ownership 29–30, 110–16
network-sourced capital 7
network ties 113–14, 169–70
networks 110–18
  elite networks 146–7
  and uncertainty 173
owners by type 89
ownership concentration 59, 70, 72
ownership development 90–1
ownership networks 6, 128, 188
ownership ties 113–14
ownership transformation 110–16
ownership types 186–7
party finance "arms race" 133–4
party patronage 190
party system volatility 190
party–business alliances 132–7
party–society connections 48–9
path to privatization 92–8
personnel networks 6, 29–30, 153–5
political competition 4–5
political parties and elections 45–6

Index

Poland (cont.)
  political party finance 188
    and business 4, 29–30, 132–7, 143–4
  political party system changes 189–90
  politicized appointments 6
  post-transition institutions 189–91
  privatization 4, 12–13, 85, 136–7
    and political manipulation 92–3
    process/methods 92–3
  redistributive consequences 3
  rule of law 183
  selective advantage institutions 3
  state authority 7
  state ownership 118
  state–economy connections 190
  state firm ownership 118
  state/private mobility of individuals 152
  transition to capitalism 3–5, 189–91
  uncertainty type 174
  variable institutional performance 168–9
  see also institutions; networks
Polanyi, K. 37–8
PolGaz Telekom 146–7
policy-making areas 31
Polish Business Roundtable (PRB) 78
Polish Confederation of Employers (KPP) 78
Polish Confederation of Private Employers
    Leviathan (PKPP) 78
political capitalism 2–3
political coalitions 22, 39, 47
political competition 11
  and networks 24
political and economic elites 24
political economy, literatures in 24
political interference 13–15
political legacies 17–21
political parties
  alliances 48
  connections to state 48–9
  finance 131–44, 188
  finance "arms race" 133–4
  and firms see firms
  public funding 49
  public regulation of 49
  rent seeking 49–50
  as representative actors 47–8
  society connections 47–9
  system changes 189–90
  see also Bulgaria; Poland; Romania
political resources, and lobbying 58
political uncertainty see uncertainty
political/economic stakeholders, interaction
    patterns 84–5

politicization
  of key jobs 149–50
  of property 147
  of the state 50
Popescu-Tariceanu, Calin 192
post-communist states, as case studies 23
post-post-socialism 84
price liberalization 12
private economy size 15–17
privatization 4, 12–13
  and bureaucracy 15
  and collective action 77
  and ownership 84
  and stakeholders 84
  and uncertainty 90
  see also Bulgaria; Poland; Romania
productivity 12
Pruteanu, George 140
PSD (Social Democrat Party) (Romania)
    9, 30, 80–1, 99–102, 137–8, 140, 192–3
PSL (Polish Peasant Party) 190
Purvanov, Georgi 141–2

"red bourgeoisie" 105
reform
  compensation costs 14
  and conditionality 11
  during transition 31–2
  EBDR reform index 1–19
  gradualism approach 11–17, 22
  and historical legacies 11, 17–22
  influence of state actors 13
  and new institutions 33
  partial reform 13
  political sustainability of 10
  shock therapy approach 11–17, 22, 31–2
relational contracting 34
rent seeking 49–50, 55–6
retail shortages 12
RMDs (management–worker partnerships)
    106–7, 145–6
Roman, Petre 99–100
Romania
  asset diversity 67, 70, 72
  asset redistribution 98–102
  banks 70
  bureaucracy and business 51–2
  business associations 72–6, 79–81
  business collective action 70–6
  business elites 138
  business fragmentation 9, 51–2
  business groups 100–2
  business leaders' influence 83

Index

business, and political parties 30, 51–2, 139
corruption 138
dominant party election 132
elite career networks 188
elite mobility 152, 155–64
elite network ties 152
elite networks 147, 186–7
elites and elections 150, 153–7
embeddedness breadth 152
employee buyouts 91
EU trade 99
exports 99
financial firms' role 60, 70
firm networks 118
firms against the state 137–40
firms and political parties 102
foreign investment/ownership 91
GDP in private sector 15–17
and IMF 100
imperial legacies 19–20
imports 99
inflation 99
MPPs (mass privatization programs) 98–100
narrow networks 132, 148–9, 152
national investment funds 106
network breadth, effects of 158–64
networks and uncertainty 173
organizations, as personal political 69, 78
owners by type 89
ownership concentration 59, 70, 72
ownership development 91
ownership, hierarchical 127
ownership networks 91, 98, 118, 128, 188
ownership types 186–7
path to privatization 98–102
as patronage state 25, 84, 164
personnel network development 153–5
political defection/migration 140
political elites 46, 137, 193
political instability 192–3
political leadership inertia 192–3
political party finance 9, 137–40, 143–4, 188
political party finance White Paper 139–40
political party financial statements 137
political party inertia 46
private ownership funds 98–9
privatization 85, 98–102, 118
    government attitude to 101–2
RAs (*regies autonomes*) 99
SOEs (state-owned enterprises) 99
state ownership 118
state ownership funds 98–9
state privatization funds 85

state/private mobility of individuals 152
transition period 9
uncertainty type 174
see also institutions; networks
Rothschild, Baron de 42, 152–3

Sachs, J. 12–13
search theory 40–1
secured transaction policy 179
selective advantage institutions 3, 36
Severin, Adrian 140
shareholders *see* firms
Shervashidze, Nikita 145–6
Shilyashki, Ivan 109–10
shock program 12
shock therapy 11–17, 22, 31–2
SIC 104–5
Simeon II, Tsar (Bulgaria) 103
SLD (Democratic Left Alliance) (Poland) 1–2,
    29–30, 97–8, 133–4, 136, 151, 189
Slovak Republic
    networks and uncertainty 173
    uncertainty type 174
Slovenia
    networks and uncertainty 173
    uncertainty type 174
Smietanko, Andrzej 146–7
SNM (National Movement Simeon II)
    (Bulgaria) 103, 142
social network analysis 194–5
Sofianski, Stefan 142
Solidarity (Poland) 2, 29–30, 96–7
Solorz-Zak, Zygmunt 97–8
Soskice, D. W. 35
stakeholder groups 87
stakeholder interaction patterns 84–5
stakeholder lobby 12–13, 15
Stamboliyski, Aleksandar 142
state borrowing 86–7
state capture 56–7
state embeddedness 148
state leaders, motivations 35
state reconception, and elites 151
state structures, and market construction 150
state type analysis
    data and methods 170–1
    variables 170–1
state–business relations 83
state–economy ties 36–7
Stoichev, Krassimir 104–5
Stoilov, Georgi 109–10
Stolojan, Theodor 99, 192
SUPP analysis variable 171, 173

"tabula rasa" approach 48
Tangentopoli scandal (Italy) 193
tax authority inspections 172
TAXINS analysis variable 172–3
Telegraf 134
Tomov, Alexander 108
Tourist Sports Bank (Bulgaria) 104–5
TPSA 3
transnational capital flow 23
TRON group 104–5
Tsvetanov, Tsvetan 191

UDF (Union of Democratic Forces) (Bulgaria)
   91, 102–3, 106–9, 141, 145–6, 152
UDMR (Democratic Union of Hungarians in
   Romania) 192
UGIR (General Union of Romanian
   Industrialists) 80–1
UGIR-1903 (General Union of Romanian
   Industrialists 1903) 80–1
uncertainty
   and broad networks 187
   and business–party alliances 133
   and cooperation 131–44
   correct balance of 39–40
   and elections 186
   and elite career networks 145–64
   and future 45–7
   and institutional development 38–40
   and networks 5–6, 10, 22, 24–5, 30–3, 50–1,
     132, 145–64, 173, 186–7

political 11, 45–6, *see also* ideological
   turnover
   and political changes 46–7
   and political competition 45–6
   and privatization 90
   types 174
Ungureanu, Mihai Razvan 192
Unicredito Italiano 96–7
USD (Union of Social Democrats) (Romania)
   100
USL (Social-Liberal Union) (Romania) 192
UtdDF (United Democratic Forces) (Bulgaria)
   142

valley of transition 31–2
Vasile, Radu 100
Videnov, Zhan 103, 105–6, 109–10
VIS-2 8–9, 104–5
VoC (varieties of capitalism) 33–6
Voiculescu, Dan 9, 81, 101, 139
voter volatility 48
voter–party attachment 47–8

Wałęsa, Lech 3
Washington Consensus 169
WBK (Wielkopolski Bank Kredytowy)
   (Poland) 94
weak ties theory 40–1
workout agreements 92

Zhelev, Zhelyu 141

Other Books in the Series (*continued from p. iii*)

Robert Bates, *When Things Fell Apart: State Failure in Late-Century Africa*
Mark Beissinger, *Nationalist Mobilization and the Collapse of the Soviet State*
Pablo Beramendi, *The Political Geography of Inequality: Regions and Redistribution*
Nancy Bermeo, ed., *Unemployment in the New Europe*
Carles Boix, *Democracy and Redistribution*
Carles Boix, *Political Parties, Growth, and Equality: Conservative and Social Democratic Economic Strategies in the World Economy*
Catherine Boone, *Merchant Capital and the Roots of State Power in Senegal, 1930–1985*
Catherine Boone, *Political Topographies of the African State: Territorial Authority and Institutional Change*
Catherine Boone, *Property and Political Order in Africa: Land Rights and the Structure of Politics*
Michael Bratton and Nicolas van de Walle, *Democratic Experiments in Africa: Regime Transitions in Comparative Perspective*
Michael Bratton, Robert Mattes, and E. Gyimah-Boadi, *Public Opinion, Democracy, and Market Reform in Africa*
Valerie Bunce, *Leaving Socialism and Leaving the State: The End of Yugoslavia, the Soviet Union, and Czechoslovakia*
Daniele Caramani, *The Nationalization of Politics: The Formation of National Electorates and Party Systems in Europe*
John M. Carey, *Legislative Voting and Accountability*
Kanchan Chandra, *Why Ethnic Parties Succeed: Patronage and Ethnic Headcounts in India*
Eric C. C. Chang, Mark Andreas Kayser, Drew A. Linzer, and Ronald Rogowski, *Electoral Systems and the Balance of Consumer-Producer Power*
José Antonio Cheibub, *Presidentialism, Parliamentarism, and Democracy*
Ruth Berins Collier, *Paths toward Democracy: The Working Class and Elites in Western Europe and South America*
Pepper D. Culpepper, *Quiet Politics and Business Power: Corporate Control in Europe and Japan*
Christian Davenport, *State Repression and the Domestic Democratic Peace*
Donatella della Porta, *Social Movements, Political Violence, and the State*
Alberto Diaz-Cayeros, *Federalism, Fiscal Authority, and Centralization in Latin America*
Thad Dunning, *Crude Democracy: Natural Resource Wealth and Political Regimes*
Gerald Easter, *Reconstructing the State: Personal Networks and Elite Identity*
Margarita Estevez-Abe, *Welfare and Capitalism in Postwar Japan: Party, Bureaucracy, and Business*
Henry Farrell, *The Political Economy of Trust: Institutions, Interests, and Inter-Firm Cooperation in Italy and Germany*
Karen E. Ferree, *Framing the Race in South Africa: The Political Origins of Racial Census Elections*
M. Steven Fish, *Democracy Derailed in Russia: The Failure of Open Politics*
Robert F. Franzese, *Macroeconomic Policies of Developed Democracies*

Roberto Franzosi, *The Puzzle of Strikes: Class and State Strategies in Postwar Italy*

Timothy Frye, *Building States and Markets after Communism: The Perils of Polarized Democracy*

Geoffrey Garrett, *Partisan Politics in the Global Economy*

Scott Gehlbach, *Representation through Taxation: Revenue, Politics, and Development in Postcommunist States*

Edward L. Gibson, *Boundary Control: Subnational Authoritarianism in Federal Democracies*

Jane R. Gingrich, *Making Markets in the Welfare State: The Politics of Varying Market Reforms*

Miriam Golden, *Heroic Defeats: The Politics of Job Loss*

Jeff Goodwin, *No Other Way Out: States and Revolutionary Movements*

Merilee Serrill Grindle, *Changing the State*

Anna Grzymała-Busse, *Rebuilding Leviathan: Party Competition and State Exploitation in Post-Communist Democracies*

Anna Grzymała-Busse, *Redeeming the Communist Past: The Regeneration of Communist Parties in East Central Europe*

Frances Hagopian, *Traditional Politics and Regime Change in Brazil*

Mark Hallerberg, Rolf Ranier Strauch, and Jürgen von Hagen, *Fiscal Governance in Europe*

Henry E. Hale, *The Foundations of Ethnic Politics: Separatism of States and Nations in Eurasia and the World*

Stephen E. Hanson, *Post-Imperial Democracies: Ideology and Party Formation in Third Republic France, Weimar Germany, and Post-Soviet Russia*

Michael Hechter, *Alien Rule*

Gretchen Helmke, *Courts under Constraints: Judges, Generals, and Presidents in Argentina*

Yoshiko Herrera, *Imagined Economies: The Sources of Russian Regionalism*

J. Rogers Hollingsworth and Robert Boyer, eds., *Contemporary Capitalism: The Embeddedness of Institutions*

John D. Huber and Charles R. Shipan, *Deliberate Discretion? The Institutional Foundations of Bureaucratic Autonomy*

Ellen Immergut, *Health Politics: Interests and Institutions in Western Europe*

Torben Iversen, *Capitalism, Democracy, and Welfare*

Torben Iversen, *Contested Economic Institutions*

Torben Iversen, Jonas Pontussen, and David Soskice, eds., *Unions, Employers, and Central Banks: Macroeconomic Coordination and Institutional Change in Social Market Economics*

Thomas Janoski and Alexander M. Hicks, eds., *The Comparative Political Economy of the Welfare State*

Joseph Jupille, *Procedural Politics: Issues, Influence, and Institutional Choice in the European Union*

Stathis Kalyvas, *The Logic of Violence in Civil War*

Stephen B. Kaplan, *Globalization and Austerity Politics in Latin America*

David C. Kang, *Crony Capitalism: Corruption and Capitalism in South Korea and the Philippines*

Junko Kato, *Regressive Taxation and the Welfare State*

Orit Kedar, *Voting for Policy, Not Parties: How Voters Compensate for Power Sharing*

Robert O. Keohane and Helen B. Milner, eds., *Internationalization and Domestic Politics*

Herbert Kitschelt, *The Transformation of European Social Democracy*

Herbert Kitschelt, Kirk A. Hawkins, Juan Pablo Luna, Guillermo Rosas, and Elizabeth J. Zechmeister, *Latin American Party Systems*

Herbert Kitschelt, Peter Lange, Gary Marks, and John D. Stephens, eds., *Continuity and Change in Contemporary Capitalism*

Herbert Kitschelt, Zdenka Mansfeldova, Radek Markowski, and Gabor Toka, *Post-Communist Party Systems*

David Knoke, Franz Urban Pappi, Jeffrey Broadbent, and Yutaka Tsujinaka, eds., *Comparing Policy Networks*

Ken Kollman, *Perils of Centralization: Lessons from Church, State, and Corporation*

Allan Kornberg and Harold D. Clarke, *Citizens and Community: Political Support in a Representative Democracy*

Amie Kreppel, *The European Parliament and the Supranational Party System*

David D. Laitin, *Language Repertoires and State Construction in Africa*

Fabrice E. Lehoucq and Ivan Molina, *Stuffing the Ballot Box: Fraud, Electoral Reform, and Democratization in Costa Rica*

Mark Irving Lichbach and Alan S. Zuckerman, eds., *Comparative Politics: Rationality, Culture, and Structure*, 2nd edition

Evan Lieberman, *Race and Regionalism in the Politics of Taxation in Brazil and South Africa*

Richard M. Locke, *The Promise and Limits of Private Power: Promoting Labor Standards in a Global Economy*

Julia Lynch, *Age in the Welfare State: The Origins of Social Spending on Pensioner's Workers and Children*

Pauline Jones Luong, *Institutional Change and Political Continuity in Post-Soviet Central Asia*

Pauline Jones Luong and Erika Weinthal, *Oil Is Not a Curse: Ownership Structure and Institutions in Soviet Successor States*

Doug McAdam, John McCarthy, and Mayer Zald, eds., *Comparative Perspectives on Social Movements*

Lauren M. MacLean, *Informal Institutions and Citizenship in Rural Africa: Risk and Reciprocity in Ghana and Côte d'Ivoire*

Beatriz Magaloni, *Voting for Autocracy: Hegemonic Party Survival and Its Demise in Mexico*

James Mahoney, *Colonialism and Postcolonial Development: Spanish America in Comparative Perspective*

James Mahoney and Dietrich Rueschemeyer, eds., *Historical Analysis and the Social Sciences*

Scott Mainwaring and Matthew Soberg Shugart, eds., *Presidentialism and Democracy in Latin America*

Isabela Mares, *The Politics of Social Risk: Business and Welfare State Development*

Isabela Mares, *Taxation, Wage Bargaining, and Unemployment*

Cathie Jo Martin and Duane Swank, *The Political Construction of Business Interests: Coordination, Growth, and Equality*

Anthony W. Marx, *Making Race, Making Nations: A Comparison of South Africa, the United States, and Brazil*

Bonnie M. Meguid, *Party Competition between Unequals: Strategies and Electoral Fortunes in Western Europe*

Joel S. Migdal, *State in Society: Studying How States and Societies Constitute One Another*

Joel S. Migdal, Atul Kohli, and Vivienne Shue, eds., *State Power and Social Forces: Domination and Transformation in the Third World*

Scott Morgenstern and Benito Nacif, eds., *Legislative Politics in Latin America*

Layna Mosley, *Global Capital and National Governments*

Layna Mosley, *Labor Rights and Multinational Production*

Wolfgang C. Müller and Kaare Strøm, *Policy, Office, or Votes?*

Maria Victoria Murillo, *Political Competition, Partisanship, and Policy Making in Latin American Public Utilities*

Maria Victoria Murillo, *Labor Unions, Partisan Coalitions, and Market Reforms in Latin America*

Monika Nalepa, *Skeletons in the Closet: Transitional Justice in Post-Communist Europe*

Ton Notermans, *Money, Markets, and the State: Social Democratic Economic Policies since 1918*

Aníbal Pérez-Liñán, *Presidential Impeachment and the New Political Instability in Latin America*

Roger D. Petersen, *Understanding Ethnic Violence: Fear, Hatred, and Resentment in Twentieth-Century Eastern Europe*

Roger D. Petersen, *Western Intervention in the Balkans: The Strategic Use of Emotion in Conflict*

Simona Piattoni, ed., *Clientelism, Interests, and Democratic Representation*

Paul Pierson, *Dismantling the Welfare State? Reagan, Thatcher, and the Politics of Retrenchment*

Marino Regini, *Uncertain Boundaries: The Social and Political Construction of European Economies*

Marc Howard Ross, *Cultural Contestation in Ethnic Conflict*

Ben Ross Schneider, *Hierarchical Capitalism in Latin America: Business, Labor, and the Challenges of Equitable Development*

Lyle Scruggs, *Sustaining Abundance: Environmental Performance in Industrial Democracies*

Jefferey M. Sellers, *Governing from Below: Urban Regions and the Global Economy*

Yossi Shain and Juan Linz, eds., *Interim Governments and Democratic Transitions*

Beverly Silver, *Forces of Labor: Workers' Movements and Globalization since 1870*

Theda Skocpol, *Social Revolutions in the Modern World*

Austin Smith *et al.*, *Selected Works of Michael Wallerstein*

Regina Smyth, *Candidate Strategies and Electoral Competition in the Russian Federation: Democracy without Foundation*

Richard Snyder, *Politics after Neoliberalism: Reregulation in Mexico*

David Stark and László Bruszt, *Postsocialist Pathways: Transforming Politics and Property in East Central Europe*
Sven Steinmo, *The Evolution of Modern States: Sweden, Japan, and the United States*
Sven Steinmo, Kathleen Thelen, and Frank Longstreth, eds., *Structuring Politics: Historical Institutionalism in Comparative Analysis*
Susan C. Stokes, *Mandates and Democracy: Neoliberalism by Surprise in Latin America*
Susan C. Stokes, ed., *Public Support for Market Reforms in New Democracies*
Susan C. Stokes, Thad Dunning, Marcelo Nazareno, and Valeria Brusco, *Brokers, Voters, and Clientelism: The Puzzle of Distributive Politics*
Milan W. Svolik, *The Politics of Authoritarian Rule*
Duane Swank, *Global Capital, Political Institutions, and Policy Change in Developed Welfare States*
Sidney Tarrow, *Power in Movement: Social Movements and Contentious Politics*
Sidney Tarrow, *Power in Movement: Social Movements and Contentious Politics*, revised and updated 3rd edition
Kathleen Thelen, *How Institutions Evolve: The Political Economy of Skills in Germany, Britain, the United States, and Japan*
Kathleen Thelen, *Varieties of Liberalization and the New Politics of Social Solidarity*
Charles Tilly, *Trust and Rule*
Daniel Treisman, *The Architecture of Government: Rethinking Political Decentralization*
Guillermo Trejo, *Popular Movements in Autocracies: Religion, Repression, and Indigenous Collective Action in Mexico*
Lily Lee Tsai, *Accountability without Democracy: How Solidary Groups Provide Public Goods in Rural China*
Joshua Tucker, *Regional Economic Voting: Russia, Poland, Hungary, Slovakia and the Czech Republic, 1990–1999*
Ashutosh Varshney, *Democracy, Development, and the Countryside*
Jeremy M. Weinstein, *Inside Rebellion: The Politics of Insurgent Violence*
Stephen I. Wilkinson, *Votes and Violence: Electoral Competition and Ethnic Riots in India*
Andreas Wimmer, *Waves of War: Nationalism, State Formation, and Ethnic Exclusion in the Modern World*
Jason Wittenberg, *Crucibles of Political Loyalty: Church Institutions and Electoral Continuity in Hungary*
Elisabeth J. Wood, *Forging Democracy from Below: Insurgent Transitions in South Africa and El Salvador*
Elisabeth J. Wood, *Insurgent Collective Action and Civil War in El Salvador*

For EU product safety concerns, contact us at Calle de José Abascal, 56–1°, 28003 Madrid, Spain or eugpsr@cambridge.org.

www.ingramcontent.com/pod-product-compliance
Ingram Content Group UK Ltd.
Pitfield, Milton Keynes, MK11 3LW, UK
UKHW021811080825
461487UK00025B/716